SOUTHWESTERN COLLEGE LIBRARY/LRC

D1118720

Where's Daddy?

To Peter, Tad, and Jonathan

HQ
759.912
W37
1994

11-30-94

Where's Daddy?

How Divorced, Single and Widowed
Mothers Can Provide What's Missing
When Dad's Missing

Claudette Wassil-Grimm, M.Ed.

SOUTHWESTERN
COLLEGE
Library
CHULA VISTA
CALIFORNIA

THE OVERLOOK PRESS
WOODSTOCK • NEW YORK

First published in 1994 by
The Overlook Press
Lewis Hollow Road
Woodstock, New York 12498

Copyright©1994 Claudette Wassil-Grimm, M.Ed.

All Rights Reserved. No part of this publication may be reproduced or transmitted in any form or by any means, electronic or mechanical, including photocopy, recording, or any information storage and retrieval system now known or to be invented without permission in writing from the publisher, except by a reviewer who wishes to quote brief passages in connection with a review written for inclusion in a magazine, newspaper, or broadcast.

Grateful acknowledgment is made to the following for permission to reprint previously published material:

Houghton Mifflin Company: Excerpts from *Second Chances* by Judith S. Wallerstein and Sandra Blakeslee. Copyright©1989 by Judith S. Wallerstein and Sandra Blakeslee. Reprinted by permission of Ticknor Fields/Houghton Mifflin Co. All rights reserved. *Macmillan Publishing Company:* Excerpts from Foreword by Judith S. Wallerstein, Ph.D. In *Impasses of Divorce: The Dynamics and Resolution of Family Conflict* by Janet R. Johnston and Linda E.G. Campbell. Copyright©1988 by Janet R. Johnston and Linda E.G. Campbell. Reprinted with the permission of The Free Press, a division of Macmillan, Inc. *Philadelphia Child Guidance Clinic:* Excerpts from *Child Custody A Study of Families After Divorce* by Dr. Deborah Anna Luepnitz, a psychologist at the Philadelphia Child Guidance Clinic. *The Analytic Press:* Excerpts from "The Non-Custodial Father" in *Fathers and Their Families*, by Stanley H. Cath, Alan Gurwitt and Linda Gunsberg, eds. Copyright©1989The Analytic Press. *Harvard University Press:* Excerpt from *Abortion and Divorce in Western Law* by Mary Ann Glendon. Copyright©1987 by Mary Ann Glendon.

Library of Congress Cataloging-in-Publication Data

Wassil-Grimm, Claudette.
Where's daddy : how divorced, single, and widowed mothers can provide what's missing when dad's missing / Claudette Wassil-Grimm.
p.   cm.
Includes bibliographical references.
1. Single mothers.   2. Fatherless family.   3. Father and child.
4. Children of single parents.   I. Title.
HQ759.912.W37   1994
306.85'6 – dc20
Design by Bernard Schleifer
Typeset by AeroType, Inc.
ISBN: 0-87951-541-4
135798642
First Edition

Contents

Acknowledgments

I want to express my gratitude to the friends and professionals who advised and supported me through the writing of this book.

First, I am grateful to the many interviewees who shared their personal stories and struggles. I wish them and their children all the good fortune they deserve.

Thank you to my friends Anita Lampel, Ph.D. whose suggestions helped me to shape the content of the book, Virginia Webster who helped me find interviewees in an area new to me, Dick Croy for his enthusiasm at crucial points, my personal editor Kristin Payson who served as my "second brain" so that I could finish the book quickly, and to my assistant Maureen Olander who energetically took care of last minute details.

Special thanks go to my editor Tracy Carns at Overlook Press for believing in the book, to my agent Meredith Bernstein who saw me through a difficult last minute transition, and to my husband Andy, my three stepsons Peter, Tad and Jonathan, their mother Susan, and my son Jerzy for teaching me about the effect that fathers, and their absence, have on their children's lives.

AUTHOR'S NOTE

All the stories presented in this book are drawn from real individual's lives. The names and identifying characteristics have been changed in order to protect their privacy.

PART I

1

The Role of the Father

In the last forty years, many women have made a historic shift, into the economy. Now it is time for a whole generation of men to make a second historic shift—into work at home.

ARLIE HOCHSCHILD, *THE SECOND SHIFT* [1]

Bo Jackson, star running back for the Los Angeles Raiders, walks triumphantly off the field, scoops up his two small sons and whirls them around in the air. He has just scored a touchdown, and his sons are privileged to sit on the players' bench to watch their father play. The commentator tells us that Bo had little relationship with his own father, and he wants his sons to know him. At several points in the game the camera focuses on Bo and his sons affectionately sharing the joy of the Raiders' certain victory. Like many of the super-fathers receiving heavy media attention, Bo is reacting to his childhood pain and trying to do better as a father than his "absent" father had done.

Newspapers and magazines abound with these accounts of both celebrities and average men taking fatherhood seriously and trying to rise above old stereotypes. Yet, contrary to the current hyped-up media image of the "new father"—who not only burps baby but actually changes the diapers—the vast majority of fathers in our culture are still very uninvolved with their children. Statistics show that about half of children growing up today will live in single-parent families at some time during their childhoods, and 90 percent of the time, mothers have custody and are still the primary caretakers. The time that men (age 20–49) spend in families with young children has dropped from an average of twelve years in 1960 to seven years in 1980.[2]

The Sad Statistics

- Today's average father will spend only seven years living in the same household as his children.[3]
- 66 percent of non-custodial fathers see their children less than once a month.[4]
- 50 percent of non-custodial fathers visit their children less than once a year (and many not at all).[5]
- 52 percent of fathers do not pay their court-ordered child support.[6]
- There were eight times as many children born out of wedlock in 1990 as there were in 1970.[7]
- When a child's father dies, there is a 40 percent chance the child will become clinically depressed.[8]

A father's absence can have an important impact on children's lives, and many men have neglected their duties as fathers. Many have not only failed to help support their children, they have failed to be part of their lives. The mothers of these children are justifiably angry, and many are genuinely concerned about the effect this will have on their children. Widows also worry about the loss of a father in their children's lives, while like all single mothers, they are struggling with new financial and emotional challenges suddenly thrust on them by their husband's death. Father-absence is a serious problem affecting more than half of the children growing up today.

Mothers whose children have been abandoned either physically or emotionally by their fathers are wondering how to intervene and lessen the damage. Fathers who have been all too absent and want to re-connect with their children are looking for guidance. Today's parents want to know what essential elements fathers provide for children. In their search, they look for answers to some very concrete variables.

How much time do children need to spend with their fathers? What activities form and strengthen a father-child bond? How is fathering different from mothering, and what do children get from their fathers that no one else can provide? Can a child who has no father grow up to be healthy and well-adjusted? What factors can compensate for a father who is absent due to death, divorce, desertion, or disinterest? What do mothers do to aggravate the distance between father and child, and what can they do to bring child and father together? How does a father in this generation need to be different from even a good father of the last generation? How does our relationship with each of our own fathers affect how we father or help our mates father? This book seeks to answer these questions. Through interviews with divorced parents and widowed and unwed mothers, I have tried to learn what are the most profound effects of a father's absence and what mothers and estranged fathers can do to halt or repair the damage.

RESPONSES TO DAD'S ABSENCE

As we know, fathers are absent through a variety of causes: divorce, death, or physical or emotional abandonment. How and why a father is absent will have an impact on the emotional and material outcome for the child. How much the father's absence is felt is a complex issue affected not only by the father/child circumstances but also by the father's personality and personal priorities. A child whose father is living nearby but who never chooses to visit him will have a greater sense of personal rejection than a child whose father has died. A child whose father lives at home but is always away on business or spends his evenings down at the office may feel more abandoned than a child whose father lives three states away, due to divorce, but sends for the child twice a year and enthusiastically spends every minute of the day with the child for two weeks. Despite these variables, children with an absent father share some common experiences and exhibit similar predictable reactions of which we should be aware.

Signs of Distress in Children Without Fathers

1. Boys are often reluctant to engage in rough-and-tumble play and have difficulty making friends with other boys.
2. Girls tend to be either very shy around men or excessively flirtatious.

3. Both boys and girls are likely to have impaired academic performances and other school problems.
4. Boys often exhibit antisocial behavior and poor self-control.

Troublesome Attitudes

1. Children blame themselves for the father's absence and suffer from low self-worth as a result.
2. Children become hypercritical of the mother and idealize the absent father.
3. Children waste time pining for the imaginary "better life" they believe they would have had instead of *actively* trying to solve their personal problems.

Studies show that when both parents are very involved with their children, those children have more advanced cognitive development, are more empathetic, have less stereotyped beliefs and more self-control. The involvement of the father in these studies was not measured strictly by the number of hours spent with the child; rather, what the father did with the child and how he felt about being with the child was significant.[9]

POST-DIVORCE PROBLEMS

Many fathers without custody stop seeing their children two or three years after the divorce, behaving as though their relationship with their children lasted only as long as their relationship with the children's mother. A ten-year study (1976–1987) by Frank Furstenberg and Kathleen Mullan Harris of the University of Pennsylvania followed a sample of 1,000 children from disrupted homes all over the nation who were representative of our nation's children in race, income, and education. More than half of these children had never been in their fathers' homes, and 42 percent had not seen their fathers at all in the previous year. Only 20 percent had slept at the father's house as much as once a month, and just 12 percent had seen their fathers once a week or more.[10]

A 1981 National Survey of Children confirmed these trends and showed that frequency of visitation also decreased considerably over time. Only one-third of children in families that had been divorced for ten years had seen their fathers in the last year.[11] These studies indicated that a vast number of fathers who did not have custody of their children certainly felt a weakening of emotional bonds.

Fathers also fail to be there for their children in terms of financial support. A 1985 Bureau of the Census survey showed that only 48 percent of mothers who were supposed to receive child-support payments reported receiving the full amount. Though an additional 26 percent did receive partial payment, another 26 percent had received nothing.[12] That's pretty uninvolved.

Carmen has not seen her father for fifteen years, since he divorced her mother when Carmen was five, and moved out West to avoid paying child support. Her memories of him are scant. She knows she must have cared about him at some point in her early childhood since she can recall hiding behind the door when he came home from work so she could jump out and surprise him. However, most of her recollections are of her father beating her mother. She has been told that the father was also abusive to her, but she has blocked out these memories.

This is not a simple case of poor memory. She recalls, in vivid detail, sitting with her great-grandfather who would read to her from the encyclopedia and exclaim over how bright she was. Her great-grandfather died when Carmen was three years old, and the father left when she was five. Therefore, Carmen must be using selective memory as a defense against painful remembrances of time with her father.

Twice in the past fifteen years her father called unexpectedly. When Carmen was about eight years old, the father called and asked if the children could be sent to him for a Christmas visit. The mother was furious with him for his years of neglect and flatly refused. The second time, Carmen's younger sister answered the phone and cursed at the father before hanging up.

When Carmen was graduating high school, she went to her father's parents and asked if they had his address so that she could send him a graduation announcement. The grandparents did not want her to have the address but said if she left the card they would mail it to him. She received no response to her graduation announcement until a year later, when her father's new wife wrote back and told her they would like to get to know Carmen and encouraged her to write. However, there was no address in the letter or on the envelope.

Right now, Carmen's mother is trying to track down the father for back child support. Carmen, who has always been a very good student, has had to drop out of college. After two years at a state university, she owes $15,000 in student loans and has had to stop and work full-time. Carmen has gone as far as she can go on state support. She could sorely use the financial backing of a father right now.

Carmen's plight and childhood experience are common among many children of divorce. Old, weak laws and poor interstate agreements have allowed many fathers to skip out on child support. Those who did support their children through the mandatory first eighteen years have been anxious to end their obligation at the time of "emancipation," and even many upper-middle-class fathers have not concerned themselves with financing their children's further education. Shame and embarrassment over their financial neglect of their children often causes many fathers to withdraw totally.

In most situations, children with an absent parent strive to find some explanation for the loss. Many children blame themselves, remembering every criticism or correction the absent parent ever made and focusing on the long list of their childish failings. For these children, the loss of the parent is not just measured in hours of shared pleasures that will be missed. Instead, the loss is seen as a judgment for all the wrongs they have done. When the absent parent reinforces this self-critical fantasy by rarely visiting the child, the child's self-esteem is reduced to ashes and his fear of abandonment is so great that he clings fearfully to the remaining parent.

EMOTIONAL ABANDONMENT

But it is not just the divorced father who withdraws from his children; for more than one generation we have seen fathers emotionally abandon their families as they become overcommitted to work. Recent studies show that although mothers who work full-time manage to spend an average of fifty minutes each weekday devoting exclusive attention to the kids, men who work full-time only average about twelve minutes a day with their children. Most men and women parenting today have no clear idea what fathers are supposed to do since their own fathers were rarely available. In the 1950s and 1960s, "business" fathers of the middle class worked ever longer hours to keep up with their peers, while working-class fathers "worked hard all day" and wanted to "relax" when they got home. The latter often meant Dad in front of the TV nursing a beer while the kids were instructed to be quiet and leave him alone.

My own father, who remained with my mother until his death, was "absent" from the beginning. He had grown up without a father and felt that he had "turned out just fine" so we didn't need one. He didn't even pretend to father us and was terrified of the pain intimacy could bring since both of his parents had died by the time he was five years old. He was a shadow in the house, so absent from any family interaction that I never even mentioned him to my school friends. In high school, when it was my turn to host a club meeting at my home, one of my classmates (whom I had known for several years) said she was surprised to see that I had a father—she had always assumed he was dead because I had never mentioned him. It was always "My mother told me . . ." or "My mother took me . . ." or "My mother asked me . . .". Never a word about my father.

I have found that many adults my age tell similar stories about their fathers' level of involvement. Therefore, many men today have only vague, confused notions of what a father should do as a parent. For generations, men have not spent much time in the home involving themselves with children. They have lost touch with children's needs and abilities. They have lost the knowledge that comes from close contact.

SOCIALIZATION FOR PARENTHOOD

Some interviews conducted by Dr. Mary-Joan Gerson, director of the New York University Psychology Clinic, reveal a great deal about men's socialization for parenthood. Men and women were asked to imagine a future child they might have and describe the child. First of all, many men had difficulty with the task, and the scenarios that finally emerged stressed a teaching or didactic function of fatherhood. While most women respondents thought first of an infant, less than half of the men pictured a child under age four. When the men did think of babies, they did not picture them as needy or dependent. Their children were most often described as being "his own person." Women seldom named the gender of the child they were describing, but men most often described boys. The men's scenarios surrounding the children were often problem-free, while the women's descriptions were more complex with conflicts and dilemmas.

When the men were asked to try to imagine the worst time of fatherhood, they pictured needing to discipline their children and worried about whether or not they could control them. The potential fathers wanted the children to be like them, while the potential mothers named important others for the children to model or felt the children should simply be themselves. The men expressed confidence that they would be good fathers some day (better than their own had been), but the mothers were anxious about being good mothers. Although the men seemed more confident in general, their fantasies were less realistic than the women's. Men generally pictured themselves playing the traditional roles of educator or disciplinarian, and had no fantasies that modeled the kind of nurturing, involved father they are expected to be today.[13] During her interviews with families, Arlie Hochschild, author of *The Second Shift*, asked fathers what they felt their role was with their children. The least involved fathers (and most of the fathers she interviewed had little involvement with their children) said they felt fathers should discipline and teach about sports, current events, or cars, or described "good fathers" as men who were "around." Despite their vague descriptions of fathering, these same men had no difficulty describing the role of the mother in great detail. According to these men "good mothers" were patient, warm, caring, physically attentive, intellectually stimulating, and emotionally supportive. As we can see, it is not that men don't know what children need or what "parents" should do, they just could not relate these traits to their own roles or responsibilities. They often drew on the images of their own absent fathers in their search.[14] For many men parenting now, fathers were the parent who left in the morning, came home for dinner, and then sat and watched TV. That's not much to go on.

Although this book will deal primarily with the effects on children of non-resident fathers and look for ways to involve or find substitutes for divorced, separated, or deceased fathers, I will include information on fathers in intact families throughout for the purpose of comparison. For father-absence is not a problem of divorce per se. Rather, it is an *attitude* or cultural phenomenon affecting many fathers in America, whether separated from their children or living in intact families. Sometimes divorce is just a legal acknowledgment of a father's abandonment. Many fathers become overcommitted to work and show no interest in their children for years before the mothers finally decide to divorce.

Linda first noticed her husband's extreme emotional absence when her children were both under five, and her father died. It was a very stressful time for her, and she remembers that her husband would not even take off work for the funeral.

"George never had time to talk. First he was too busy with graduate school, then he was too busy with his job. He never ate dinner with us. He would get home about 8 or 9 at night. He travelled a lot. In January and February of each year he was gone for the whole two months and the rest of the time he was gone for a few days every week. He never even had time to give me his travel schedule. His secretary used to *mail* it to me! If we went on vacation George usually took along a briefcase full of work and would call in to the office.

"George never played catch with Gary and so Gary never got interested in sports. The kids played in the band like I had, but their dad didn't think it was anything important to go see. In all the years they played, he only went once or twice. For years it was just the kids and me.

"I felt like we should join a church as a family but I could never get George to go. So I just went ahead and joined with the kids myself. In fifteen years he never went with us except maybe for Easter. He felt put out when I asked him to come the Sunday I was accepted into membership. We've been divorced for almost two years, but someone at church just asked me last Sunday where my husband was, because it was Easter. They hadn't noticed my husband wasn't around, because he had never been around.

"Since George never wanted to talk I usually waited until things were at a crisis level before I would tell him about anything. Then when I would say we needed to talk, he would roll his eyes like it was this great imposition. We only talked if there was a problem. We never sat down and talked about our day.

"When George got his computer, he stopped staying long hours at the office and just came home and worked on the computer. He was here, but we saw no more of him. I don't feel like I ever had a husband, nor the kids a father. I had probably grieved over the marriage for five years before we actually got divorced.

"So when George got notice of a transfer, I just decided not to go with him. My friends were my support system. I didn't want to go off and start all over with no one for company but him. Now that we're divorced he's still working long hours, but he calls the kids. They actually feel like they have a father now. He's helping them with their college expenses. My daughter has told me that he is so different on the phone. I guess it's the loneliness."

FATHER AS CARETAKER

Psychological researchers Michael Lamb and David Oppenheim agree that the much acclaimed "new father" presented by the media is still largely a fiction. They looked at studies done on fatherhood during the 1980s and focused on the question, "What does the average American father do, and how has that changed over the last several years?" Here are some trends they discovered.

Fathers and mothers still parent quite differently, with the largest discrepancy being in the area of responsibility. In the vast majority of cases, mothers still take primary responsibility for the child. When fathers do help out, they depend on the mothers to tell them what the child needs them to do. Although fathers appear more actively involved with the children in dual- career families, one study showed that fathers whose wives are employed do not spend any more time with their children than fathers whose wives are home all day with the children. Instead, the children simply have less time with their mothers, thus somewhat equalizing the time children of dual-career parents spend with each parent. A comparison of working men and women shows that when men have leisure time they most often choose to spend it in some personal pursuit such as golf, whereas working mothers usually spend their leisure time in activities that involve their children.[15]

So, it is not just children of divorced or bereaved families who suffer from father-absence. For the divorced mother it may be some comfort to know that even if she had stayed married to her child's father, that child might not see very much of Dad anyway. As we have seen, some fathers wake up to the importance of their children only after they have lost them through divorce. In some families I interviewed, particularly the joint-custody families in California, the fathers typically spent one or two nights a week plus every other weekend with their children, devoting their full attention to the kids during the visitation. Not many fathers in intact families do this. Of course, just as joint custody is still the exception, divorced fathers who see their children frequently are still in the minority.

AN HISTORICAL VIEW

Have men always played such a distant role in their children's lives? History tells us no. In colonial America children were nurtured by their mothers until they were about three years old—when they could reason—and then were turned over to their fathers for their education. The father would teach his children to read and write and later taught his sons his trade. But the Industrial Revolution created a division between work and home, and the division of male and female responsibilities became very rigid. The father was no longer at home so all work there (which included nearly all child-rearing tasks) became the domain of the mother. While women were home with the children learning to form emotional ties, men's new economic roles took them out of the home and curtailed their day-to-day contact with their children.[16]

Father no longer had time to be the teacher and moral leader of his family, although he often kept the unsavory role of disciplinarian. ("Wait till your father gets home!") The father then had to depend on his job to bring him status—how much he earned and what position he held were the measures of his worth. To bolster his own ego, he felt he had to devote more and more time to his economic role. And as he spent less and less time at home, the emotional family door closed on him.

To grasp the magnitude of the father's changing role in the family, it is helpful to look at changing custody practices from the 1700s to the present. During colonial times, and on through to the middle of the nineteenth century, the father was automatically awarded custody of the children in the event of a divorce. But by the late 1800s, due to the changes in the family caused by the Industrial Revolution, custody was automatically granted to the mother. Because of the new roles demanded of fathers in the changed economic system, they had become estranged from their children and, at that point, had lost the skills and bonds that make good parents.

Men had been doing what society expected of them when they retreated into the breadwinner role. Then when divorce became the norm and judges automatically awarded the children to the mothers, most fathers passively accepted their new designation as non-parents. *Just as women were shut out of the marketplace, never yet to gain equal status with men, fathers were shut out of the family.*

It is the oddballs—the fathers who had strong feelings for their children and were enraged at their loss—who have upset that social norm and initiated change. In California, where joint custody has become the rule, some women confessed they would rather give up the father's financial support in order to regain more control over their children. Many custodial mothers in states where joint custody is practically outlawed want to have total control over the children while the father pays the bills. In response, fathers seem to be saying, "If the children *belong* to her, why shouldn't *she* pay for them?" Each side has tried to deny the complexity of these social changes and their inevitable consequences. Meanwhile, the welfare of the child has gotten lost in the shuffle.

CHANGE ON THE HORIZON

For the present, women seem to be carrying most of the burden for children emotionally, financially, and physically. They are getting tired, and that makes a qualitative difference in everyone's life. Remember the old traditional family where Mom was waiting at the door to pamper Dad at the end of his hard work day? What happens to mothers who are now playing breadwinners? Moms come home just as exhausted and burnt out from their full-time jobs as dads do. It is nearly impossible for many moms to give their children the special attention they need to feel loved and important or to work through a childhood crisis.

But there is an alternative. Men and women can each work toward becoming whole people. They can share all the responsibilities and all the rewards. Women have been headed in that direction since feminism gained strength in the 1970s. They have been the catalyst for many great changes in the family. The initial stages have been rough. Divorce, to a large degree, has exemplified men's unwillingness to change and women putting their feet down. So women, seeking some of men's power, have begun to take over male roles and responsibilities. Now men, wanting some of women's satisfactions, are beginning to become more androgynous too. The fathers who are winning back a place in the family are not just tough and assertive (traditionally masculine traits) but are also sensitive and empathic (traditional female traits).

James E. Levine, the founder of the Fatherhood Project, who has been studying the changing family role of men since 1973, admits that the case of the new father is overstated in the media, but he points toward a number of indisputable and remarkable changes that have taken place. Perhaps most striking is the fact that twenty years ago less than 10 percent of men were present at the births of their children, while today the number is over 90 percent. Men have also begun to take off from work following the births of their children (30 percent of the Fortune 1000 companies now offer paternal leave, although only 1.3 percent of fathers actually take it). The visibility of men dropping off and picking up their children at childcare, the increase of men in pediatricians' offices and parenting classes, and the installation of baby changing tables in the men's rooms of airports and rest stops also attest to the changes finally taking place in men's behavior toward their children. "We are seeing an evolution, not a revolution," states Levine. "It is a mistake to overdramatize the new fatherhood, but it is also a mistake to say that men are acting the way they always have."[17]

WHAT WE HAVE LEARNED FROM DIVORCE

Divorce is not the only cause of a father's absence, but the circumstance of divorce is an important source of information for all parents concerned with a father's absence. Though we will be looking at how a father's death affects children and the problems of the child of unwed parents, many of the problems that arise when a father is absent due to divorce are common to all children who do not have a father living in the home. Regardless of their personal position, readers can learn something useful in all the chapters of this book. However, I highlight the problems of fatherhood and divorce since this is a problem that affects about half of the children growing up today. Divorce has never been so widespread, and there are no role models for parents or lawmakers to follow. We have been making it up as we go along, and we have made our share of mistakes.

When "divorce fever" broke out in the 1970s, our lawmakers were not prepared to anticipate the complex consequences of divorce in a "liberated" society. Most states were too shortsighted to consider the needs of the children in the years following divorce. Women were often left with too little money to raise the children even when child-support was awarded and paid; and lawmakers had not thought ahead to how they would respond to men not paying their court-ordered support. Until the mid-1980s, many men were easily able to avoid paying support. This pernicious "freedom" also allowed many men to avoid remembering they had children at all.

Beginning in the 1970s, it was a time for women to become aggressive and militant in order to defend and represent the needs of their children. The efforts of feminists to bring this shame to the nation's attention began paying off in the 1980s when laws were passed that made child support more equitable and collectible. It is far more difficult today for a man to default on child support. Children are beginning to get money from absent fathers on a more regular basis.

But men cannot be legislated or threatened into *caring* about their children. What can we do to encourage fathers to spend more *time* with their children? How can we support the forming of a bond between father and child? This type of concern calls for a different mode of action.

Behavior always has a cause, and when we begin to understand what has caused a behavior, we can begin to change it. It is an oversimplification to imagine that so many men have neglected their children because they are cold-hearted and selfish. Summing up men's behavior this way does not lead us toward a solution. Railing at Daddy's irresponsibility will not bring him back into his children's lives. Another way must be found.

I have interviewed more than fifty families to try to discover what causes some dads to lose contact with their children as well as what inspires others to maintain or renew their emotional bonds. I was interested in both understanding fathers' behaviors and discovering if there were ways to change them. In my search I have found a number of success stories that can teach us a great deal.

Negotiation and bridge-building between two polarized parties calls for sincere conflict-resolution efforts. The first step we need to take is to understand the fathers' feelings, motives, and needs. The second step is to examine with an open heart and mind how women change their own behavior so that they can further the father/child relationship. This takes the ability to let go of past angers and be truly open to new approaches.

At points in this book I may seem to sympathize with men too much. I show what is happening for them emotionally that causes them to abandon their children. I may look like I am making excuses for them. I am not. Their neglect of their children is wrong. But we all change more easily when we understand what has been pushing us to behave destructively. I offer these explanations and stories to the reader so that men can better understand the feelings they have blocked, and so that women can see the *whole picture* and act accordingly.

I have tried to be neutral, to take no side except perhaps the children's. Unfortunately, whenever we approach a controversial subject we find people locked into opposing positions, each blocking out any sympathy for the other side. This is a *stage* in problem-solving that is sometimes necessary. Often when we need to initiate change, if we consider both sides of an issue fully, we can become paralyzed. Generals know this. They don't encourage soldiers to think about the families of the enemy. Football coaches know this. Those who would move us to political action know this.

As I showed earlier drafts of this book to sample readers, some men found my chapters on obtaining child support too strident, while some women found my passages explaining men's behavior to be "too easy" on the men. I found that by attempting to be neutral, I had offended both sides. For these people, if I was not with them, I was against them.

However, I believe that in our heart of hearts we all know that there are two sides to every issue. When we wish to build relationships between human beings, we must allow ourselves to consider fully what all people in the situation are feeling. This is far more difficult and painful than naming one side good and the other side bad.

I am calling on you all to be your wisest selves as you read this book. Put the best interests of your children above all else.

SUMMARY POINTS

- Contrary to the current hyped-up media image of the "new father," the majority of fathers in our culture are still very uninvolved with their children.
- Studies show that when *both* parents are very involved with their children, those children have more advanced cognitive development, are more empathetic, have less stereotyped beliefs and more self-control.
- The rejected children of divorce do not just experience the lost hours of shared pleasures, they see Dad's rejection as a judgment for all the wrongs they have done.
- Studies show that men generally picture themselves playing the educator or disciplinarian but have had few models of the kind, nurturing father they are expected to be today.
- Father-absence is not a problem of divorce per se; uninvolved fathers are the cultural norm, and the laws governing custody show that fathers are expected to be uninvolved.
- In most families, mothers still take primary responsibility for the children; when fathers do help out, they wait for the mothers to tell them what to do.
- Since the Industrial Revolution, most men have been out at their jobs losing their day-to-day contact with their children, while most women remained at home with the children learning to form emotional ties. Fathers were effectively shut out of the family.
- In order to reverse the trend of father-absence, we must consider fully what men are experiencing and proactively create a change in societal attitudes and "rules of conduct" that allows men's greater involvement in childrearing.

2

Why Don't Dads
Get Involved?

"I remember my closest friend told me my son would be better off if I forgot about him and got out of his life entirely. I think the best thing I ever did was to ignore that advice."

— A DIVORCED DAD

When we learn that 50 percent of men without custody virtually stop seeing their children two or three years after divorce[1] and 26 percent avoid paying any child support,[2] we wonder what kind of monsters men are that they could have so little feeling for their own offspring. It calls up all our self-righteous indignation, and we can't help feeling that women are morally superior. But this reaction ignores the complexities behind men's feelings. We are a generation coping with a new phenomenon. Divorced dads are operating without role models, and many men have made short-term decisions that they regretted in the long run. Regardless, the children of divorce who have had to endure Dad's indifference feel deeply rejected.

Debbie was eight when her parents divorced, and her sister was three.

"At first we used to talk to him on the phone a lot, but then he began calling less and less. He never knew what to say to my little sister because he never really knew her. He used to talk to me first and then ask me what he should talk to her about.

"Then I began to realize we were usually the ones calling him. I decided not to call him anymore and see how long it took him to call me, and I noticed that it took him four months.

"When he lost his job he couldn't afford to come see me or to pay our plane fares for us to go see him. Up until last Thanksgiving, when I started college near him, I had only seen him once in three years. He had come out the night of my high school graduation. He was only here for a day. When I went to pick him up for the graduation, my sister came with me and he said to me, 'Why don't you introduce me to your friend?' My sister was so hurt that he didn't even recognize her. I lost a lot of respect for him at that point and I've only just recently forgiven him."

There is no simple answer to why many divorced men show little interest in their children, stop seeing them entirely, or fail to support them financially. If we wish to change this pattern, we must open ourselves to understanding the forces that cause men to lose contact. It is not a simple matter of men's callousness or moral inferiority. As Debbie goes on with her story, we realize that the distancing breeds on both sides until that delicate thread of contact is broken.

"Part of the distance was me too. I never knew what to say to him as I was getting older. Like when I first got my period, I never said anything to him, but then my mother mentioned it in a telephone conversation and my father was really hurt that I hadn't shared that with him. Also, about that time I was getting really close to my mom's boyfriend because we had been living with him for about five years."

When stepfathers enter the scene, many fathers think that the children are better off. Some feel shut out, and others pull away gladly, relieved that some other man has taken over their burden. But this is only one of the many factors that can contribute to men distancing themselves from their children.

Many men have very deep feelings of love toward their children, but even that does not mean they will stay in touch with them. Fathers frequently complain that their ex-wives make visitation with their children difficult. In a study of 560 divorced parents, researcher Julie Fulton found that nearly 40 percent of the mothers with custody had refused to permit their ex-husbands to see their children at least once, and their reasons for denying visitation had nothing to do with "the children's health, safety, or wishes." Fulton observes, "Custodial parents are attempting to make a new life for themselves and their children, and many of their decisions and actions serve to keep the other parent at a distance."[3]

Fathers also experience the pain of being the "occasional" parent who feels he has little control over the children's lives; the guilt over failing the children that damages his self-esteem to the point that he comes to feel the kids are better off not seeing him; and the residual conflict from the marriage that must be struggled through whenever there is contact with the ex-spouse. Other fathers may have been brought up with the culturally trained macho belief that children are women's work and women's concern and are having trouble changing this belief. In this chapter we will explore all these causes—pain, conflict, feelings of inadequacy, and indifference—and raise our awareness to the male's viewpoint in divorce in an effort to sort out what we can and cannot change.

PAIN

David and his wife had agreed that they would start a family before his wife turned thirty-three, the age of declining fertility, but when Miriam reached her early thirties she expressed hesitance about becoming pregnant. She was very successful in her career and had become very active in a lot of social and civic activities while David was very busy with graduate school. She had been finding all this so satisfying that at that point she was considering not having children. This was a shock to David, and he couldn't hide his feelings of deep disappointment. Miriam gave in and became pregnant.

For many years David had pictured himself in an armchair with several small children wiggling on his lap and snuggling up against him. He was the father of many in his dreams. Most men I have interviewed across the years, some of whom turned out to be very loving and conscientious fathers, have not had any fantasies about fatherhood until their wives were pregnant, and even then, many fathers had no fantasies about children at all.

So David began fatherhood with an exceptionally strong desire to have a child. When Ben was an infant, David was very active in his care—changing diapers and doing whatever needed to be done. However, David had traditional ideas about mothers and children and had hoped Miriam would want to spend a few years at home. Consequently, he was upset when his wife went back to work full-time, without even discussing it with him, when Ben was just a few months old. He felt it was bad for Ben, and this caused a lot of tension. "I felt helpless and really shut out of things. There was nothing I could do about her working and the way I believed it affected my son. I felt sad that Ben was missing the experience of having a mother at home with him." Part of David's fantasy of fatherhood included a mom at home taking care of the child during the daytime. (As he looks back now he feels that Ben was in good quality daycare, and the experience was not harmful.) David would have been an ideal candidate for a stay-at-home dad, since his wife was so dedicated to career, and childcare was a higher priority for him. However, at that time in the early 1970s, fathers who stayed home with kids were considered failures, and mothers who would let fathers be caretakers were considered cold and rejecting. It never occurred to David and Miriam to go against social mores. Instead, they resolved their differences in a more socially accepted way: they divorced when Ben was two years old.

Miriam found herself a job one hundred miles away and took the son and left. In their parting conversation David remembers telling her that he would insist on being part of Ben's life, and she said, "I might move to Alaska or California. I don't know where we'll go." David felt threatened by this statement and backed off to keep the peace. David wanted his son, but this was 1975, and his lawyer told him that he did not have a chance at custody. David related,

> "When I was first separated from Ben I couldn't bear to date anyone with children. I tried it but when I would see someone else with their kids I would get all choked up. I just missed Ben so much. I was grieving for him.
>
> "I remember my closest friend had gotten divorced and he told me that Ben would be better off if I forgot about him and got out of his life entirely. But I couldn't bear to do that. I think the best thing I ever did was to ignore that advice."

Fifteen years ago, getting out of the child's life was considered by many to be the right thing to do. Even recent books on fatherhood recommend that "good fathers" will drop out of the child's life rather than keep a conflict going if the mother resists the father's efforts to see the child. Albert J. Solnit, professor of pediatrics and psychiatry at Yale University School of Medicine, compares joint-custody practices to Solomon's decision to split a child in two and give half to each of the mothers that claimed him. He applauds the father of one of his clients for giving up the battle to keep his visitation rights.

> "In one instance, a father was given liberal visitation rights by the court, but the mother hated the visits and ordered her ten-year-old daughter, Jane, to refuse to visit.
> . . . "Jane's father was not an angel. He was furious with his former wife but realized that his wishes to litigate, to gain revenge, to bring about visits as ordered by the court—to win a Pyrrhic victory—would have created a huge psychological burden, possibly a trauma, for Jane."[4]

I was once guilty of this thinking myself. I have been married to a "divorced dad" for the past sixteen years and have watched him struggle with this uncharted territory since his youngest child (who is now a junior in college) was preschool age. Many of those years were difficult for me as a stepmother, but truly wrenching for him as a non-custodial father. I have seen the pain of my stepchildren, the struggle of their mother, and the agony and confusion of their father. Although I certainly have lost my objectivity at times, of all the players I probably have the most balanced view of this family drama, which is representative of the one many in our generation are creating extemporaneously.

Shortly after we married, my husband was transferred out of state to a military installation one thousand miles away from his children. He was financially strained by the divorce, and I was a full-time student (financed by money I'd saved before the marriage). It was very hard for us to afford plane tickets for his children twice a year as his divorce contract allowed, but most years we managed it by making a lot of personal sacrifices. Though he couldn't get custody of his children, his ex-wife had tried to be generous by designating that he could have them for their entire summer vacation each year. However, I limited the summer visit to a couple of weeks because we had only a one-bedroom apartment, a very small space for two parents and three boys under age nine. And, I must add, my husband expected me to care for the children while he continued to work, their visit notwithstanding. If my husband had not remarried, summer-long visits would have posed even greater difficulties. Childcare, when it existed, had long waiting lists an occasional parent couldn't access, and he could not have taken summers off from work.

My husband was not a very competent parent but he was a very enthusiastic father, and he loved his children with a passion. He mourned them deeply that first year, often weeping inconsolably. He had constant nightmares about strangers stealing them and harming them. I tried to understand what he was going through, to comfort him, and to offer helpful advice. I stretched to remember what experience I had had that was comparable and how I had coped with it.

Like my husband who grieved for his children, I had mourned my brother and sister. I had been very close to them because I had the major responsibility for their daily care when I was an adolescent. Our parents were very dysfunctional and absent much of the time. My youngest brother was ten years younger than I and had actually called me Mommy when he was a baby. My sister was born when I was fourteen. My family was very troubled and living at home was killing me psychologically. On the advice of my college psychologist, I moved out when I was twenty-one. I feared for the well-being of my two siblings under twelve, and I felt tremendous guilt in leaving them. So much so that I eventually moved across the country to get away from my family and sort through my own emotional problems. I had no control over their lives anymore, and it was empty torment to be near them and helpless. I had as little chance of getting custody of them from my parents as my husband had of getting custody of his children (which he had wanted). In 1975, the courts awarded custody to the mother unless she was extremely unfit (which my husband's ex-wife was not).

Drawing on my similar experience, I gave him the best advice I could. Try to forget about them and get linked up with some kids who are here. Like many stepfathers who have become estranged from their own children, but take a very active interest in the children of their new mates, I'd adopted the philosophy of "Love the one you're with." I'd been a teacher when I first moved away from my siblings, and I had always "adopted" my students and taken them on outings.

This was very healing for me. I could do a lot for the children I took a special interest in, while I could do little about my brother and sister except stay in touch with them by phone and letter and visit once a year.

Emotionally, I distanced myself a great deal. This numbed the pain, a pain I couldn't live with on a daily basis. I had dated men who had tried to keep in close touch with their children and some who had not. The brutal reality was that the more distant divorced dads led calmer, less crazy lives and seemed to be in a lot less pain.

DISTANCING AND OTHER DEFENSES

Distancing is generally a good and healthy defense mechanism for dealing with highly charged emotional conflicts in which we have no power to change the circumstances. Although I'd been unusually attached to my brother and sister, the bond was still not as tight as a parent's. My husband had far greater difficulty distancing from his children, and his nightmares continued for years. One year, when we did not have money for their plane fares at Christmas, my husband fried with guilt and became very depressed. Those first few years were terrible for him. Then he did begin to pull away emotionally.

When we had our own child, he welcomed the chance to love the one he was with. It's simply much safer to be fiercely attached to someone you see every day. And it's much more rewarding to spend money on someone who is present, so you can see his face light up when you buy him new shoes, or get a hug when you take him out for ice cream. By contrast, though my husband never missed a single child-support payment in fifteen years, there was little joy in sending this money. It was like making the car payments on a very expensive car that someone else was driving and that you only got to borrow once or twice each year.

Add to that the fact that the person who gets to drive the car every day is someone you consider an "enemy"—the person who has perhaps hurt you more than anyone else in your life—and one can understand the resentment that many men feel. These complex factors all contribute to the ambivalence men feel about their children after divorce. I believe that most of this apparent "coldness" is a defense mechanism to ward off the depression and despair that men feel when they have so little control over their children's lives.

At the same time, I don't think this distancing is an exclusively "male" thing. I think it's a numbness that comes out of being the non-custodial parent. Women without custody often behave similarly. I interviewed women who have not seen their children in years, one because she had left them and dared not go back, another whose daughter had been "stolen" from her by her ex-husband while she was in the hospital recovering from a car accident. Both these mothers had learned the strategy of distancing. The latter, Marlene, had never had enough money to sue for the daughter's return.

"My daughter was five when I lost her and she just has no desire to see me now because she's been fed a line by my ex. I can't say what's said because I don't know. I'd left her father because he was messing around and he was in the military and gone nine months out of the year. I saw no need to stay married to him. I had my daughter early in the marriage and she'd always been with me because he was never around. But then when I left my husband, he all-of-a-sudden wanted her. He started visiting her on weekends, and then he got out of the service. Meanwhile I had hooked up with Bert and had Lenny. When I had my accident my ex came and took our daughter and then filed for custody. He could provide for her and I couldn't. Also, he had possession of her at that point, so he got her."

This is a California divorce that took place in the 1980s. Unlike many more conservative states, at that time, mothers in California had to show they had some means of supporting the kids or they stood a good chance of losing them. There was no assumption that Mom would get the kids and Dad would provide the funds. Often the one with the biggest paycheck got the kids, both because the high-earner could provide more materially, and undeniably, because the richer one could afford to pay more for a lawyer, and go on fighting until he had his way.

"It's been three years since I've seen her. I just can't afford to send for her, and now he and his new wife say she doesn't want to see me. My daughter's fine, she's healthy, my ex is a great father now. I've sent her cards but I don't think he gives them to her."

Though Geoffrey Greif and Mary Pabst in their book *Mothers Without Custody* report that non-custodial mothers, as a group, were more faithful to their children than non-custodial fathers, 44 percent of the mothers reported that spending time with their children was very awkward and difficult for them. A large national survey showed that only 33 percent of non-custodial fathers continued to visit their children once a month or more, but 69 percent of non-custodial mothers were seeing their children that often. However, non-custodial mothers had many of the same complaints as non-custodial fathers. They often felt shut out by the lack of continuity in visitation with their children or by obstructive attitudes of the father. Mothers who had little involvement with their children felt guilty, but those who had the least involvement felt the least guilt. They had "let go" of their children without regret.[5]

SENSITIVITY HELPS

Marlene, the woman who lost her daughter above, later remarried and had a son, Lenny. She remained too financially strapped to seek her daughter and eventually left this husband who was out of work more than he was employed. But she was scrupulous about helping her son keep contact with his father. She and Lenny's father, Bert, have had a strong commitment not to keep each other away from Lenny, because both had "lost" their relationship with previous children. Bert had two children somewhere "up north." The mother had moved away with the children and failed to tell Bert where she was.

Marlene, because she had so unfairly been deprived of her daughter in her first marriage, had one of the most cooperative and accepting attitudes of any of the divorced women I interviewed. Her relationship with Lenny's father had always been stormy. They had separated seven times in seven years before they finally gave up on the relationship. But in custody matters, Marlene trusted Bert.

"We have no formal custody agreement for Lenny and we've never needed one. Wherever it's best for him to live at the time is where he goes. We've each been the parent who was cut out at some time. The parent the kid lives with has the most influence.

"I've never even asked him for child support. I wanted Lenny. During a fight I once told Bert that the only thing I wanted from him was that one little seed. And I got it."

Bert has not been the most enthusiastic father for Lenny. He showed little interest in him as an infant.

> "I think it's because he lost his other two so young and there was nothing he could do about it. He didn't want to get attached. But I just kept calling on Bert when I needed help. When Lenny gets to be too much for me I call up Bert and make him take him. I say, 'You deal with it for awhile.' Now he realizes that he's always going to see Lenny, so we're over that hurdle. Lenny knows both parents want him. When Lenny gets to be too much for him, or Bert and his new family are out of money and they can't afford his food, I'm ready to take Lenny back."

CONFLICT

The breaking up of a marriage is a time of great conflict. Most often one party instigates the divorce and the other spouse is shocked and angry. He or she feels wronged and abandoned. Even the spouse who wanted the divorce feels and expresses a lot of anger. The departing spouse may have initiated the divorce because of long-standing anger, or may be feeling guilty about wanting freedom from the marriage and therefore is trying to justify leaving by trumping up some "wrongs" to be angry about. Whether or not there is a lot of anger, there is still a lot of conflict as the two partners must negotiate both the division of property and the custody of the children. Throughout the complex negotiations both partners are in a lot of psychological pain over the death of the marriage.

Even the healthiest couples will go on experiencing a lot of anguish and conflictual feelings for eighteen to twenty-four months after the separation. (When the conflict lasts beyond twenty-four months, this is generally an indication that the conflict between the ex-spouses is unusually severe, and they should definitely seek counseling to help them become more accepting of the divorce and less antagonistic.) Two years is a large portion of childhood, and children are deeply affected by parental conflict. Indeed, divorce experts agree that the most damaging aspect of divorce is persistent conflict between the parents. Parents tend to pull the child into the conflict and pressure the child to take sides. This is a terrible emotional burden for the child, and children often begin to do poorly in school. Other immediate effects of living with their parents' ongoing conflict include temper tantrums, withdrawal, sleep disturbances, bed wetting, lying, and a lot of acting-out behavior during the period of transition at visitation time.

When Debbie was five her mother told her that her father had been having an affair. Debbie stated,

> "I didn't realize what a betrayal that was at the time, because I was so little, and now that I'm old enough to understand, it seems a little late to get mad at him."

This affair apparently prompted the talk of divorce that hung over the family for three years.

> "They used to fight a lot, and it was violent fighting. I would leave the house and go sit at the neighbors'.
>
> "After the divorce my mother would talk against my father all the time. There was a period of time when I stood up for him a lot, but it was horrible arguing with her. I think my mother's comments have really hurt my sister's relationship with my father because she never really knew him. She just knows what my mother says about him. My father never says anything bad about my mother. I told my mother that he never says anything and it isn't right that she slams him all the time, and my mother says, 'That's his choice.' I guess she thinks he doesn't say anything about her because she's perfect.
>
> "There have been a lot of times that I've felt angry at her for keeping me from my father. I've said to her, 'You demand so much loyalty that it ruins my relationship with my father.' Like, my mother got remarried and I'm not allowed to tell my father because she's afraid he'll stop sending the support check. I was in my mother's wedding and I was a bridesmaid and all that. When my father would call me I'd have to pretend that nothing was happening in my life. She's told me, 'If you tell him and he cuts off the support check, I'm going to be really angry.' And yet, I worry that my father will find out and then he'll wonder why I haven't told him. I feel really terrible. It's like being between a rock and a hard place."

As we will see later, the issue of money keeps coming up in Debbie's story. There are many conflicts over money when parents divorce. Indeed, this subject is so heated and complex I have devoted two whole chapters to it. In Chapter 10 we will look at how to make men financially responsible without involving the children in the battle. For now, we will explore other areas and aspects of conflict in divorce.

Debbie has gone to a college that is halfway between her parents' houses. She is now much closer to her father and can drive there in one day. This has ended their long period of separation. But the conflict between her parents is far from over.

Debbie told me that her father had strongly encouraged her to come for a visit, "He was really good about it, and he's already planning on me coming for next Thanksgiving. I may spend my Christmas vacation there." When Debbie visited with her father's new family for a long weekend, she got to know them for the first time. They had fixed up a guest room for her and told her that that was her room. They invited her to come live with them if she liked.

> "That would really upset my mother. She couldn't handle it. Loyalty is the number one most important thing in her life. She uses the word 'betray' a lot. I have to try to make her think things are her idea so that she thinks I'm being loyal to her by doing what she says. She'll say to me, 'If you want to spend Christmas with your father that's fine. We'll miss you, but if you'd rather be with your father . . .'" She says it's fine but it isn't really."

CHILDREN IN THE CROSSFIRE

Judith Wallerstein of the Center for the Family in Transition in Corte Madera, California, who has spent the last fifteen years following divorced families to study the effects of divorce, writes of ongoing conflict:

> The consequences are frequently tragic. The persistent quality of the conflict, combined with its enduring nature, seriously endangers the mental health of the parents and the psychological

development of their children. Ironically, under the guise of fighting for the child, these parents may succeed in inflicting severe emotional suffering on the very person whose protection and well-being is the presumed rationale for the battle. Moreover, as we have seen all too often, the conflict may erupt into child-stealing and violence that destroys lives.[6]

Unfortunately, children are often the best "tool" for inflicting pain on the ex-spouse. Parents frequently fight over visitation privileges, and visitation pick-up and delivery are often times of open conflict.

David, whom we met earlier, had "reasonable and seasonable" visitation rights as described in his divorce contract and a verbal agreement that he could have his son every other weekend. Holidays and summer vacations were split fifty/fifty. David told me, "I would drive two hundred miles round trip to pick Ben up and bring him back to my house on Friday nights, and then another two hundred miles to take him back again on Sunday." This visitation distance had been imposed on David at the time of their separation, when his ex-wife had decided to get a job one hundred miles away. Although David's ex-wife had been the one who relocated, she never offered to drive one way to facilitate visitation.

> "From the beginning I was insistent about being a part of Ben's life. About every two years my ex-wife would become uncooperative about my visitation and I would tell her that my lawyer would contact her if she persisted. Then she would be more cooperative again. For example, once I remember I was at her house at six o'clock to pick him up as always. There was no one home and my ex-wife had not said she would be late. It was nine o'clock by the time she got there and I had been worked up about it for hours. I was tempted to leave—with a kind of 'I'll show her!' attitude—but I realized Ben and I would be the losers so I stuck it out."

David felt these were her passive-aggressive attempts to get him to give up on visitation, but he would not allow himself to be discouraged.

> "I don't think she went out of her way to keep Ben and me apart but visitations were inconvenient for her at times and she

would want to cancel my weekend or keep him on a holiday that
we had agreed was mine. I know it wasn't always convenient for
her, but it wasn't convenient for me to drive one hundred miles to
see him, either. Convenient or not, I felt Ben needed to see me
and I needed to see him."

Though many divorcing spouses cool down after two years, much
damage has already been done in terms of making visitation a time of
intense negative feeling. Some dads, who have been driven off by a
mother's anger or who have avoided visitation because of the fear of
their own anger erupting into violence, have already lost touch
emotionally with their children. It is hard to bring them back. If
children are to have contact with their fathers after divorce, these
parental conflicts must be worked through, and dads may need to be
"invited" back into their children's lives by a more welcoming
mother after the conflict has cooled.

Wallerstein describes the children caught in this crossfire of
parental conflict as feeling very anxious and emotionally isolated as
they try to sort out how they can avoid taking sides in a conflict
between two parents who are so preoccupied with the conflict itself
that they forget about the emotional needs of their children. Though
it has had its rocky moments, David and Miriam's divorce has been
fairly low-conflict overall. As we listen to their son Ben, now sixteen
years old, we realize that even in the best of circumstances, kids feel
torn. Ben was nine years old when he and his mother moved to
Cincinnati an additional three hundred miles away from his father.
He recalled:

"Right before we moved it finally hit me that my mom and
dad weren't ever going to get back together again. It was a really
hard time for me. I didn't talk to my mom or dad about it. I would
talk to my friends, and my teachers noticed I was upset. I wasn't
doing as well on my schoolwork and I pulled into myself. My
teachers were really good about it. They let me know that a lot of
kids feel that way and they mostly just listened a lot."

Ben had other insights during this period that helped him cope
with his parents' ongoing conflict.

"I learned a long time ago not to let my parents put me in the
middle of their arguments. They would each give me messages

for each other which were often just hostile criticisms, and I would pass them along without realizing what I was doing. When I was about nine I began to realize what was happening, and I stopped passing along these messages.

"Sometimes my mom and dad tell me how much money they are each providing for me, and they had an argument about insurance a few years ago. I knew that whatever they decided, I'd be all right. I feel like in the end they'll always provide for me, so I just let them work it out themselves. If they are about to decide something that I wouldn't like, I'll get involved and give my opinion, but otherwise, I just stay out of it."

Ben has finally reached an age and a level of understanding about his parent's conflict that allows him to distance himself and not get emotionally caught up in their subtle tug-of-war. He is a good role model for other children caught between battling parents. Of course, it would be better if the parents did not put him in the middle in this way. We understand each parent's need to have the son recognize what each does for him financially. However, in their preoccupation with defending themselves, they have failed to notice that their child already comfortably believes they will both responsibly care for him. They are burdening the child with an unnecessary defense.

DESTRUCTIVE CHEERING SECTIONS

Unfortunately, custody disputes and bad feelings have often been provoked or supported by "external" participants, such as in-laws, new spouses, extended kin, counselors, and legal profession-als. This whole host of "others" usually mean well and are trying to be supportive of the parent, but they may do more harm than good. Janet R. Johnston and Linda Campbell, counselors and au-thors of the book *Impasses of Divorce*, explore the negative effects of these other parties as well as other factors that aggravate the con-flict between divorcing parents.[7] As Johnston and Campbell explain, these negatively biased "helpers" have usually only heard one dis-torted side of the story—often when the divorcing parent was most hurt and angry. Indeed, extended families can get so emo-tionally wrapped up in the conflict that the conflict sometimes grows to resemble tribal warfare! The mother or father who might otherwise be ready to "move on" emotionally becomes frozen in their most hateful stage by the encouragement of this negative cheering section.

Counselors and legal professionals who have had little contact with the other parent often have a lot of misconceptions. These professionals each have their own motivations and tasks in their relationships with their clients. As these professional agendas distract them, they are not necessarily focusing on what is best for the children involved. For example, therapists are trained to be supportive of their clients, and if they see a powerless, depressed, or abused spouse, they are likely to encourage an uncompromising aggressive stance that only prolongs post-divorce disputes. Or, to encourage a client to become more self-sufficient and detached, they may advise the client to avoid as much contact with the ex-spouse as possible. Though this kind of advice and support may be what is best for the divorcing parent, it may aggravate the distance and hostility between the parents or between the children and the non-custodial parent, and therefore be destructive for the children.

Lawyers are programmed to be even less helpful in "keeping the peace" between the divorcing parents. They are trained in adversarial approaches — in which one party is assumed to be the bad guy — and are predisposed to winning for their clients at any cost. Stories are common of lawyers advising men to ask for custody, whether or not they want it, because they can often get the ex-wife to settle for less money. Meanwhile, opposing counsel advises women to postpone the divorce or ask for more money than they actually want in a kind of open-market "bargaining" stance. Divorcing spouses who might want to negotiate are advised not to speak to each other about the matter because it will weaken their positions. Lawyers, paid by the hour, get richer as the conflict draws on, and less money is available to the children when the court battle finally ends.

Johnston and Campbell have even seen cases in which the lawyers were most preoccupied with beating the opposing counsel due to competitive feelings over previous lost court battles involving other clients. A lawyer who is distracted by other concerns (such as making his mark as a tough attorney) cannot focus adequate attention on the needs of the child. In all fairness, there is a new crop of lawyers that has had special training in mediation, child development, and new divorce laws; they are more aware and can offer more constructive guidance. But there are still many lawyers who are entrenched in a legal system that sees everything in terms of black and white, winners and losers, good guys and bad guys. And whoever wins, regardless of the *means*, is seen as the good guy.

New marriage partners also have a very biased viewpoint and cannot be truly objective about what is in the best interests of the children. New partners will naturally have strong loyalties for their spouse and are unlikely to disagree with any of their partner's opinions about his or her ex-spouse. If Mom says the father is unfit to have the children for the day, her new partner will agree with her rather than challenge the fairness and objectivity of her opinion. Then Mom takes her partner's agreement as further proof of her ex-spouse's unfitness as a parent. Mom is also prone to romanticizing the great job her new partner is doing as a stepparent and may focus on all of Dad's bad qualities to prove he is an incompetent parent.

In addition, a new stepparent often has very vulnerable feelings about his parenting skills and may run the natural father down in an effort to make himself look better. Meanwhile, in Dad's household, his new partner may feel jealous of his contact with his ex-spouse and may discourage visitation with his kids. As Marlene's story shows, there are also great complications and lots of opportunities for conflict that arise when we blend families.

"Lenny is nine years old now and he wants to argue about everything. He pushes and pushes. He makes me so angry sometimes. I wish there was somebody else to take over. But when I take him to his Dad and Lenny has a fit, his Dad leaves and the new stepmom has to deal with it. She's got her own two kids, so how can I send her one more?

"At the same time, there's no one-on-one with Bert and Lenny. The new stepmom won't allow it. She won't ever let him go off with just Lenny. The other kids always have to be included. Yet, when Lenny is here the other kids have more time with Bert, so why can't Lenny have that opportunity sometimes? I tried to talk to her about it but there's jealousy there or something. I don't know, but maybe Lenny represents sex with another woman."

As we can see, new partners are not neutral parties. If conflict persists between you and your ex-spouse, all new partners should be involved in any mediation efforts that take place.

FEELINGS OF INADEQUACY

Kelly Houseman's husband, Clay, was anxious to have children. They got married in June, and in January he was adamant about starting a family. They were twenty-four years old. Kelly was a day-care director, and her husband was the manager of a local business. When her daughter, Karen, was born the following fall, they bought a home that really stretched their budget. They needed Kelly's income for the house payments. A year later she gave birth to a son and continued to work full-time. Shortly after the birth of their son, her husband lost his job.

While her husband was "trying to find himself" they paid a full-time babysitter, but his period of unemployment stretched on and on. Clay seemed to have a fear of caring for the children, and they had savings set aside to pay a sitter, but Kelly most felt his lack of parental support in the night. Her son Tom was a colicky baby and would often cry for hours. Her husband made no move to take charge of the situation. The kids were her job, and Kelly would often be up most of the night with the baby and then have to go teach all day on very little sleep. Finally, Clay got another job, but he worked evenings and would come home at 3 A.M. As Kelly paced the floor with a crying baby on each hip, her husband would walk past her and go to bed. When she began to complain about his lack of help, he began to stay away longer and longer hours.

Clay had grown up in a family with eight children, and his mother did not work outside the home. She devoted herself to her children and waited on them hand and foot. This was his concept of the woman's role, and he didn't know how to incorporate a working woman into this formula. "He meant well but he just really didn't know what to do with the children," stated Kelly. Clay rarely played with the children he'd wanted so much. He simply could not relate to infants. A few times Kelly tried leaving him with the kids while she went out, but after a half-hour he would track her down and tell her she needed to come home. His concept of father did not go beyond breadwinner, and his self-esteem as breadwinner had been damaged by his long term of unemployment. So Clay worked longer and longer hours and became more and more estranged from the family. Kelly recalled:

> "There was no relief for me. I was the one in charge day in and day out. And I was working with small children all day. I needed a break."

As the pressure built between Kelly and her husband, he turned to drugs. When she realized that the habit had gone beyond his control, she asked him for a divorce.

> "Getting divorced was the best decision I ever made. Something inside me changed. I felt like I had choices. I still didn't have help with the kids, but I felt less stressed. I was back in control of my life.
>
> "Our visitation agreement was vague, just reasonable and seasonable. But there wasn't any argument over it. He just rarely came to see them and I wished he would spend more time with the kids. For the first year and half they hardly saw him at all.
>
> "He'd say he was coming to get them and then call back a couple of hours later and say something came up. Or he'd just show up two hours late. The kids would be sitting there ready to go the whole time. They would fight with each other and then get mad at me.
>
> "It would be weeks between phone calls and he would always give the excuse that he was working long hours. The kids would get very upset. When he gets into his work everyone has to go on hold. I told him, 'We're tired of being on hold. You've either got to decide you're going to be a father, or you're not going to be a father. But this being a father once every other month when it suits your schedule just can't go on.'
>
> "I would feel very angry and resentful at times but I tried to channel that so that the kids wouldn't see it. Regardless of how I felt about him, he was their father and he would always be their father."

Clay's behavior is typical of many men. His desire to have children was fervent and sincere. But he had no role models for fatherhood in this "liberated" generation. He didn't earn enough money to be the breadwinner, but he had no idea that, if his wife worked, as his mother hadn't, he should help out around the house and care for the children. His total avoidance of fatherhood, after pushing so hard to have children, makes his fear and feeling of inadequacy evident.

I heard this tale again and again—how the reality of children does not fit in with the father's fantasy of how it is going to be. These fathers grew up with the fantasy of the man of the house sitting in his easy chair while the wife tends the children and his physical needs. Many men just add in a wife arriving home at about the same time as he does (with a paycheck in her hand) and the bliss is enhanced through the money she brings in.

Kelly explained:

> "It wasn't easy getting Clay more involved with the kids. It took a *lot* of patience. I knew the only way my kids could have a 'normal childhood' was to get him involved. I knew I had to get him to see that before it was too late. I felt close to my father and I wanted them to have that. Of course, if he hadn't cared enough to listen to me it wouldn't have worked. My ex-husband really did want to be a good father, although he had no idea how to go about it.

> "I learned early that I shouldn't nag about it continually or he'd just stop listening to me. I had to grit my teeth for awhile. Sometimes the kids would think the sun rose and set on him and that would be hard to bear. But after awhile they would get angry at him ignoring them. Then I would call him up and say, 'You are missing the boat. You wanted these kids and you say you love them, but you're not showing them that. They don't understand your not having time for them.' I told him that time was running out. My daughter was starting to withdraw. She didn't want to get close to him when he was just going to ignore her. She was nine years old, and she didn't know any other way to defend herself emotionally.

> "It finally broke through to him. He went into a daytime job, and he started to see the kids much more."

We will hear more about Clay Houseman's transition in Chapter 4.

SOCIAL SKILLS

Ironically, however, fathering is not all the new father needs to know. Even those who learn to be far better fathers than their own had been find themselves disappointing their children because they lack social skills that have become second nature to women because of the divergent ways males and females have been socialized. In traditional marriages, women have long been the social secretaries, responsible for keeping track of the "family calendar." Even today most intact couples assign this role to the woman. (Though some women under thirty report younger men have better social skills.)

When men divorce they usually have little experience keeping track of social plans and have had no male role model for this behavior. Unless a man carries an appointment book for his profession, he generally relies on memory. This may work for regularly scheduled visitations, but important occasions (other than birthdays and major holidays) are easily forgotten.

Joe, a construction worker in his late thirties, illustrates this dilemma beautifully. He has been divorced six years and has two boys, ages eleven and fourteen. He has paid child support regularly and has seen his sons at least every two weeks since the divorce. His affection for his sons is obvious when he speaks of them and when I have seen the family together. The boys exude a confidence that their father loves them.

Joe's own father was harsh, violent, and emotionally distant. He was an automobile mechanic who spent no leisure time with his family except for two vacation days a year, when the family went to the beach. Most nights the father was off drinking. When he was home he insisted his sons help him with yard work, home repairs, and auto repairs. This man also built a house for the family when Joe was between the ages of six and eight. Joe was taken along many Saturdays to hammer nails, which he rarely did "correctly" by the father's assessment. The father never complimented any of his children on a job well done and was short-tempered about and critical of their attempts to meet his standards. He never had casual conversations with them, and he carried the adage "children should be seen and not heard" to the extreme—not even speaking to them when Joe and his older brother sat down to lunch with him in the solitude of the partially constructed home.

Joe's affectionate jostling of his sons and his efforts to draw them into conversation are a striking contrast to the way he was fathered. Yet, as I comment to Joe that he has done far better than his own father, and better than most divorced fathers, he is relentlessly self-critical. "My kids don't know how my father treated me and they don't know anything about other kids who don't see their fathers at all. They just know when I'm there and when I'm not."

He recounts with regret missing his son's graduation from junior high—an event that he knew beforehand was very important to his son. He simply forgot until the day after. He drove over to see the son and apologized, telling him that he was very angry with himself and disappointed about missing the graduation. His misery and self-recrimination about this are real. He says there have been many other incidents like this in which he "forgot." "I just have a terrible memory," Joe states solemnly. We could acidly point out that Joe's forgetfulness is no excuse—it isn't, and he already knows this. But why is it that he cannot remember such details that are even deeply important to him? It has to do with his socialization.

If he were still married to their mother, she would have reminded him. Most women keep track of acknowledging accomplishments and relationship matters. When a man has no woman to remind him, he is often as lost as the woman who has no man to remind her to change the oil in the car. We should all be "full people," but it's a lot harder now that we have abandoned the division of labor. It's more like each being two people.

Social skills and nurturing behaviors traditionally have not been part of a boy's training for manhood. When the couple is still intact, there are opportunities for the mother to guide and teach the father about how to be a more nurturing and considerate parent. But once that link is broken, the man is on his own, left with only the skills he has developed. These may not include remembering and acknowledging important social occasions. Joe has not only neglected his boys at times, he also never writes to his sister or sends presents to his nephews. When he has lived with a woman for a period of time, his social IQ seems to take a leap, but as soon as that relationship dissolves, his social skills drop back to base level.

Is there anything the child's mother could have done to prevent the graduation-night disappointment? Joe's ex-wife probably grew tired of being his social secretary long ago. We can hardly blame her if she did not want to call and remind Joe of the graduation ceremony to be sure he made it. In a world in which all parents are responsible, "together" people, each person should only be responsible for themselves. She may have been too busy arranging an after-graduation party to give any thought to her ex-husband's propensity to forget the dates and times of social events.

But there are hidden agendas too. What mother would not take some satisfaction in seeing an irresponsible dad exposed, so her own caring looks all the more shining by contrast? As one woman candidly admitted to me, "Part of me really ate it up that my son always preferred me." It is difficult to resist the temptation to let Dad fall flat on his face, but one must consider what is in the best interests of the child. At best, it is a tough call between reminding the ex-husband of what he should do to make the kids feel most loved, and allowing the children to experience some disappointments at their father's hands to prepare them for the many times ahead when their mothers cannot protect them.

INDIFFERENCE

In this chapter we have seen some situations in which men appeared indifferent but were actually genuinely concerned about their children. We have seen men pull back for a variety of reasons that seem less cold when we understand the story from the father's point of view. Nonetheless, Wallerstein's fifteen-year study of divorced families shows that some men seem to be truly indifferent about their children's well-being or futures. Indeed, some fathers seem to have a pathological lack of concern for their children. We are stunned again and again by many of the fathers' insensitive responses at Wallerstein's ten-and fifteen-year follow-up interviews.

Dale Burrell, a twice-divorced father who moved around the country following his career goals, seems representative of the glib fathers who fail to understand the impact their lack of contact has on their children. Shortly after his second divorce Wallerstein spoke to him about his children. His comments and Wallerstein's interpretations were as follows:

"Noah is four," says Dale. "He's okay—he'll have a broader perspective on life." (It occurs to me that this is a strange way to talk about a four-year-old.) "You know," Dale continues, "I stayed in this marriage longer than I might have because of my previous divorce. I really wanted this one to work. Steve [his older son by his previous marriage] came and lived with us last year — it was his idea to come — which was fine with me, but it was also his idea to go back. I think things haven't worked out for him. But he was a great asset to us, as a built-in babysitter."

I ask again about the other children.

"I saw Tanya and Kyle three times in the past two years," he says. "Whenever I'm traveling near the Southwest, I stop by for a visit. In 1979 to 1980 I saw them all four or five times."

"Did that amount of contact feel good to the kids?"

"I think they felt pretty good," he says blandly. "I don't think they'd want a lot more. They're more interested in their friends at this age."

Once again I have the feeling that it is hard for Dale to talk about his children separately or about his separate relationships with them.

"I have a theory about fathers and kids," he says. "Me, I have four kids and each represents a fantasy of mine. Steve is doing the same thing I did after high school. He's working in a bowling alley while he figures out his next move. Tanya is into art. Kyle is into music. Noah will get all the love in the world." . . .

There is no evidence that Dale is aware of how much he has disappointed his children. If he understood, he might have done things differently so as not to hurt them, for he was a good, caring father before the divorce. What his children see as painfully intolerable rejection represents his way of defending himself, of shutting out potentially disturbing stimuli, of maintaining his own equilibrium. He says, "Things will work out. I have no regrets. Everything is fine." Divorce is much more difficult for his family than it is for him.[8]

Wallerstein, who has interviewed Burrell's children separately across the years is aware of how desperately his children have missed him. By contrast, she sees that many men are so emotionally distanced from their children that for them "out of sight" is truly out of mind. Tragically, some men will have reached the point of no return in their emotional separation from their children, but as the stories in the next two chapters show, many fathers' feelings for their children can be rekindled.

SUMMARY POINTS

- Many men find each separation from their children so painful and the negotiations for visitation so difficult that they ultimately stop seeing their children.
- Some men seem truly indifferent about their children. However, we must remember that non-custodial parents of both sexes find it difficult to keep up a sense of rapport with their children and become discouraged. Their indifference may well be a defense mechanism against the pain of loss.
- Adult children of divorce, and twice-divorced parents who have experienced the "other side," often have a special sensitivity that helps them understand and support the child's relationship with the father.
- Infrequent visitation does not necessarily mean that the father does not wish to see the child. Because divorce is often accompanied by intense conflict, the father may be staying away in order to avoid encountering the mother.
- Extended family members, new marriage partners, lawyers, and therapists often become a destructive cheering section that works against the resolution of conflict between the parents.
- Social skills and nurturing behavior have not been part of men's training for adulthood. Many men feel inadequate about their parenting abilities and consequently avoid caring for their children both before and after divorce.

3

Involving Dad

"As I remember it, it was a peaceful separation. My parents never talked against each other, and I never felt deserted by my Dad. Now I see how my mother had allowed that relationship."

— AN ADULT CHILD OF DIVORCE

As we have seen, it is not always easy for dads to stay in touch with their children. Some must arrange visits and try to keep up a relationship across long distances. Others may live nearby but find that the lack of day-to-day contact aggravates their shyness and awkwardness with their children. Therefore, mothers may need to take a very active role in helping the fathers stay involved. This can be a tremendous test of character when Mom's bad feelings toward Dad make her wish he would just disappear. Nonetheless, mothers who want to encourage the father-child bond need to discover what will make it easier for the father to re-establish or keep close contact with his children. Since each man is different, moms need to determine when they should aggressively pursue the relationship on behalf of the children and when they should take a "hands-off" approach. David, below, has taken a lot of initiative and needed no encouragement from his ex-wife. Indeed, he may have resented her suggestions since he takes a great deal of pride in his creative solutions to fathering his child long-distance. However, most men not only have few ideas about how to maintain closeness with their children, they may be much more easily discouraged than our tenacious David.

DADS WHO STAY IN TOUCH

Even with the mother's cooperation, the most determined fathers can experience a lot of difficulties staying in touch, particularly if they live a great distance away from their children. Fortunately, studies show that the frequency of contact with the father is less important than the quality of the contact. Of course, some very determined fathers let nothing stand as an obstacle. Though he was a long-distance dad, David seemed to manage both quality and quantity!

Ben, who was two years old when his parents separated, has no memories of living with his father.

> "My earliest memories are in Wilmington where my mother got a job when my parents divorced. Every other weekend my dad would come get me and take me back to Pennsylvania. He used to take me camping, fishing, or hiking; or we would just bum around by my dad's house. I always looked forward to it.
>
> "We've always talked frequently, like once or twice a week, and sometimes we'll talk for hours. He's always been there. We've never really lost contact even after I moved farther away. He never embarrasses me by repeating something I told him in front of other people. I never have to tell him what's private to me—he always knows."

How did Ben's dad manage this closeness despite their geographical distance? When David divorced, he found a book on how to be a "long-distance" dad that he felt helped him tremendously.

> "The book said that even something as insignificant as a sticker in an envelope can be a meaningful communication to a kid. I would send him a couple of mailings a week with a note, a cartoon, or a picture I drew.
>
> "When Ben was about nine years old the space shuttle went up, and we pre-arranged to be on the phone together. Ben still mentions this as something we did together though I was actually a thousand miles away at the time."

David always made an effort to be present for Ben's special events. He saw Ben's graduation from kindergarten and went to his piano recitals. This required some persistence, or as David calls it, "proactive parenting." The mother rarely volunteered to tell him when these events were to be, and David would have to listen to Ben carefully in order to be aware of special events. For example, when he learned that Ben was taking piano lessons, David repeatedly asked Ben if he had a recital coming up any time soon.

"Another suggestion I got from the book was to make direct contact with Ben's teachers. Each year I would arrange a conference with his teacher so the teacher would know that Ben had a dad who was very interested in his activities. I would give them stamped self-addressed envelopes so the teachers could write to me and tell me how Ben was doing, and I would sometimes help Ben with his homework over the phone.

"The teachers were generally very cooperative and one even changed the time of a classroom party to accommodate me. A few times Ben and I made a gift for the class or I went in and led an activity with him. I made myself visible to his classmates. I wanted them to know that he had a daddy. And I felt Ben was proud to show me off.

"When I would go down for Cub Scout activities, Ben would drag me around by the hand at the pack meetings and introduce me to everybody. We worked on his pinewood derby at my house and I made sure I was there for the race. Later I would go along on the camp-outs.

"Ben is on his way to becoming an Eagle scout now. We've done a lot of his badges here, and he's very proud of these special badges he has that the rest of the group doesn't have."

David's conscientious efforts stand in contrast to Joe's (Chapter 2) sense of helplessness. David is a professional who works with paper, whereas Joe is a construction worker who works outdoors with machines. A high school dropout, Joe has always felt intimidated by schools. For Joe to be as pro-active as David would require many deep changes. He carries few phone numbers and would feel uncomfortable contacting his children's teachers or group leaders whom he has not met before. Since Joe only lives about twenty miles from his sons, his problems with "being there" for his children are primarily psychological or social.

During Ben's childhood, David lived one hundred miles away, then a thousand miles away, and now about four hundred miles away. These distances notwithstanding, David has seen a lot of Ben. Though Ben is now sixteen years old and has lived four hundred miles away since he was ten years old, David has seen Ben about once a month as well as during his school vacations. Up until this year, when Ben felt he needed to get back home sooner to see his girl-friend, David has had him for about a month in the summer. They talk on the phone at least once a week, and since Ben has been an older Scout, he has finally begun to take the initiative to keep his dad informed about father-son events. Now that Ben is older, there are new opportunities for father-son sharing.

"The last time my wife and I went down to visit Ben we double-dated. I had told Ben that I wanted to meet his girlfriend and we realized that our favorite family restaurant was also Ben's girlfriend's favorite restaurant. It just seemed natural to invite her to go with us."

David feels very good about his relationship with his son and wanted to offer this reassurance to other long-distance dads: "One thing I have learned out of all this is if you really want your kid to have a daddy, it's possible."

What Dads Can Do

1. Dads can take proactive measures to stay involved in their children's lives. Short letters and frequent phone calls can keep the connection alive.
2. Dads can contact the children's teachers and activity leaders and ask how they can get involved on a regular or occasional basis.
3. Dads can educate scout leaders, youth group leaders, and others about keeping both parents informed of all activities and special events.
4. Dads can arrange to pick-up or drop-off their children at neutral locations such as school or a neighbor's if they wish to avoid contact with the mother, while staying in touch with the child.

5. Dads can explain to their children why they find it difficult to stay in touch with them so that their children do not see their absence as a personal rejection.

NEUTRAL PARTIES

There are a number of times in David's narrative when we realize how much neutral parties can smooth things over and help the father make contact without stirring up the conflict that seems to perpetually exist between most divorced parents. When David sends letters to his child at the babysitter's, Ben is freer to enjoy this special acknowledgment from his dad. But much of the time kids are in a bind with divorcing parents. Whether the child is with Mom or Dad, there is the constant fear of hurting one parent if he talks too much about the other parent. Similarly, if the child acts very excited when he gets a card from Daddy, he may sense that he has hurt or betrayed Mommy and that dampens the fun for him. Communicating through a neutral source solves this problem. As David considers the power Ben's mother has as a gatekeeper, we realize what a relief it must be to have some neutral parties to communicate through. Teachers, babysitters, Scout leaders, and impartial grandparents and neighbors can all serve this important function.

"Staying involved in Ben's life wasn't all easy. I had to be quite persistent. I couldn't count on my ex-wife to keep me informed. When fathers aren't proactive the kids can really miss out. The mother is a gatekeeper and she can let the father in or she can keep him out in a million subtle ways.

"I remember that I once gave Ben stationery to write to me with stamped, self-addressed envelopes. He took them home and he never used them.

"So then I took some to the babysitter's and I got letters from him. I don't think his mother forbade him to write to me, but she didn't encourage him either."

Terry, den mother to seven Cub Scouts, shared her experiences negotiating with divorced parents. Four of the boys in her den came from divorced families, and although they had been signed up for Scouts by their mothers, three spent a significant amount of time with their fathers. The den was in California, where shared custody is becoming the norm, and the boys had varying arrangements by which they spent different weeks or different weekends with their fathers.

"All the boys in the group were very enthusiastic about Scouts and would get very excited about the trips we'd planned, but when the day of the trip would come [usually on the weekends] at least two wouldn't show up each time. At the next meeting they would explain that they were with their dads.

"My first response was to get very angry at these dads (whom I hadn't even met) and agree that they were just as irresponsible as the mothers had said. But then one Saturday one of the boys showed up at my house when we had no activity planned. Greg had brought his father over just to meet me.

"The father explained that he had heard so many nice things about me from Greg that he wanted to come introduce himself and ask if there was anything he could do to help. I realized that I had misjudged this man. I thought, it may very well be that he is always unreliable in cooperating with the mother's plans, but he and I have no negative history together.

"At the next meeting I had extra copies of all the notices about our activities. I made a general announcement that if anyone had parents that didn't live in the same house, they needed to take a notice for each parent and put each parent's name on the top of the sheet to make sure each parent got a copy. Of course, I later learned that some of the notices weren't delivered, so then I had the boys give me the addresses of the fathers, and I began mailing them notices. The fathers started showing up with the boys when it was their weekend. I was friendly and concentrated on helping them feel included.

"The reverberations from this were incredibly rewarding. I found that I could have good relations with both parents and I could sense how relieved the boys felt now that I had taken the position of the 'go-between.' The boys began to admit more positive feelings about their fathers and a couple of the mothers even began to see their ex-husbands in a new light."

Terry's story is very instructive about the positive potential of neutral parties, but many leaders are too confused about the new family arrangements to know what to do. You, as a parent, may have to educate them. Getting communication going directly back and forth between the dad and the child's activities helps alleviate some of Mom's burden.

If your children belong to any youth groups in school or at church, or participate in sports or Scouts, approach the leaders about sending notices to fathers. If you are a father reading this, you don't need to be told how it feels to be treated like a second-class citizen in these matters. Introduce yourself with a friendly and welcoming attitude. Don't worry about what your ex-spouse may have said about you. Just *show* the leader who you are. She'll get the picture.

If you are a mother in this situation, regardless of how your children's father has behaved about these things in the past, remember that he can have a very different relationship with a neutral party. Tell the leader that your child's father would like to have a schedule too, so that he can make advance plans for the times the children are with him. Even a dad who spends too little time with his kids might be drawn in by one of the club's activities.

Some ways work better than others to get Dad more involved in the children's activities. Typically, if a divorce or separation has been particularly conflictual, your ex-partner will be suspicious of anything that comes directly from you. If you hand-deliver the notices, your ex may see this as one more of your criticisms or demands. Likewise, if you have your child deliver a notice you have obtained, your ex may interpret this as another "manipulative" move to use the child to communicate with him. Don't ask your child to ask the leader, and don't discuss the matter with the leader in front of your child. Make a separate call and plant the suggestion, telling the leader that he or she might get more cooperation if everyone was informed about activities. State it as an "operational suggestion" — not one you are making because your ex is so uncooperative or your relations with him are so bad. Rather, explain it as the "modern" thing to do in the case of divorced parents. Suggest that the other parents would probably appreciate this too. Then provide the leader with your ex's mailing address.

Even if Dad does not live nearby and is not likely to be the chauffeur for activities, there can be side benefits to his receiving notices or newsletters. He'll know what his children are doing, see what their activities cost, read about fund raisers that he may be able to help with, and just generally feel more included.

Your attitude will also let the leader know that he or she is free to "be friends" with your ex. Many leaders will reject the other parent out of a misguided sense of loyalty to the mother. Try to let them know this isn't necessary. Your child needs to feel that both his parents are reasonable people who care about his or her welfare.

If you have not yet reached a point where you have neutral feelings toward your children's father, it might be best to arrange neutral pick-ups and drop-offs. Many divorced parents choose to have Dad pick up the kids at school or the grandparents' house, or Mom will go next door to the neighbors' when Dad is due. Also, if the father has a compelling need to make a clean break with the children's mother, it will be difficult for him to visit the children in her home. Some mothers unconsciously use visitation pick-up and drop-off to try to have more contact with the children's father, when such contact may be very threatening to him in his stage of emotionally breaking away.

When an over-anxious mother is very insistent about the father seeing the children, he (who is trying to establish himself as an independent man again) may no longer feel that he has made the *decision* to see them. He may react to her insistence that he see the kids more by going away until he feels the way is clear for him to *choose* to see the children. Neutral parties can often give the father a way to see the child without his feeling "controlled" by his ex-wife.

What Moms Can Do

1. Moms can encourage Dad's involvement by finding activities that help him link up with the children.
2. Moms can try to emphasize some of the father's positive traits so that boys can feel good about themselves when they resemble Dad and girls can see the good in men when it is time for them to date.
3. Moms can assure the children that they have not driven Dad away, and his absence does not mean he does not love them. She can explain that Dad is just avoiding her or painful memories of the marriage.

4. Moms can maintain contact with Dad or his family so that the children know where to seek him out when they are older.
5. Moms can take good care of themselves and build a strong network of supportive friends so they can provide a stable home life for their children.

BUILDING BRIDGES

Though some dads may seem impenetrably indifferent, moms must be careful not to give up too easily. Building bridges between children and their estranged fathers can take great patience, persistence, ingenuity, and willingness to take risks. Dads drift away for various reasons, and they have great difficulty finding their way back. It is human nature to avoid our problems instead of working toward solutions. As we listen to Lenny, we see how easily his father gave up on him, but we also hear the yearning for his father's love that his mother could not ignore.

Lenny had been living with his father much of the time for years, but then there were blended-family problems that drove Lenny away. His dad and his stepmom would get into fights about how each was treating the other's kids. Lenny told me:

> "Once my stepbrother and I were fighting, and he started calling me names and pushing me around. I pushed him back and then ran into the house. My stepmom saw him chasing me and hitting me, but she sent *me* to my room. I complained to my dad when he came home from work but then they got into a big argument. I was thinking it was all my fault, and I felt bad. I was hoping they would just talk to each other about it."

After a while Lenny wanted to go back and live with his mother, because he was tired of getting into fights with his stepmother.

> "I told my mom and she asked me to go out and play and she talked to my dad. Then my mom told me to get my stuff. Before I left I went in and hugged my dad and told him I'd see him in a while. He asked me why I wanted to go, and I said I didn't want to cause any trouble between him and my stepmom. He said it was my decision and that was that."

Marlene didn't know if Bert was hurt or just preoccupied, but he showed no interest in Lenny and arranged no visits. Two months passed. Marlene began to notice Lenny being depressed a lot and getting in trouble at school. I asked Lenny what he remembered about this time.

"I thought my dad was mad at me or something. Like maybe I hurt his feelings. I felt really sad and I was a little worried that maybe I would never see him again. I was afraid that he didn't want to talk to me or something, but my mom said, 'Why don't you call him? You haven't heard from him in awhile.' So I called him and he said, 'Long time, no see.' Then we arranged for me to go visit him for the weekend."

Although Lenny is back in touch with his dad, the step-sibling problems persist and the relationship is a constant struggle. Nonetheless, Marlene isn't willing to give up the fight. She keeps pushing Lenny's contact with his dad, not because she enjoys the challenge, but because her son needs her to, and that's reason enough for her.

Kelly Houseman's efforts at getting her ex-husband involved with her children have proven even more rewarding. Once the children's father found a comfortable niche in their lives, Kelly's efforts had a snowball effect. Kelly got Clay more and more involved with the children by helping him link up with their sports. Clay was always a good athlete and this was one area in which he felt competent.

"In the beginning, all Clay knew to do was to take the kids over to his apartment and watch TV. And of course they would get bored. It wasn't a very good visit. But when he started to get involved in the kids' sports, things really started to change.

"I had invited him to the games and then I became a tennis coach and his pride was a little hurt that Mom, not him, was coaching his son. Our kids are really good at tennis and so pretty soon people he ran into would tell him what a great match his son or daughter played and he began to feel he was missing something. Sort of like missing your kid's first steps. So he began to come to the matches.

"Clay didn't know anything about tennis but when Tom went into baseball, Clay started to show up at practices every now and then. The coach was glad for any help he could get. Clay began to step in as the pitcher or catcher or something like that. Since he had always been good at sports, it was just a natural way for him to get involved."

Though Clay's relationship with his children has steadily improved, the greatest winner in this family is Clay's new son by his second marriage. Clay was no better with this child during infancy, but he now brings "little brother" along to most of his older children's games. He is learning to father, slowly but surely.

Kelly has kept an impressively calm attitude throughout. As we will see later, she has had many justifications for cutting off her children's contact with their father, but instead she has repeatedly chosen to do whatever she could to encourage the father-child bonds. Her attitude is such a contrast to most divorced parents that I searched for the reason that fueled this difference. She explained how her own childhood experiences had influenced the way she handled the divorce and visitations. Kelly told me:

> "When I was about ten my parents separated and they handled it beautifully. They didn't talk against each other. My father wasn't living with us, but he was there when it counted. I only went to his apartment twice in all that time, but I remember him coming to see us at the house, and he was always there on family occasions. As I remember it, it was a peaceful separation. I never felt deserted by my Dad.
>
> "Now I see how my mother had *allowed* that relationship. I see so many divorces where the mother does not allow the children to have that kind of relationship with their father."

PUSHING DAD AWAY

There is no doubt that there are some dads who should never see their children. Fathers who are physically abusive or who have sexually abused any of the children and have not been through a rehabilitative program and shown genuine remorse and a willingness to change should be barred from seeing their children. Mothers are justifiably concerned, too, about releasing their children to men who are frequently intoxicated or involved in illegal drugs. We have all heard or read stories about fathers who take their children to drug blow-outs, or leave them in an empty apartment to care for themselves. Unfortunately, these fathers often continue to have visitation rights. This is a serious and tragic problem that many divorced mothers face, but it is beyond the scope of this book.

What we can explore are the qualms many mothers feel about allowing their children to visit with dads whom they see as neglectful or irresponsible. We must keep in mind that in the conflict that follows divorce, there is a tremendous temptation to vilify Dad. Since we are used to thinking in terms of winners and losers, many mothers regard their getting custody as the judge's assessment that they are the "good parent" and therefore the father must be the "bad parent." In fact, many times the judge is following some other criteria such as the "tender years doctrine" that supports the philosophy that children belong with the mother unless she is unfit.

However, it is not uncommon for an estranged wife to suspect that Dad is a poor parent. Sometimes this is true, but more often than not this is a distorted view, inflamed by the post-divorce conflict. We all know from pre-marriage dating that many relationships go through a "honeymoon" period in which the loved one is over-idealized. However, when relationships turn sour or we become attracted to someone else, we suddenly start to see all the faults (and then some) of the former loved one. This is a defense mechanism similar to the one teenagers use in breaking away from their parents. When we need to separate from someone we have loved, we unconsciously exaggerate their every flaw so we can break away without guilt or longing. Similarly, in the tremendous stress that follows divorce, we may each recognize that we are at our worst—short-tempered, disorganized, irritable, and preoccupied with self. We know we are not always like this—we are not "ourselves." We expect to calm down and be better people (and better parents) when we have recovered from the crisis. Yet, when our former partner acts irresponsible or edgy we think, "Ah ha! Now his *true* colors are showing!"

To aggravate the problem, divorcing spouses usually bring out the worst in each other. A mother may come away from confrontations with her ex-spouse frustrated and embarrassed that her "worst self" has once again been triggered. She may be stable and supportive with the children when she is alone with them, but as soon as Dad shows up to get them, she loses it. There is naturally a lot of tension in this situation, and Dad is bound to lose his temper, too. If Mom cannot be objective about all the stress *everyone* is under, she may even convince herself that Dad's previous civil and even kindly behavior was "all an act." Further, she often assumes that Dad will treat the kids the same way he treats her. If he leaves slamming the door and shouting at her, she worries that he will scream at the kids and shove them around all weekend. If Dad's unresolved conflicts cause him to be unreliable about returning her calls, she extrapolates that he will probably neglect the kids. What Mom may fail to sort out is that Dad may be a lousy "lover" but he can still be a good parent. After all, he is not angry at the children, and he doesn't need to escape them.

When the children come back from their visit with their fathers, mothers should be careful not to prod the kids for information. Vulnerable, hurting parents naturally want to feel they are superior at some things, and there is a tremendous temptation to try to discover ways we are a better parent than the ex-spouse, but we should try to "hang loose" about reports that Dad has fed them cereal for dinner. They will survive.

MOM'S ATTITUDE ABOUT DAD

When Dad is not around, for whatever reason, Mom is left to explain or describe him to her children. Some avoid the subject entirely, like one unwed mother I interviewed who has never discussed "Dad" with her eight-year-old son. But most make some attempt to tell the child about the father. Even in the case of death or divorce, the child often depends on Mom to tell him or her what Dad was like. If you are a mother who must fill your children in on what Dad is/was like, give what you say careful thought.

Remember that when you describe your children's father to them or complain about him, they are learning something about men and your attitudes about men. Your son, who inevitably identifies with his father, may feel you hate him, his maleness, if he hears you talking hatefully about his father. Adding to the boy's emotional burden are the many times other relatives have told him he is "just like his father." Vanessa Riley models a neutral forgiving attitude that leaves room for her son to benefit from his father's attention. When Vanessa learned she was pregnant, she was thirty-three years old and unmarried.

> "When I told Larry I was pregnant, his attitude was that we should 'do something with it.' And I thought, 'I'd rather keep the baby and do something with you.' But he did hang in there and was around a lot for the first three years of Kirk's life. We tried living together after Kirk was born, but I didn't want to marry him. I didn't have the feelings for him that would make a marriage work. I felt he was irresponsible and too self-centered.
>
> We both led very independent lives even when we lived together. If I wanted to go somewhere, I just took the baby and went. I had the attitude that I had no obligation to him. He was the father of my baby, but it was *my* baby, not *our* baby. I was distant, but it wasn't just me. Larry was always hard to get close to. That was one of the reasons I didn't want to marry him. It would have driven me crazy."

Larry moved out when Kirk was three. Vanessa knew the relationship would never meet her needs and she asked him to leave.

> "He was never abusive but he drank too much and I didn't want my son to see his father that way. I would get phone calls at three o'clock in the morning to come get him because he was drunk and couldn't find a ride home. It was ugly for about two months after we separated because he said I was trying to take his son away from him. He was really very upset. He had a nervous breakdown and went into the hospital. When he came out of the program he seemed calmer and we haven't had any problems since."

He kept in touch with Kirk, and the separation has remained amicable.

> "Larry is still rather immature. He is the 'party father' or buddy. He doesn't discipline Kirk and he thinks I'm too strict."

Despite Larry's history of heavy drinking, Vanessa has not worried about Kirk's safety with him.

"He lost his license long ago for driving under the influence, so he never drives drunk, because he never drives at all."

Vanessa has accommodated visitation by driving her son to see his father and going to pick him up even though it takes thirty minutes each way. Larry has continued to drink sporadically and once Kirk called her to come get him, because Larry had passed out, and Kirk was scared.

"My husband and I had a long talk with Larry that time and told him that he would not be allowed to continue seeing Kirk if that were to happen again. We were all civil about it. I try not to let a lot of things upset me. I felt that Larry really did care about Kirk and would not endanger him. They were at home. He had friends over, they were drinking, and Larry had gone overboard."

The incident happened four years ago, and there has been no trouble since. It is not easy to trust such "imperfect" men with our children, but Vanessa has tried to keep a sense of perspective. She knows she could get all worked up about Larry's irresponsible behavior, but she prefers to step back and see his love for his son. By not harping on the father's faults, she can allow Kirk to love what is best in his father.

Likewise, mothers need to use caution when discussing fathers with their daughters. Many girls who have listened to their mothers' negative remarks about their fathers have grown up believing that men cannot be trusted. They have trouble committing to a relationship with a man and frequently change partners when they begin to become attached. It is better to communicate, with compassion, that the American family has gone through many changes in this generation and men have not yet learned how to be part of the solution. At the same time, daughters need a realistic vision of their fathers so that they do not reject every man who woos them in adolescence and adulthood.

Often in the case of a deceased father a lot of idealizing goes on, and it's important to mention the father's faults in a neutral way, with a "nobody's perfect" attitude, to keep the image of manhood one that your son could achieve. If you can talk about things Dad could do that would be more helpful, *without rancor*, you may teach your son something to strive for as a father, and your daughter something constructive to look for in a man. But tread lightly. It's a situation that has the potential to be very destructive.

With an abandoning father the task is much more difficult because you may be so angry that you are hyper-aware of his faults. Again, be guided by your children's need to form a constructive image of men and fatherhood, not by your need to unload a lot of your anger and marshall support for yourself. Take your anger and your needs to lunch with your friends. At home emphasize the father's positive qualities. (He must have had some. Why were you attracted to him?) With all the talk of genetic links and early learning, your children will inevitably look for their father in themselves. If all they hear is negative, this is all they will find in their own souls. Use your description of Dad as another way to teach them to love themselves.

I think Kelly Houseman's story, below, is a good example of putting things in perspective and looking at the long-range effect of what we say to our kids. After Clay Houseman left Kelly, he still felt responsible for supporting his children, but his job did not pay much. Because of the financial pressure, he got involved in illegal gambling and ended up being sent to prison for three months. Kelly related:

> "That was more devastating for me than the divorce. The divorce felt positive because I was putting a stop to a bad situation and getting a hold of myself again. But Clay's downfall was all negative. He wasn't the type to do those things and I was sad to see him sink so low.
>
> "I had trouble deciding what to tell the kids. They were five and six years old. He would be missing for months and they would eventually hear that their father was in prison because it's a small town. So we decided we'd better tell them ourselves. Clay was able to come talk to them before he went to jail, and we just sat them down and told them that he had done something wrong and now he was going to have to pay the price.
>
> "Going to prison really woke him up and changed him. I took the kids to see him. I think we made four trips."

As I listened to Kelly's story, I was thunderstruck by her stamina and compassion in handling the situation this way. I reflected to her what a dramatic example of forgiveness and acceptance this was for her children. Surely, these kids won't ever have to worry about their mom's unconditional love if they have witnessed her compassion toward a divorced father who went to prison. And I find not one grain of foolishness in her decision. She did divorce him when she needed to. She is not a sucker, or a rescuer. It's not as if she lent him money to run away from the law. Her attitude was, "He did something bad, he was doing the only thing he could to make up for it, and we, as a family, don't hate him for making this mistake. He's down and out, and we will do what we can to comfort him as he gets through this difficult time." It's all about human values. She has an admirable compassion and objectivity that inspires my deepest respect.

"I think that every sacrifice I've made, everything I've done was worth it. Because I want my children to understand that people make mistakes. They might do horrible things that they shouldn't do, but that doesn't mean that they are necessarily bad people. I believe that it shows what the power of love and caring can do. I really think that if we had chosen to move at that time, and just cut him out of our lives, he may have never pulled himself up again.

"So many people think that when a father goes to prison the best thing is to just move away or end all contact. And maybe if he had been an abusive father, or I knew he couldn't change, that would have been best.

"But he had never harmed them and who knows what situations they'll face when they are teenagers? I don't want them to be afraid I'll throw them out if they get pregnant or get in some other kind of trouble. I want them to feel that they can come home and talk to me about it."

WHEN DAD WON'T RESPOND

Sometimes fathers just turn their backs and refuse to have anything to do with the children. Mothers often become angry when their efforts to bring their ex-spouse and the children together constantly meet frustration. In this case, it is best to remember we can never control the behavior of another human being.

Rae Ann certainly went above and beyond the call of duty in her efforts to try and get her ex-husband to "connect" with their son. Rae Ann had divorced her husband Hank when her son Jesse was two-and-a-half years old. In retrospect, Rae Ann worries that she was too pushy in keeping her son in touch with his dad. She automatically dropped Jesse at his father's every Saturday for a visit, whether the father had requested it or not. Determined that she would not make the mistake of her mother and run down Jesse's dad, she cheerfully told Jesse each week that he was going to have a great time with his father. Rae Ann had noticed Jesse's reluctance to visit his father each weekend, but she tried to ignore the signs.

> "I tried so hard to build up a good father-child relationship that I would say, 'Oh good, Daddy's coming. Won't this be fun?' But then Daddy would take him and make him spend the whole day in a restaurant. And that wasn't fun, so that must have been very confusing to Jesse."

Jesse remembers his father's awkwardness during their early visits.

> "At first I saw him about once a week, then once a month during the first five or six years after my parents divorced. He would take me over to one of his friends' houses and they would sit and talk. It wasn't very worthwhile, in my opinion. I don't think he was capable of being a father. I don't hold that against him. I think he liked me and would do anything for me, he just didn't know what to do with a child."

Looking back, Rae Ann has changed her view and would like to advise newly divorced mothers.

> "Don't go overboard in any direction. I think the mother should just be neutral, and let the kid tell you how he feels about the father and the visits. Just do active listening."

The best we can do, if we are hoping someone else will change, is to leave the door open in case they do. We have seen how Kelly and Rae Ann constantly pushed their ex-husbands to keep in touch with their children. These mothers are very sensitive to this issue and are wonderful role models because they were each children of divorce. They know how a child feels when the father is not part of his or her life. Though Rae Ann did not manage to keep her ex-husband in touch with their son, her persistence did manage to bolster her son's self-esteem. Considering that Jesse's father didn't want to pay child support and gave up seeing him when his mother pushed the issue, I am surprised at Jesse's quiet assurance that he was loved by his father and that his father "would do anything" for him. I asked if he had ever worried that his father didn't care about him.

> "Oh, no, never. My mother always told me that he liked me, and he wanted me to visit. Even though he didn't really know what to do with me, I knew that he wanted to see me. He would hug me and he always seemed glad to see me."

We can hear in Jesse's story the reassuring talks his mother must have had with him. Though Rae Ann has some fear that she pushed contact with his father too much, Jesse has not been damaged. But this is not always the case. If the father really wants to avoid contact with the child, pushing the child on him can cause the child to encounter open rejection again and again. How does a mother decide how much to push and how much to protect her child from possible rejection?

One way to protect the child's self-esteem is to offer explanations for the father's behavior that make it clear he has not left or refused to get in touch because the child is "defective." Explain the father's background or current problems that prevent him from being in touch. What was his childhood like? What sort of father did he have? What work or money pressures is he under now? Even if you feel that the father really could afford the time or money to come visit and that his childhood pain is no excuse, it does not help your child to hear this. Something is keeping him away, and it is not some foul trait in your child. That should be cleared up immediately and forever, even if it means you must sympathize with the father's hang-ups.

Because many fathers have a hard time dealing with their ex-wives, it is usually wise to encourage the children to make direct contact with him. It's good for them to write letters or call and just chat with their father about what is happening with them. These communications should not mention money! As I will explain in

Chapter 9, money should be kept as neutral as possible by making finances a problem between the father and the "powers that be." Mention of money is sure to put a damper on the child's communication with the parent. The strain on the parent-child relationship is obvious when we hear Debbie talk about her phone calls to her father:

"I think my parents shouldn't have dragged me into the money thing. If I were giving advice to divorcing parents I would tell them that they should keep in mind that their kids want to love both parents equally. It's hard for the child to love their absent parent or to feel their absent parent loves them when they have to call and ask for money all the time. It seemed like every time I called my father, I wanted to tell him I loved him, but instead I was asking him for money. I felt like he probably didn't want to hear from me anymore."

Keep the father informed about the kid's lives through light, newsy letters or phone calls. Send pictures of the children or pictures they have drawn. If you must communicate about money sometimes find some way to clue that those letters are different. In your letters about the kids meant to spark Dad's interest and affection, begin by saying, "Just wanted to share some news about the kids." Then share good news (and any bad news that has nothing to do with money and for which your ex-husband cannot be blamed). When you've run out of such news, stop, seal up the letter and send it. If you need to address financial issues, write a separate letter that begins, "I need to talk with you about money . . ."

Sometimes it's practical for you to call Dad to let him know about important things happening in the kids' lives. If he visits at all, call the next week to let him know how much they enjoyed the visit. If you sense your ex is uncomfortable talking to you, call and tell his new wife, or mention it to any of his relatives or co-workers you can comfortably contact. Spread good will. Don't sit back smugly waiting for Dad to forget their birthdays again so they can see what a "#%&@!" he is. Send him a gentle reminder in plenty of time for him to remember their birthdays. Tactfully mention that the best time to reach them by phone is before school or some other time that you know is also easy for him to call. Then don't prime your child to receive the call. If he follows through, just let the child be surprised.

Encourage the children to call Dad or send a card on *his* birthday. Don't try to punish Dad by letting them forget Father's Day. The kids are the ones who will feel bad if they don't send Dad a card.

Of course, not all attempts to bring Dad and the children together will be successful. Some dads are either so cut off from their feelings or so uncomfortable talking to children that phone calls may be discouraging and depressing experiences for your child. When even letters to these dads do not get responses, it may be time to let the children drop out of the direct efforts to contact Dad.

But this does not mean you should give up. Mom can still carry on the effort on behalf of the children, without making them aware that Dad has not answered her letters or asked about them. With the most resistant of dads this may all be one-way communication for awhile, but there is merit in just letting him know what your address is so he can find the children when he is ready. If he has left without an address, make sure his parents or siblings know where you are. Though Rae Ann has regrets about pushing the father-son relationship as hard as she did, and Jesse's relationship with his father was not very satisfying, particularly during adolescence, there is a somewhat happy ending to the story. Rae Ann had helped Jesse stay in touch with his paternal grandfather. One day during a visit to Grandpa, when Jesse was grown and the father had been paying back child support for a few years to finance Jesse's college education, the grandfather relayed the message that Jesse's father would really like to see him. Father and son are now in contact. Jesse told me,

> "For the past seven years we've had virtually no contact until a couple months ago. We've just started seeing each other again but it's a whole different situation. I don't think of him as my father, I think of him more as a friend. I see him every few weeks when I come home from college and we just go out and have a good time.
>
> "We've never talked about those seven years. I don't think it would help the situation any to bring it up. What's done is done. Clear up until the point that I started seeing him again I had been thinking a lot about all the bad things he did. But now I choose not to look at that because it's over with.
>
> "He's a fun guy to be around now. The first few times I visited him I did it out of courtesy. It was really uncomfortable, but now

we are more relaxed with each other. I want to see him now. I enjoy being with him."

Jesse is very low-key about this new contact with his father and is even cautious in describing it. Without seeming aware of the potential for being hurt in the relationship, he insists that his father is just a man he's getting to know. He was protected by his mother's past assurances that his father cared about him. In this way, Rae Ann's plan to spare her son pain and smooth the way for the father-son relationship has worked. The father's clear efforts to revive his relationship with his son seem to confirm what Jesse had been led to believe all along.

It has become a self-fulfilling prophecy in the most positive sense. Jesse was led to expect love from his father, and so when he finally encountered his father face-to-face, despite his father's seven years of apparent neglect and disinterest, Jesse was willing to approach his father with a "spirit of goodwill" and openness that is very uncharacteristic of a child of divorce. A more bitter, more rejected-feeling child could have responded to the father's overture with anger and hostility and "proven" his father to be uncaring by driving him off. But by expecting love, Jesse made it a reality.

Like Jesse's father, your child's father may someday want to make contact, and you want to make that as easy as you can. Avoid making any blaming statements to your ex about your children's behavior or circumstances. Guilt is one of the most common factors that keeps dads away. There is a stage when guilt will spark a man's sense of responsibility, but just beyond that comes a stage when guilt makes him too ashamed to ever show his face again. If you want him to come around someday for your children's sake, you've got to find a way to lessen that shame. Forget about whether or not he *should* be ashamed of himself and suffer for it! Keep your child's ultimate well-being in mind.

SOLO PARENTING

What if Dad just won't visit? Is the child doomed or can Mom raise a healthy child alone? Studies show that in the extreme disruption and chaos following divorce, both parents are so distracted by their pain that they are far less effective parents. Since mothers are the custodial parent in 90 percent of the cases, the children are deeply affected by their mother's diminished stability and capability. With no father in the household, the mother has no "supportive other." She is on her own to manage the finances, keep up with household tasks, train children to take gradually increasing responsibility appropriate for their ages, monitor children's schoolwork, and teach them to be healthy respectful people. This is all a tremendous load for any parent of either sex to take on alone. (If Dad never helped Mom with these tasks before divorce, now she can thank her lucky stars she learned to be so self-sufficient!)

It is no wonder that following divorce most children experience missed appointments, irregular meals, and erratic bedtimes. During this time parents tend to expect less from their children, both in terms of behavior and help with household chores. Mothers are typically less affectionate, especially with their boys. The parent's low expectations and diminished coping ability combine to create an unstable home for the children.[1]

Aside from the special influence and contribution of a male to the household, much of what children lack when Dad moves out can be provided by the single mother. The sooner Mom can organize and simplify the many demands on her time, the quicker she can become a calm, steady parent again. Divorced kids suffer not so much from a lack of male company as they do from having fewer adults around who are available to be the nurturers, guides, and limit-setters children need to feel safe and secure.

Children are experiencing their own pain and sense of loss following divorce. Their school performance often suffers and they may begin to have fights with friends. To gain control over their own lives, kids need their home to be a "port in the storm." The sooner Mom can create this environment, the quicker children can recover. Fortunately, most fathers do maintain contact with their children in the first two or three years after divorce. By the time the children must face the emotional crisis of Dad's diminishing interest, Mom should have had time to regain her emotional stability.

The transition to single-parenting is tremendously demanding and cannot be done without sources of emotional support. Mothers need to get out and seek the company of other parents through organizations such as Parents Without Partners and other groups like

Scouts or churches that offer activities for parents and children together. Mom must form a network of friends who can at least serve as telephone parents—adults she can call for a second opinion on parenting decisions and in times of crisis.

BE THE BEST YOU CAN BE

There is no reason to assume your children will be permanently damaged because the father has minimal or no contact with them. Fathers do provide important stimulation, support, and discipline in children's lives. The child of a disinterested father is at a disadvantage. Father-absence is a handicap and mothers must seek appropriate correction or compensation. Just as the mother of a blind child would learn about the handicap and what she can do to organize the child's life to reduce the negative effects of that handicap, the mother of a father-absent child can learn methods that will lessen the damage from a lack of "fathering." By being a reliable, competent parent, and overcoming the female's culturally trained tendency to be overprotective, Mom can supply much of the stimulation, support, and discipline her children need.

If Mom shows she can make small repairs and is comfortable pursuing a career or functioning as breadwinner, both her male and female children will have a good role model for "androgynous adulthood." Mom can also look around her for opportunities to bring her kids into contact with good men. This will be discussed further in Part II.

So far we have discussed the problems children of divorce suffer from their fathers' absences. In the next four chapters we will learn how father-loss affects children born out of wedlock and children whose fathers have died. There are many interesting similarities and some very important differences. Through the stories of these children we learn about the importance of grieving the loss of Dad, the drive to understand who he was so the children can better form their identities, and the need to talk and reminisce about him. For these reasons, divorced mothers and children of divorce will find much of the information on these families that share the experience of father-loss both relevant and enlightening.

SUMMARY POINTS

- Studies show that how often the father sees the children is less important than the quality of the visits.
- The mother often serves as a "gatekeeper" and can make the father's contact easier or more difficult by her attitudes and willingness to be cooperative and flexible.
- Dads should take pro-active measures to stay in touch with their children. They should not only visit, phone, and write but also contact the children's schools and activity leaders to learn about the children's special events.
- Moms should help children understand why Dads lose touch and actively try to build bridges between Dad and his children by encouraging the children's positive opinion of Dad and helping them discover interests and activities they can all share.
- Post-divorce conflict brings out the worst in everyone, and divorced parents tend to magnify all the worst qualities of their estranged spouses. Moms who worry about Dad's competence must keep in mind that Dad can be a lousy "mate" but still be a good parent.
- Neutral parties can help the father stay in touch without stirring up parental conflict. Teachers and activities leaders need to be educated about this important role they can play.
- When Mom models forgiveness and acceptance of Dad, the children know they will be forgiven for their own mistakes.

4

Uncommitted Fathers
and Unwed Mothers

■

"I tend to think of Chip as two different people—who he was then and who he is now. I don't really know him now and I try to keep an open mind. I was really different then, and maybe he is really different now."

—KIM, A TEENAGE MOTHER

■

Out-of-wedlock birthrates have more than quadrupled in the past thirty years. In 1960 only 5.3 percent of children were born to unmarried mothers; in 1970 the rate had doubled to 10.7 percent of the births in this country; and in 1986 a surprising 23.4 percent of this nation's children were born to unmarried parents. The birthrate for unwed Hispanic parents was even higher at 31.6 percent, and 61.2 percent of black children were born out of wedlock in 1986. Though the number of children of divorce in this country has doubled since 1970, the number of children of unwed parents has increased eight-fold![1] Each year in the United States, 500,000 babies are born to teenage mothers.[2] In the case of the pregnant teenager, we often have three children's futures at risk: the mother's, the baby's, and the teenage father's.

THE ISSUE OF CHOICE

An Oscar award-winning film produced by the Children's Aid Society of California, entitled *Teenage Fathers*, raises an important issue for the fathers of teenage pregnancy.[3] The pregnant female adolescent has a number of options open to her: abortion, adoption, or keeping the baby. If the teenage girl feels she cannot handle the stress of carrying the baby to term, she can elect an abortion. This would leave her free to go on with her career plans or look for a better relationship. It gives her a chance to say, "I'm not ready for this." If she has strong convictions that prohibit abortion as an option, she can still choose to avoid the physical and financial responsibility of a child by giving her child up for adoption at birth (or at any point afterward). If she feels mature enough to care for it, she is also free to keep the child.

What do each of these options mean for the teenage fathers of these babies? Abortion would allow him to avoid paying high medical bills at a time when he is trying to finish high school, and adoption would save him from eighteen years of paying child support. However, if the mother chooses to keep the baby, he faces not only years of financial obligation, he must also deal with his role in the child's life. What if he doesn't feel ready to be a father? The teenage father is often far more immature than his female partner. Like all teens, he has little sense of the consequences of his actions. When he is "caught" because his girlfriend becomes pregnant, he feels bewildered. He feels as much of a victim as she does.

A generation ago, it was best for the mother to have full responsibility for the choice because chances were that she would end up fully responsible for the child. A teenage boy who was not ready to marry and become a father could usually escape pretty easily. He could deny that he was the father, and no one could prove otherwise. If it was obvious that he was the father (because the girl had dated no one else and had an impeccable reputation), he could generally still escape responsibility if his parents didn't "force" him to marry the girl. Today, paternity can be proven with indisputable genetic tests. The boy and girl each made a decision about whether or not to have sex, and each, by neglect or design, decided not to use birth control. However, once the girl becomes pregnant, only she gets to decide the consequences. Ready or not, the teenage boy becomes a father.

IMPACT OF EARLY FATHERHOOD

Who are these young men and how capable are they of being fathers? On the whole, most of these young fathers have not learned to manage their own lives yet and are certainly not ready for father-hood. Immature adolescent fathers are likely to lack a sense of commitment to mother and child, have little incentive to learn to be a good father, and will often feel jealous of the baby. Most teenage boys are self-centered, poorly skilled at planning or working toward future goals effectively, and more concerned with the here and now. The teenage father is no different.

They have been caught at an exploratory stage and now must suddenly skip a few developmental levels to parenthood. The normal progression for men (and now for most women) is to complete their education, acquire a good steady job, become financially indepen-dent, get married, and then have children. Each step represents taking increasing responsibility for self and ultimately leads to a mature outlook by the time of parenthood. Yet, research shows that most males do not become mature enough to make good choices about career, values, or family life and commit to those choices until they are in their twenties. Indeed, only 20 percent of male college students show this ability.[4] When all the developmental transitions are squashed together into one triply intense transition that is her-alded by social disapproval instead of supportive celebration, the pressure can be unbearable.

At the same time that young boys are trying to become indepen-dent of their parents, the thought of tying themselves down to a wife and baby seems an unbearable curtailment. Nonetheless, about 20 percent of unwed adolescent fathers do live with their babies,[5] and more and more adolescent fathers are maintaining contact with their co-parent and child.

The dropout rate for boys who become fathers in high school is twice as high as those who don't (43 percent vs. 23 percent). Teenage fathers in tenth or eleventh grade and those who are one year or more behind in school are most likely to drop out. Boys who complete high school do get better jobs and earn more than boys who don't,[6] and a high school diploma is considered the minimum requirement for most jobs.

In studies that compared young men who were headed toward the same educational goals, those who became fathers early never "caught up" to those who postponed fatherhood.[7] Thus, they end up in a "catch-22" situation: if they end their education now and take an unskilled job, a few years down the road they will be despised for being such poor providers. We must ask then: Have we "set things up" so that it is foolhardy for a young father to choose to marry the mother of his child? Can we develop programs that help him stay in school and meet his financial obligations under these very difficult circumstances?

THE TEEN FATHER'S ROLE

Unwed fathers can be a major source of support to their babies' mothers, a source of constant conflict, or a blank spot in their babies' lives. Many factors affect the likelihood of teenage fathers remaining in contact with the mother and their child. Were the mother and father each other's *exclusive* sexual partner before the pregnancy? Have either of them, even now, reached a stage where they are ready to be sexually faithful to one person? How committed were the mother and father to each other prior to the pregnancy? How does each family feel about the other mate? How long the couple dated or were sexually active with one another will influence the father's degree of attachment and sense of responsibility as well as the mother's willingness to let him remain involved with her and their child.

At one end of the scale we have the teenage father who has been having intercourse exclusively with the teenage mother to whom he has felt very committed. Whether or not they marry is then influenced by how each of the couple's parents feel about early unions. A boy who has been committed to one girl at the time she becomes pregnant is more likely to make a commitment to be part of his child's life, whether or not he decides to marry the child's mother. Pauline and Rob, a teen couple I interviewed, did marry. Their families have been very supportive, but the going still hasn't been easy.

Pauline became pregnant during her senior year in high school. She had been dating Rob, the father of her child, for three years, and then they had broken up when she moved twenty miles away and started attending a different high school. She did not do well at the new high school, so a few months later she moved back to her old town with her mother and began attending her old high school again. She walked the same halls as Rob, but they never spoke. Pauline had missed many periods but kept telling herself she was not pregnant, she was just getting awfully fat. When rumors began to circulate among the students that she was pregnant, Rob came to her and asked if the baby was his. She broke down and admitted to Rob and to herself that she was pregnant, but begged him not to tell anyone, especially their parents.

Disturbed and concerned about the health of Pauline and the unborn baby, Rob overrode Pauline's wishes and told his mother. All the parents (with the exception of Pauline's natural father who disowned her) were wonderfully supportive and continued to be so throughout the delivery and the baby's early months. Rob and Pauline decided that they wanted to marry and have the baby. They had broken up previously over jealous fights, but with a baby on the way they felt more securely committed. Rob told me, "We talked about it a lot for two weeks and then decided that we wanted to get married."

At the other end of the scale there is the promiscuous male who has no interest in becoming a husband, let alone a father. Developmentally, he is obviously at a very self-centered stage and is not much use to anyone until he has completed this stage. Though he can be held financially liable for a child he fathers, if he earns no money he can hardly pay child support, and he is likely to see the threat of having to share money he earns as all the more reason not to start earning money.

Kim, who was only thirteen when she became pregnant, has had to cope with this kind of immaturity. Her ex-boyfriend Chip, who was fifteen years old at the time she became pregnant, was very dominating, controlling, and verbally abusive. Though Chip was her boyfriend, Kim was actually a victim of "date rape." She had not wanted to have sex, and he repeatedly forced her. Physically much too weak to resist, she would respond with total passivity and hope it would be over soon.

Despite the cessation of her periods, Kim believed Chip when he told her she was not pregnant. She blocked it out of her mind until, when she was five months pregnant, her mother noticed the signs. "We never asked for child support payments from Chip or anything," Kim told me. It was a volatile situation and they wanted the fewest strings attached.

"During my junior year of high school I made friends with Chip again. I hadn't spoken to him for almost three years. Chip apologized to me for having treated me so badly and that meant a lot to me. I realized that his father was alcoholic and his parents had always been fighting. He'd seen his dad hit his mom, so he had really poor role models.

"Although he doesn't seem to know what to do with Brian, I think he really does care about him. But I don't think Chip is very mature yet. He acts more like Brian's playmate than his father. Sometimes I worry that when Brian is older he'll decide he wants to go live with his dad because his dad lets him do whatever he wants. That would kill me. I would have to let him go. But I would hope that once he got over there he would figure out that it's not good for him."

Since graduating high school a few years ago, Chip has not worked. When Chip turned eighteen he inherited some money held in trust for him from his father. Within a year he had blown all the money on cars and rock concerts. According to Kim, Chip is strung out on drugs much of the time. Though he is almost twenty-one years old, Chip is currently still living with his mother and contributes nothing to the household.

Kim could have sued for a large portion of Chip's inheritance, while he had it, but she didn't want to take anything from him. She believes this will protect her from any future claims he might make on the baby if he takes an interest in him later. (This is actually not true.)

New laws regarding receipt of welfare and Aid to Families with Dependent Children (AFDC) require that the father be named and pressed for financial support whether or not the mother's family desires this continued connection. However, many policy makers and service providers question the wisdom of adopting policies that encourage the father's involvement even when the mother or her family oppose it. At the same time, father advocates stress we should not ignore the father's needs and interests, thus helping the family shut him out, because this may ultimately be bad for the child. Therefore, some social agencies have begun to address the problems of the father. These will be discussed in the next chapter.

THE TEEN MOTHER'S ATTITUDE

Whether we feel sympathy for the unwed father or not, we need to acknowledge that some young men are simply not ready for fatherhood. The girls who decide to keep their babies, despite the boy's lack of readiness, need to develop realistic attitudes about this. Megan, who was seventeen when she learned she was pregnant, serves as a good role model. Her complicated story is representative of the complexities the modern unwed teen must consider.

Megan's long-term boyfriend, Blake, had gone off to college, and the relationship had not survived the weekend commute. Hurt and alone, she began dating Donny, a boy she regarded as "just a friend." The relationship turned sexual too quickly, and they parted. Megan, who was having trouble getting along with her parents at that point, left home and went to live with Blake near his college campus. While there she realized she was pregnant and that the child must have been fathered by her sixteen-year-old friend Donny.

Having grown up in a Catholic family, she ultimately found abortion unacceptable, and her very supportive parents made raising her child seem attainable. Marrying the baby's real father was out of the question, and she also recognized that it was not his decision to keep and raise the child. So she has taken full financial responsibility for the child, and she wants full legal custody also. She processed those developmental stages very rapidly and comes across as a mature, responsible, loving mother. Megan told me:

> "I never had an opinion on abortion before. The place where I went for my pregnancy test was very anti-abortion though I didn't know it at the time. The girl who gave me the results of my test was twenty years old and in college full-time. She told me that she had a two-year-old son that she had conceived during her senior year in high school and talked about all the financial aid I could get. She was the first example I saw of what it could be like to have the baby. So I went back and told Blake I was pregnant and he said, 'Well let's contact Donny and he can pay half for the abortion and I'll pay the other half.' And I said, 'What if I have it and then give it up for adoption?' He said, 'No. You'll hold that against me forever.' And I said, 'Well, I'll hold it against you forever if I get an abortion.'
>
> "When I told my mom she flipped out, but she said she'd tell my dad. He just came in my room and cried. I told him I hadn't decided yet if I was going to have the baby and my dad said, 'I'd rather you cut my arms off, than have an abortion.' They've always been very pro-life. I knew I had to have the baby.

"Now my life has done a complete turn-around because of my baby Keith. When I left home, I wasn't coming back. I was going to drop out of school and get a job. I can't imagine where I'd be if I hadn't gotten pregnant. I had gotten into drugs. There I was in a really destructive relationship with somebody who dumps me because I wouldn't have an abortion. But Keith has brought me back to my family. My mom and I are closer now. I'm getting ready to go to radiology school. I feel so grateful to Keith for making me get my life together. I feel better about myself than I ever have before in my life."

SINGLE MOTHERS BY CHOICE

Some unwed parents are responsible adults who have chosen to keep a child alone and some of these children are even planned. As women postpone childbearing, many single women find themselves going beyond the recommended time for safely taking the very reliable pill and experiment with slightly more risky birth-control methods. Coils can slip out of place unnoticed, diaphragms are ineffective when a woman's weight fluctuates more than ten pounds, and foams were never guaranteed to be 100 percent effective. For whatever reason, even cautious, mature women can get pregnant by accident. Many single women reaching the end of their prime child-bearing years also consider having a child alone. And though these fathers may be reluctant to play that role, the children will often be graced with one stable parent.

Vanessa (whom we met in Chapter 3) had always wanted a child but during her ten-year marriage she could not conceive. Medical tests had shown that her husband was sterile, and he wouldn't agree to artificial insemination. This was one of the reasons that caused their separation.

Vanessa began dating and found that she had become pregnant by a man she would have never considered marrying. After wanting a child for so long, she wasn't about to get an abortion. She was working full-time for a good salary and was able to support herself and her son. She remarried five years later.

"While Larry [Kirk's father] was living with us he helped pay the bills but I have never collected child support from him."

While Vanessa was on her own with Kirk, she felt they were doing fine as a unit of two.

> "It was difficult at times. Sometimes Kirk felt more like a responsibility than a joy. Not that I didn't love him. But I had my work and I was just getting my own life back together after two essentially bad relationships. I had to find myself again.
>
> "Before I had Kirk I was sure I could handle it all easily. I had enough money and I thought that was all there was to it. But emotionally it was a lot harder than I thought. He was the kind of kid who wanted to be with you all the time. There was no sitting and relaxing."

Still, she had a steady income, good childcare for Kirk and lots of experience with small children to help her discipline and keep their lives consistent and orderly. Weekends at Larry's are still "party weekends," where there is no set bedtime and Kirk can eat all the junk food he wants, but Vanessa doesn't let this bother her. The way she sees it, through Larry she received the greatest gift she had ever longed for—a child. Having been without a child for so long she doesn't have the heart to deprive Larry of visitation, and she wouldn't want Kirk to be cut off from Larry if Kirk wanted contact. She has a civilized, easy-going attitude about the whole thing.

Vanessa had demanded no child support because she was fully aware that she had the power to keep the child or abort it, and keeping the child was a choice she made without Larry's consent. Though many of the teen mothers I interviewed had this attitude, they are not financially independent from their parents yet and may later regret they were not more aggressive about forcing the fathers to pay support. But for now, all these women seem to regard their children as gifts or privileges, not burdens.

Mary, a special-education teacher who adopted as a single mother in her thirties, also considers her child to be a rare treasure. Unable to get pregnant during her six-year marriage, she continued to yearn for a child after her divorce, but there were no new marriage prospects in sight and she appeared to be infertile. She learned about a private adoption network that would allow her to adopt as a single mother. Though few single mothers are given infants by social services, Mary was fortunate enough to get a biracial baby at birth through private contacts.

Mary's child Rachael, now eight years old, was born prematurely as an emergency C-section and may have suffered a shortage of oxygen during the birth. She has had learning problems: dyslexia (a reading problem) and apraxia (a communication problem). Rachael is of normal intelligence and can understand others easily, but cannot form replies that show her understanding. "School has been very difficult for Rachael even though she is in a special class," Mary explained. "I had thought being adopted and being biracial were going to be the problems in her life. But these are small concerns compared to her educational handicaps." All in all, Rachael's learning difficulties, adoption concerns, and biracial conflicts seem like more pressing issues than father-absence.

PUTTING IT IN PERSPECTIVE

There is an important lesson for us to learn from Mary's experience. A child who has no father involved in his or her life may be disadvantaged, but father-absence is just one of any child's problems. Many children have school problems, health problems, or problems with peer relationships. The absent father is often just one of a cluster of problems. When there are no men available to a child, Mom can still help the child gain stability in other areas of his or her life. We must look at the whole picture before we erroneously pronounce our children hopelessly damaged because their father is not around. Mary has not been very concerned about Rachael lacking a male role model.

> "In a way I have some advantages over families where there is a father but he just isn't around. One married friend of mine, who keeps counting on her husband to help with the kids, is constantly frustrated because he backs out of things at the last minute. But I can choose the adults in Rachael's life and reject the ones that we can't count on. I work with kids and I know they blame themselves when their fathers don't come around or want to spend time with them. I have more control over the adult influences in Rachael's life at this point and she seems to benefit."

Mary experiences the normal problems of parenting alone and not having another partner to share crises with.

"The worst time I ever had was when Rachael was small and she was very sick with a severe respiratory infection. She was having a lot of trouble breathing for weeks and finally the doctor suggested I bring her into the emergency room. I'd had an exhausting day at work and I was just so worn out. I called a friend to come help me, but she couldn't come. I felt so alone and overwhelmed. I really needed some support and there wasn't any available."

Mary has joined an informal single-adoptive-parents group. It is a support group with about ten parents who have monthly adult outings without kids where they can meet and network. They exchange stories about the trials and joys of being a single adoptive parent and trade phone numbers so they have another adult to call when they are at their wit's end or just need a second viewpoint. It is also a social group where parents and children can get to know others who share common ground. Rachael has opportunities at group birthday parties and picnics to see that there are other adopted multiracial kids who have only one parent, so she doesn't feel like one of a kind.

On a bad day, who or what can a single mother turn to when she has overwhelming problems with her child? Mary can hope for support from her friends, but if they are having a bad day too, it may not be possible for them to help. So Mary has learned the importance of expanding her network. As she sagely points out, in some ways she is better off than mothers whose husbands are always gone on business, or divorced mothers whose ex-husbands don't show up when they say they will. Mary knows she is alone, and she is the only person she can count on. If she gets help, life has gone beyond her *expectations*. Therefore, she feels grateful and blessed when she receives a helping hand, and it is just another day when she doesn't.

Mary also has no grudge against men to pass on to her daughter. Since Rachael does not know her father, she has no preconceived notions about men—good or bad. Instead, her impressions of men will be formed by the ones she meets. Mary can help her meet warm caring men through church, her circle of friends, or other social organizations. Unlike other children with an "absent father," Rachael is a bit like that proverbial blank slate, and Mary can help her draw her own picture of "father."

HOPEFUL SIGNS

As our stereotypical notions of fatherhood change, the pressures on teen fathers change too. Now that mothers contribute financially in about 80 percent of homes, and more and more men are taking a nurturing role, teen boys are freer to be nurturing and less pressured to prove all by bread-winning. Research shows that fathers who are more emotionally expressive (though traditional in other ways) produce more androgynous and therefore less rigid boys.[8] In addition, more and more teenage fathers are remaining involved with their teenage partners. Over 70 percent of fathers in the Teen Mother and Child program at the University of Utah are either married, engaged, or living with their partner at the time of delivery. Other studies on financially disadvantaged fathers also show 50 to 70 percent involvement.[9] Three forces have recently converged to alter our perception of the adolescent father:

1. New research shows that a father's involvement is important to the child's development.
2. Young parents of both sexes have begun to request programs for fathers.
3. Social service providers are beginning to realize that current programs which increase the distance between the teen mother and father, and thereby often push him out, perpetuate the welfare-mother syndrome.

As of 1982, federally funded programs sponsored by the Office of Adolescent Pregnancy have been urged to address the psychological and vocational/educational needs of these young fathers. Some goals of these programs should be to:

1. Help adolescent fathers learn decision-making skills so they can make responsible realistic decisions about pregnancy, childcare, and their vocational/educational choices.
2. Encourage young fathers to become involved in the pregnancy and parenting process.
3. Increase the socioeconomic independence of adolescent families.
4. Decrease the repeat pregnancy rate by educating about contraceptive use.

According to researchers Frank Bolton, coordinator of Psychological Services at the Arizona Department of Economic Security, and James Kahn, of the Teen Mother and Child Program at the University of Utah, when adolescent fathers are given emotional and social support, rather than being assumed to be self-centered, irresponsible, immature kids, they often respond by becoming seriously concerned about their responsibilities to their children and make an effort to contribute financially.[10] At the same time, the teen father will probably need to keep his financial support goals low, and the adults who surround him should not compare him to older fathers and expect instant maturity. His fledgling efforts to be a responsible father need to be respected and encouraged so that when he is developmentally ready to take on more major responsibility, he is still emotionally strong.

The Teen Father Collaborative launched by Bank Street College in 1983 has begun to develop and experiment with programs that meet teen fathers' needs. They established eight sites throughout the country to serve adolescent fathers.[11] Many of these programs combine mental-health counseling, peer counseling, and employment counseling to help meet the young men's multiple needs. Some offer on-site childcare classes and organize outings for teen dads and their children. Fathers are taught practical well-baby skills such as feeding, diapering, and bathing their infants, while building relationships with other young men in their situation. Most enter the program through the teen mother's programs, but efforts are made to advertise and attract teen dads to come on their own initiative. Boys reported being drawn to the programs by presentations in schools, public-service announcements, and active recruitment efforts at local teen hangouts.

Half of the participants in the Bank Street programs were fathers and the other half were fathers-to-be. Of those who participated, 55 percent were making some financial contribution for their child. At a one-year follow-up, most of these young men felt most grateful for their one-on-one relationships with a male counselor who had helped them not only with personal explorations but also with employment advice. Some found the peer counseling (where young men listen to each other and offer support or advice) the most meaningful. The peer-counseling network made the teen dads feel less isolated and many got together with each other and their children outside of group meetings. Most felt the parenting-skills classes were helpful and increased their confidence in caring for their children.[12]

SUMMARY POINTS

- Unlike the mother, the teen father who does not feel ready to be a parent has no power to decide to abort the child or put it up for adoption.
- Research shows that most young men are not mature enough to make good decisions about career, values, or family life until they are in their mid-twenties. Hence the adolescent must skip over many developmental steps when he is hurled into the role of father.
- Adolescent fathers are caught between a rock and a hard place. If they forego further training and education now to support their children, they will be caught in the role of poor provider indefinitely.
- Now that unwed mothers are free to choose between abortion, adoption, or keeping the child, they seem to feel more powerful and less victimized. The unwed mom often sees the child as a positive force in her life.
- Older single mothers who have achieved financial security are less concerned about having a father's involvement. At the same time, they often do not have the negative feelings about men that divorced moms express.
- Some social service agencies are beginning to realize the importance of offering programs that address the needs of the unwed father. Career counseling, parenting classes, and peer-group sharing with other young fathers help these unwed fathers adjust to their new roles constructively.

5

Motivating Unwed Dads

"I feel that there is a positive healthy relationship that can develop between father and child, and whatever we can do to make this happen is all to the good. Establishing paternity lays the foundation for all the rest."

—GARY KREPS, WEST VIRGINIA STATE
CHILD ADVOCATE OFFICE[1]

Though we have made tremendous progress toward helping the teenage mother bear her child in a new atmosphere of openness and acceptance, many people still hold very negative, stereotyped ideas about the teenage father. Our social and legal agencies often regard him as a criminal and take a punitive rather than supportive approach to involving him in the family. In Oklahoma the process of establishing paternity is essentially adversarial. The father is summoned to court even if he is willing to acknowledge paternity voluntarily.[2]

Many father advocates and researchers feel the cumbersome, confusing, and punitive aspects of many of the procedures to establish paternity or child-support payment have created understandably negative resistance in the unwed fathers. Instead, we need to convey acceptance, respect, and support by society and social agencies through more positive approaches that emphasize the father's rights, and give these fathers credit for contributing whatever they can to the child's well-being.

By looking at feedback from unwed fathers involved in more innovative programs, we can see what works best with young fathers. Teenage fathers report they most often seek help from parents, siblings, or friends rather than teachers or other professionals. They felt most useful preparing for baby's arrival by purchasing clothing or fixing up a room rather than by reading parenting books. We need to offer programs to these young men that address their very concrete needs, not only in terms of baby, but also in terms of their desire to someday become "providers."

Unfortunately, in most cases there is resistance to spending money on programs for fathers. Funding is scarce, and the unwed mothers who must feed and house their children are more visibly in need. Social service agencies attract few males, so not only is the male viewpoint under-represented, there are few male workers to greet the reluctant teen father when he does show his face. At the same time, adolescent fathers are much less likely to seek help on their own than teen mothers, and overburdened social workers don't have time to "drum up business" by aggressively reaching out to teen fathers. Some programs that do start up fall apart quickly because there has not been enough revision of the programs to truly address the teen father's needs.

Yet, research shows that the public's money is best spent on strategies that can attract and then educate absent fathers or reluctant fathers-to-be. Some methods that have worked include:

Strategies to Get Dads Involved

1. Poster campaigns and media spots that promote paternal responsibility in a positive light.
2. Parenting classes designed specifically for fathers offered at high schools, junior colleges, churches, or community groups.
3. Information and education offered at prenatal classes about the importance of the father's role and his responsibilities.
4. Informative pamphlets and flyers distributed to and by health-care workers, social-service professionals, gynecologists, pediatricians, and other professionals who come in contact with new fathers.
5. Birth registration efforts that encourage the father to have his name put on the birth certificate.
6. Legislation to require the Social Security numbers of both the mother and father on the child's birth certificate.[3]

Like all teens, adolescent fathers need practical vocational counseling and training programs to prepare them for the world of work. On top of this, they need instruction in how to be a "father" to the child whether they live with the baby or not. Although very few will seek out this kind of help on their own, many can be encouraged to participate by offers of free legal advice or job placement. Before the baby is born, the father should be encouraged to attend free parenting classes and other prenatal information sessions such as those offered by the Childbirth Education Association. Unmarried dads should also be encouraged to attend prenatal visits to the doctor and hear the child's heartbeat. Fathers' support groups and workshops designed to address fathers' needs should be implemented.Male counselors are particularly effective with these young fathers. We must keep in mind that current attitudes toward adolescent fathers are likely to make them suspicious, defensive, and even hostile to social-service workers or other "helping" people. Programs can be administered in "neutral territory," such as universities, hospitals, high schools, community mental health centers, churches, or other community agencies such as YMCAs or boys' clubs.

The best approach might be to encourage the teenage father's continuing relationship with his child while emphasizing that he need not make a commitment to the mother. Much effort should be put into helping him feel free to keep these relationships separate. The attitude of the teen mother is very important here, because the teen father is likely to feel guilty about impregnating her and will naturally wish to avoid her unless she makes it clear he can see the child without paying an "emotional price" each time.

Megan, whom we met in Chapter 4, has an exemplary attitude. Though she saw less and less of Donny as she tried to finish school and work a part-time job despite her pregnancy, Megan was careful not to become "enemies" with Donny. As we have seen, Donny's feelings after the baby's birth were obviously ambivalent. He attended the christening, and Megan reported that he danced around with Keith, saying, "My baby is going to be mellow." Megan showed me photographs of Donny feeding the baby on his christening day. "He called himself 'Dad,' " she told me, "but then at other times he completely denies it."

Beyond the problem of child support, if the teenage parents do not marry, how involved the father will be still has to be negotiated.

Donny has denied paternity, but Donny's mother acknowledges the strong family resemblance and considers Keith to be her grandchild. Though Donny stays away, Grandma comes to visit whenever she is in town. According to Megan:

> "Right now we're in the middle of establishing paternity. We're both supposed to go for genetic testing next week. I'm just doing it with a doctor, not with a lawyer or anything. I'm paying for half of the testing and Donny's mother is paying for the other half. His mother just wants him to recognize his responsibility. It's not a question of child support, we both just want him to acknowledge that Keith is his son. Someday when Keith says, 'Who is my father?' I can say, 'Donny is your father.' "

Megan wants to wait until Donny is eighteen before she has him sign a release giving her full rights over Keith. She explained,

> "I worry that someday he might get married and his wife can't bear children and he'll come back and decide he wants Keith. I just want it to be settled once and for all."

Megan shows good sense here and some ability to look ahead. She is considering her child's emotional future as she strives to establish paternity, though her vision may be dangerously short-sighted in terms of the child's financial future. There may come a time when Donny can pay child support and his son can benefit.

According to a booklet prepared for social-service professionals by the American Association for Marriage and Family Therapy Research and Education Foundation, there are a number of factors that influence how likely unwed fathers are to stay involved.[4]

Factors Influencing Unwed Fathers' Involvement

1. *Proximity*. Fathers who live nearby have more contact with their children.
2. *Outreach to father at time of birth*. Studies show that the father is most likely to acknowledge paternity and commit to the child while he is in his "honeymoon" period with his child.
3. *Male outreach workers*. Unwed fathers respond better to male social-service workers who sympathize with their need for employment or parent education.

4. *Father's employment status*. Fathers with a steady source of income were more likely to be willing to pay support.
5. *Supportive community*. Fathers were more likely to get involved with their children if the grandparents and their friends encouraged and supported their involvement.

ESTABLISHING PATERNITY

The unmarried teenage couple has one advantage over divorced parents trying to share a child—they don't have years of bitter exchanges fueling their disagreements. The father may not be ready for most of the responsibility of fatherhood, but attempts to help him bond will improve the chances of his staying in touch. The couple can view their future relationship as co-parents, and in line with that, it is not unreasonable for the father to be encouraged to attend the birth and infant-care classes offered at the hospital. The more he knows about the child and parenting, the more likely he is to keep in touch.

An innovative new program begun by Gary Kreps, of the West Virginia State Child Advocate Office, is based on this premise of helping fathers bond at birth. Hospitals in Charleston, Huntington, and Kingwood have begun a program to let unwed fathers know what their rights and responsibilities are. When Mr. Kreps learned that eight out of ten unwed fathers attend the birth of their children, or come in during the first day or so to see the baby, he saw the hospital as a place to reach out to the unwed dads. The fact that such a high percentage of unwed fathers want to see their children shows the tremendous sense of connection they must feel at the time of the birth. Kreps realized that this was an ideal time to ask the fathers to acknowledge paternity, because five years down the road many of these young men come to feel so disconnected from their child that they even begin to convince themselves that the baby probably wasn't theirs anyway.

Kreps designed booklets for both the mother and father that clarify for each of them what their rights and responsibilities are to the child. Many fathers who live in dread of their responsibilities (and would deny them) are pleasantly surprised to learn that they also have rights. The booklet also explains how important it is to the child to know who his father is and what an impact the father can have on his child's life. Another important point that comes across in the booklet is that the mother is not eligible for full state financial aid unless a father is named. The teen father who has no job or means to provide for his child learns that by simply declaring paternity he gives his child's mother the right and means to receive full financial aid from state agencies. It is something concrete the young father can do to help out his baby financially.

Kreps has designed a Declaration of Paternity form for the father to sign that is a four-copy document. One of the copies is given to the father so that he has a paper to prove he is the father of his child. Like carrying a picture of one's girlfriend or other loved one, the father can show this form as physical proof of his connection to his child. It engenders a sense of "pride of ownership." It has the psychological benefit of symbolizing the young man's fertility and manhood through fatherhood. Kreps finds unwed fathers very responsive to this paternity document at this stage of their relationship to their child. Most of the young men are excited to learn they have rights, and the document feels like proof of these rights. They are in a honeymoon period with their newborn child, when the novelty of fatherhood has not yet worn thin, and they have a desire to be responsible. Since their relationships with the mothers may have been relatively short-lived, these men experience fatherhood without the marriage burnout that many divorced fathers feel after a drawn-out, angry relationship with an ex-spouse.

At the same time, the pamphlet and the Child Advocate Office nudge the boy toward taking responsibility. He is encouraged to get a part-time job and contribute something to his child's support, emphasizing that every little bit helps. Though the money he is obligated to pay out of a part-time minimum-wage job is often rather insignificant in terms of the mother's total financial needs, a pattern of giving to his child will be established.

ENCOURAGING PATERNAL RESPONSIBILITY

However, it is beneficial to establish paternity aside from and before thinking about child support. Though the father is usually most willing to admit to paternity during the first year, he is often least likely to be able to provide child support then. Some innovative programs give the young father credit for paying child support if he attends parenting classes, completes high school, attends job training, or does other things to improve his employability or parenting skills. The Teen Alternative Parenting Program in Indianapolis has implemented such a program in an effort to change the nature of the relationship between the child-support system and unwed fathers from a stance that is perceived as adversarial to one that is supportive. The fathers have been very enthusiastic in responding with their "in-kind" contributions (training rather than child-support dollars) to the child's support.[5] Gently encouraging the father to give what he can, rather than berating or punishing him for not providing money when he has scant financial resources, allows the father to stay around and become attached to the child. Studies show that today's unemployed young father may very well be tomorrow's successful wage earner. Data from the National Longitudinal Survey of Labor Force Behavior of Youth (NLSY) show that 60.6 percent of young absent fathers who were poor in 1980 were earning a decent wage six years later.[6] Kreps explained:

"We want to establish rapport and help the father learn a sense of responsibility. As an employee of the Child Advocate Office I do have to be concerned about getting child support from fathers. Though the bottom line is to get him to acknowledge paternity, what's more important to me is that I know how it affects a child to grow up without a father. Research shows that the sooner an unwed father acknowledges the child as his own, the greater the probability that he will stay in touch with the child.

"There's no coercion involved. We've found that by just making it convenient for them to sign the Declaration of Paternity, four out of ten are quite willing to do it. We try to simply make Dad aware of the fact that he is a father, and he has rights as well as responsibilities, regardless of his age. Hopefully we can get the fathers to start doing small things to help the mother, such as taking the baby and babysitting so that Mom can get out, or even bringing over a box of Pampers.

"I feel that there is a positive, healthy relationship that can develop between father and child, and whatever we can do to make this happen is all to the good. Establishing paternity lays the foundation for all the rest."[7]

Underlying Kreps's comments and his premise for the program is one basic idea—to teach a sense of responsibility to fathers. Why is this something that needs to be taught? Why have boys not absorbed the concept of a father's responsibility from our culture? Frank Furstenberg, professor of sociology at the City University of New York, explains the source and likely consequences of an alarming trend. As women have established themselves as money-earners, they have freed men to take a more active role in the nurturing aspects of parenting. Unfortunately, the result instead has been that men see themselves as having no important role. As men now see it, if they do not provide for their children financially, then the mothers will, and failing that, welfare can.

Some social theorists have already decided men are a lost cause and concentrate on encouraging programs that better prepare women to be more financially secure.[8] It is as though we have put all our eggs in that one basket. There is so little federal money going toward educational and social programs that somewhere along the line we left out the men in our planning. Programs like Kreps's, on the other hand, say, "Let's not give up on fathers!" By making the effort to push them to take responsibility, we also reestablish their status as an essential part of the human community.

Just establishing paternity has many long-reaching benefits for the child of unwed parents. Some may not seem very relevant or important when the father is sixteen years old or unemployed, but these conditions are subject to change, and the man will be the child's father for the rest of the child's life. Here is a list showing some of the benefits children are eligible for once paternity has been established.

The Child's Legal Rights

1. *Child support payments* which, though they may be meager at first, could be substantial as the father matures.
2. *Social Security benefits* are available to the child if his father later dies or becomes disabled.
3. *Military dependent benefits* (which include free health care and use of government-funded discount stores) are awarded to all children of service personnel.

4. *Health insurance* through the father's employment.
5. *Dependents' benefits* from worker's compensation programs.
6. *Right of inheritance.*

In addition, the child who knows his or her father can learn about the medical and genetic history of the father and the father's family. If the father's name appears on the document, the child could seek him out when he or she is older, even if the father has discontinued contact.

THE GRANDPARENTS' INFLUENCE

In most cases, the teenage mother has custody of the child, and her parents provide the greatest degree of financial support. If the teen father contributes money, it is probably minimal compared to the grandparents' contribution. Therefore, the mother's parents often feel a sense of ownership toward the new baby that can leave the father feeling shut out.

Both the teen mother's and teen father's parents can have a tremendous amount of influence on the role the father will play in his child's life. At one end of the spectrum, there are the maternal grandparents who recognize the difficulties of a teen pregnancy but feel very positive about this new life in their midst and regard the father as no more guilty than their daughter. They may have an attitude of good will and objectivity that strives to do what's best for all these "children" involved—mother, father, and baby. The father's parents' attitudes are also influential, though they have less power in the situation.

Why was Rob (in Chapter 4) so ready to take responsibility for fatherhood? What sort of family did he come from? Rob's parents are still together, and they had already seen one of his older sisters through an unexpected teenage pregnancy. "My mom was happy for her because she knew my sister loved the guy, and they wanted to get married," Rob explains. In Rob's experience, teenage pregnancy is a happy event, so he felt confident that his parents would stand behind him, and, he was glad to marry Pauline and do what he could to provide for his child. "The baby was there, and I had to be ready," he states simply. Rob is an actively involved father. He changes diapers and gets up in the middle of the night to warm the baby's bottle. "We've only gone out once in the last month and a half," Rob tells me, "because we hate to leave the baby." Pauline's mother is now living with a boyfriend who is extremely supportive of Pauline and Rob. John helped them find a little cottage on a river. The cottage is cozy and the setting is beautiful. It is a lucky find. Rent and utilities cost only $200 a month. Still, the couple is struggling financially, and they are each suffering from post-graduation blues. In this town where the young couple has not been able to make friends, Pauline's mother and her boyfriend are also babysitters and companions to Pauline and Rob. "We get to go out on John's boat and do other things with them," Pauline told me. "And that's really nice because we can't afford to do much."

The most helpful social support adults in contact with teen parents can give is gentle guidance, reinforcement of their impor- tance as parents, tangible assistance in the form of financial help or relief babysitting, and emotional support.

At the other extreme there may be maternal grandparents who are angry about the pregnancy and the financial burden on them as a result. They may never have liked the grandchild's father and see him as an evil boy who seduced their good daughter. They may want him out of her life and the grandchild's life entirely, or they may push for him to quit school and pay as much child support as possible. At the same time they may make it impossible for the father to visit the child, sometimes even pressuring him into signing away his right to visit at any future time. They may threaten to cut off all support to the mother if she has anything to do with the father or permits visitation. As we saw in Chapter 2, grandparents may become part of a negative cheering section that brings out the worst in each of the new parents. This increases the adolescent mother's power as "gatekeeper."

Few adult men would be willing to face a group of hostile in-laws each time they wish to see their mate or child. Certainly we cannot expect teen fathers to have a greater degree of assertiveness and emotional stamina. If the young father is to stay involved with the child, mothers and maternal grandparents must try to stay focused on the "best interests of the child." Kim, whom we met earlier, has obviously gotten some good guidance from her parents. Even though her son's father is still not capable of behaving like an adult father, she is keeping the door open.

"I don't have very good feelings about Chip and sometimes I do make little sarcastic comments. But my mother has said to me, 'Kim, don't say anything. It'll get back to him.' And I know it's not good for Brian. Of course, I wouldn't tell Brian how horrible his father acted toward me way back when I was in junior high school. I tend to think of Chip as two different people—who he was then and who he is now. I was really different then, and maybe he is really different now.

"I don't discourage Chip from seeing Brian. When he's older, I don't want him to feel that I took his father away from him. He can be the one to decide then if he wants to see Chip or not.

"But Chip breaks his promises to Brian all the time. Even a simple movie. He promises him and then he just doesn't show up to take him. I think Brian does love Chip and Chip does love Brian, but Chip is still not mature enough to handle it."

WHEN DAD GROWS UP

Ray and Kerry were teenagers when Kerry became pregnant. They were both still in their "wild carousing" stage, not very ready to settle down. Ray was bright but had never taken school seriously and was lucky to have graduated high school. Kerry had to drop out to have the baby. Ray didn't feel ready to marry but thought he should, so they got married by the Justice of the Peace two months before Kerry gave birth to Jeremy. Ray and Kerry fought constantly, and after the baby was born, Ray just couldn't take the pressure, and he left.

Kerry made no effort to contact Ray, and he made no effort to contact her. About a year later, he heard she had moved out of state. When Ray was in his early twenties, he met and fell in love with Monica, a woman a few years older than him, who was recently divorced with a six-year-old son, Darrin. Ray had done a lot of growing up. At his construction job, he'd been noticed as being a good worker and a quick learner. His boss, an older man, had encouraged Ray to go back to school and take some management courses. Ray was being praised at work and school and appreciated by Monica and her child. He moved in with them and became a very active second dad.

Being with Darrin rekindled Ray's yearning to know his own son, who was now almost three years old. Also, Ray had failed to divorce his first wife and now wanted to marry Monica.

With the help of a private investigator, Ray finally tracked down Kerry, and a long costly court battle began. Under temporary orders, Kerry was required to allow Ray to visit and to let her son go for weekend visits with his father twice a month. However, Ray had to pay expensive plane fares to visit his son. When Ray arrived at Kerry's house the first time, she was not at home. She never came home that weekend, and Ray had to fly back without seeing his son. He spent more money on lawyer's fees to force her to comply with the visitation order. At one point, Kerry cashed in a plane ticket Ray had sent for Jeremy and moved again.

Kerry finally got tired of running, and Ray paid for them all (himself, Monica, Jeremy, and Kerry) to have psychological examinations as the courts tried to decide who should have custody of Jeremy. While the custody was being contested, Ray spent a fortune on plane tickets flying Jeremy back and forth so he could establish a relationship with him. But when the big day in court finally came, Kerry was awarded sole custody of Jeremy, and Ray was given a child-support bill and all lawyer costs. Ray and Monica were thousands of dollars in debt, and Ray could no longer afford to send for Jeremy. He now sees him twice a year, a week at Christmas and in the summer. Ray, meanwhile, has become closer to Darrin to soothe his loss. So Darrin is the biggest winner in all this, and Jeremy the biggest loser.

This is a typical divorce story of high conflict, so why do I include it here? I think that Ray's age and stage of life at the time his child was born are the most significant factors here, for later evidence shows that he could be a very good father, even though he showed an alarming lack of interest in his son as an infant. Ray could have avoided searching for his son, but he chose to seek him out, knowing full well he would be expected to pay child support once contact was re-established. Now that he had a steady job he did not mind. But he expected to gain some rights along with this responsibility.

Although we should acknowledge that all of us are capable of change and should not be judged by our previous behavior, it is especially true of men and women in their teen and young adult years. Even Kim stands ready to accept that Chip may grow up as she has. Boys generally mature later than girls, so it is understandable that a relatively mature girl would remember her child's father as being totally irresponsible in contrast to herself.

But most people, male and female, grow and learn with time. It is essential to give a young father a second chance when he is older, for not to do so is to hurt the child he fathered.

SUMMARY POINTS

- Most current approaches to the unwed father are punitive. Instead, we need to convey acceptance, respect, and support so young fathers feel appreciated for giving what little they can, until they can give more.
- By offering free legal advice or job placement services, we can attract teen fathers and help them develop a sense of responsibility and pride in fatherhood.
- Unwed fathers are more likely to stay in contact with their children if they are approached at the time of the birth, are counseled by male social-service workers, can find paid work, and are encouraged by friends and family to stay involved.
- The unwed father needs to believe that declaring paternity will have some personal benefits for him.
- It is important to maintain contact with even very immature fathers who show little interest in the child and have no financial help to offer. Most of these fathers mature and eventually earn enough to make a substantial financial contribution to the child.
- Some unwed mothers and their families mistakenly believe that by not establishing paternity or accepting money from the father, he will lose all rights to the child. Instead the child loses all rights to the father's future income.
- Since the parents of the mother are often her main support, they have a great deal of power to encourage or prevent the father's involvement. Grandparents need to be accepting of the unwed father and actively encourage his involvement with the child.

6

Who Was My Dad?

> *"I used to have a feeling of longing for my dad because I'd spent a lot of time with him. That longing didn't stop until I was in high school. Now I long for him sometimes because there are so many things I'd like to ask him."*
>
> — MICHAEL, A BEREAVED SON

How deeply a child is affected by the death of his or her father depends on many circumstances. Though psychologists believe that the death of a parent is the most devastating life stress a child can experience and there is great potential for long-term psychological harm, most children can recover and lead fully productive lives. Some are even strengthened by the experience of coping with such a great stress early in their lives.[1] However, there are a number of very important factors that influence how much impact a parent's death will have.

In judging the child's grief, the parent must remember that as adults we generally have many deep friendships and ties. A child's world is much narrower. While the surviving parent has lost his or her main support, the child has lost one of the two people he or she depended on totally. In the child's vision a god has been shattered. If this parent could die, what's to stop the next one from dying soon?

Factors Influencing Childhood Bereavement

1. The cause of death (sudden death due to heart attack, accident, suicide, or murder, or a slow death from cancer or some other chronic disease).

2. The grief reaction of the surviving parent and how well she can tolerate her child's grief reactions.
3. The quality of the child's relationship with the father before he died and the role he played in the child's life.
4. The quality of the child's relationship with the mother.
5. The age and developmental level of the child and his or her ability to grasp the concept of death.
6. The emotional health, strengths, and weaknesses of the child prior to the death of the parent.
7. Emotional support available through friends, family, group affiliations, or organizations.
8. Financial circumstances following the death and their impact on where the family will live or how many of their old routines and activities they will be able to continue.[2]

Regardless of the circumstances that surround the death, 70 percent of children who have lost a parent showed strong symptoms of bereavement during the first month after the death, and a year later about 40 percent were still showing deep signs of grief. Typical symptoms were feelings of sadness, the lethargy of a depressive mood, irritability, poor concentration (and school performance), fatigue, low self-esteem, dependent, clingy behavior, and sleep disturbances. The first few weeks are particularly difficult for everyone as daily routines (such as dinnertime without Dad) constantly remind everyone of the deceased parent. Interviews with parents and children in the same families have shown that parents tend to underestimate and underreport the disturbances in their children. Though many parents believe their children are doing fine, most children experience a lot of symptoms of depression and anxiety following the father's death.[3]

The first year is usually the most difficult for everyone, and for the most part the older the child, the quicker the recovery. However, for some children who are too young to immediately grasp the meaning of death, there may be delayed grieving.

THE VERY YOUNG CHILD

When any child in the family is very young, as was Katy O'Rourke when her father died, the rest of the family must actively provide the memories in later years. Her sister Melody seems to be the only family member who realizes how much her sister Katy missed. "I feel most sorry for my sister because she was only four when he died," Melody explained. "She only saw the sick side of our father, if she remembers him at all."

Because of the mother's fear that talking about Dad will stir unbearable sadness in her children, the O'Rourkes have rarely discussed the father in front of Katy. As a result, Katy has never really had an opportunity to express her grief. Katy reported, "I remember when I was growing up, people would ask me where my father was and I would be afraid to answer them." She felt so close to tears at the mention of him that she feared she would embarrass herself if she tried to speak of him.

> "In fifth grade someone asked me about it and I started crying. My fifth-grade teacher had known my father and she started talking about him in front of the whole class. We were having a discussion about fathers and she asked if anyone didn't have a father. I raised my hand and everyone looked at me and I got up and ran out of the room."

We discussed why fifth grade might have been such a difficult year for her, and Katy speculated that it may have been because girls started to talk about their dads more as they became more aware of boys. Males were the subject on every girl's mind.

Children like Katy, who are under age seven at the time of the father's death, often suffer the most long-term damage. Children under two years of age have no concept of death, and preschool children are working through early identity struggles as they begin to identify with their same-sex parent. Their own developmental struggles, coupled with the loss of a parent, creates a lot of inner turmoil. Most young children under stress misbehave, becoming whiney, uncooperative, or aggressive. These grief reactions are alienating, and the children may be rejected by friends, teachers, and the surviving parent. In addition, young children still need a lot of physical care, and this puts extra stress on the bereaved parent and strains the mother's relationship with the child, just when that child most needs reassurance. Younger children are also often kept away from the funeral and shut out of the grieving process. They may be further confused by the flowery abstract explanations of life after death offered in the name of religion and are better off if they gain a more concrete understanding of death.

Katy can remember no details about her father, but overall she remembers him as being loving. She never asked her brother and sister about her father. After the fifth-grade teacher spoke to her about her father Katy avoided the subject all the more strenuously. "I didn't want to hear about it. It was just too painful," she told me.

The mood of my talk with Katy was somber. Although she feels she can handle the subject of her father much better now than she used to, her pain is just below the surface. She is yet very vulnerable. Since the mother fears stirring up dark feelings in her daughter, a therapist could serve as a "pain moderator" leading them to experience only as much grief as they can handle at each session.

AFTERSHOCKS

Delayed mourning may be present in older children too. They often show the greatest number of disturbed symptoms six months after the death when the changes and consequences have been felt. Studies show that boys tend to express their grief by acting out, while girls are more likely to express their grief in words. Boys who had lost fathers were at high risk for depression in adolescence, whereas adolescent girls whose fathers had died were likely to be shy and anxious around boys.[4]

If a child has been very close to his father he may have long-standing pride and comfort in being just like Daddy. However, this will inevitably raise his fear of dying, just like Daddy. When the cause of Dad's death is believed to be hereditary, this fear can be very intense. It would help the child to have tests to see if he has inherited the disease and for him to learn all he can about preventing or controlling it.

The O'Rourke children had all had the non-tropical sprue which ran in the family and had ultimately caused their father's fatal illness. As they all followed their father's peculiar wheat-free diet, they were reminded constantly of their genetic link to a man who had died so young. Ten years after Mickey O'Rourke died, when the children all simultaneously came up with a negative test result, there was truly cause for celebration. What a relief to be able to say, I may be like my father (especially in the son Michael's case since he looked so much like him), but I will not die like him!

On the other hand, if the child has had a distant relationship with his father, and particularly if there has been a lot of conflict, he may worry that he has succeeded in "wishing Daddy dead." This fear is especially prevalent in four- or five-year-old boys who have felt in competition with Dad for Mom's love. Mother may need the help of a therapist to sort through all these confusing feelings with her child. The young child needs to understand what powers he has and does not have for "wishing Dad away" or "wishing him back."

The early adolescent is also very vulnerable to guilt feelings because he is generally caught at a stage when he is trying to break away from his parents. However, if the father dies when the child is fourteen or older, the child has usually completed his separation from the parent and entered a stage of comradeship with Dad that allows him to let go more easily.

GRIEVING

Many mothers worry about their grief frightening their children and do all their crying in private, keeping a "stiff upper lip" when the kids are around. Mothers have a right to grieve privately, however, they should sometimes show their grief in front of the children, so that the children know that grieving is allowed. School-age children may need to be drawn out and helped to talk about their feelings of loss. Unfortunately, some mothers are so uncomfortable with feeling their own deep sadness that they are very upset by their children's expressions of grief and may try to distract or cheer the child up.

Shirley O'Rourke shows the confusion that many widows feel about how to handle the father's death. Her husband Mickey died of primary billiary pserosis when his three children were all under twelve. His disease was first discovered shortly after his third child was born. One of the complications of the disease was brittle bone syndrome, and his bones seemed to crumble at the slightest impact. His oldest daughter, Melody, recalled,

> "One time we went grocery shopping and he picked up a bottle of milk and it broke his wrist. The last year he was alive he

went from being 5' 10" to being 4' 10" and his weight went down from 160 to 80 lbs."

Her mother Shirley added:

"The best the doctor and medicines could do was to keep him alive as long as possible. He was able to work and Prednisone gave the kids six years to know their father before he died.

"About a year before Mickey died I was in the family room with the kids one Sunday afternoon, and I think I told them to keep their voices down so they wouldn't awaken Dad. Michael said to me, 'Is Dad going to get better, Mom?' And I said, 'No, he really isn't going to get better, he's only going to get worse.' Their eyes teared up and Melody asked, 'Is he going to die?' I said, 'Yes. Sometime he will. It won't be today or tomorrow. I don't know when it will be. We can pray for Daddy to be more comfortable, but there is no point in praying that Daddy won't die because he can't get better with this disease.'"

Shirley did an excellent job telling the children about their father's terminal condition. Though the stage was then set for further open communication about the father's dying, she later let her own discomfort with the subject of death get the better of her. When the father finally died, a tacit agreement that they must not talk about it fell into place. Our first clue to this is the mystery that surrounds Michael's whereabouts on the night of his father's death. Though ten years have passed since Mickey died, no one knows where Michael went. Mrs. O'Rourke told me,

"I don't know where Michael went. There was so much confusion that I never asked him. We've never talked about it. I can talk to my friends about that day, but I just can't bear to talk to my kids about it. I've always felt that if they would want to talk about it, they would bring it up. And now that they're older, the only time we are all together is Christmas or some other vacation when we're supposed to be having a good time. I just want them to have a happy life and I don't want to bring up sad events of our past."

Where was Michael the night his father died? One of his sisters had also reported to me that Michael had been missing, but no one knew where he had gone. When I interviewed Michael separately, I asked him what he recalled from that night.

"The night my dad died is a real vivid memory for me. It was about 7:30 at night and it was already dark out. I was in the living room and my mom went to help my dad because he was gagging or something. I got scared and I left on my bike. I rode around the neighborhood and I kept circling back. After about a half-hour I saw an ambulance there. There were all these people standing around. A little while later the ambulance left and then all the people left.

"Once everyone was gone I decided to come in. My grandmother was there and she was making a pot of beans. My mom and my grandfather were at the hospital. My grandmother told me that my father would be all right. But then my mom and my grandfather came back and we all had to sit on the couch. They told me that my dad had died and then all these neighbors and friends started coming over. I just went in the back of the house. The next day my mom asked us if we wanted to go to school and Melody stayed home but I went to school. I never missed a day. I didn't want to be at home because there were all these ladies there crying.

"My mother had a closed casket so I never saw my father dead. In some ways, he's still alive to me. I didn't want to see him dead. It would have added sorrow to see him dead. I wanted to remember the happy side. We'd already had enough bad times."

Michael avoided the sadness at the time of his father's death, and he still avoids it. On the surface, this "family pact" has protected everyone, but when talk of the parent's death is taboo, all conversations about the lost loved one are inhibited. Not only do we lose the tremendous lessons which can be learned from how someone faces death (and I have the impression that Mickey faced death courageously), many family stories that might touch on the taboo subject are lost from the family history.

Although a mother is wise not to burden or overwhelm her child with her needs, there is nothing wrong with mother and children having a good cry together. A family visit to the grave also shows that Dad can be thought about and talked about. If Mom feels unduly depressed and can't sort out how much grief is a "normal" amount, she should seek a therapist or self-help group for widows to get a sense of perspective. When therapists work with grieving children they keep these goals in mind:

Helping Children Grieve

1. Create a safe place for children to express their feelings about their loss fully and freely.
2. Understand the many ways children show their grief, including acting out behavior and declarations that they don't need anybody.
3. Help the child understand the facts about the father's death.
4. Help the child adjust to economic changes and gain a sense of security in new surroundings.
5. Help the child and parent understand each other's grieving styles so they can be alert to when they each need support.[5]

Children sense their parents' unexpressed emotions and will be all the more disturbed if Mom tries to hide her grief. They need an example of someone allowing herself to feel the pain, and then recovering from it.

Though it may be tempting to pack up the children and run off to Grandma's or flee the house that holds so many memories, children of any age are better off if the surviving mother can make no changes in their lives for the first year or so. The death of a parent is enough to adjust to without also having to adjust to a new town, new school, and new friends. The mother needs to save all her strength for coping with her own grief, adjusting to her new financial circumstances, and helping her children work through their feelings. She doesn't need the extra stress of moving.

As in any family, each child experiences every shared event in a slightly different way. In the O'Rourke family each child has had one great disadvantage in connection with their father's death. Katy's disadvantage was that she was so young when her father died that everyone assumes she wasn't very affected by it. Michael had the big disadvantage of being the only male in the family, and boys probably need a father even more than girls. Melody's disadvantage was being the oldest, so that when her father was very sick, she had to take care of Katy, and her mother leaned on her a little too much. Also, the father had had to be moved to Melody's room because the bed was more accessible. Melody recalled, "I was mad that my dad had taken over my room and jealous of the attention he was getting." This resentment of Melody's is pretty understandable since in most homes eleven-year-olds are getting the lion's share of attention, not their parents.

After her father's death, Melody showed troubling symptoms. Her teacher had told Shirley that Melody's work was suffering and she was withdrawing from her classmates. Shirley was aware that she had relied on Melody too much during her husband's illness. Shirley was worn out from the years of caring for her husband and was feeling overwhelmed by the thought of raising three kids alone. She decided to seek counseling for herself and Melody. The therapist saw each of them separately and was able to help both Shirley and Melody through that very difficult first year.

TALKING ABOUT DAD

Katy wanted to offer this advice to bereaved families: "The mother should be open to the questions her kids ask and maybe tell stories about the father. She could bring out pictures and talk about what he was like. I'd want to know both the good things and bad things about my father."

As we all know, the mere act of talking about our problems, whether or not our listener can offer any sage advice, relieves the pressure and tension that bottled-up feelings cause. Talking about the deceased allows a healing calmness to soothe the bereaved. "I always had a good strong network of friends," Mrs. O'Rourke told me. "While Mickey was sick, friends would call me to see how we were doing. They would usually call when the kids were in school and I felt free to talk. I couldn't get out much, particularly in the end because Mickey needed so much care, and I felt like those phone calls really held me together. I felt bad that the kids didn't have anyone to talk to about death, because kids their own age couldn't really understand what they were going through."

Shirley is right. The average child cannot even conceive of death, let alone offer appropriate solace to a bereaved friend. As the

O'Rourke children pointed out, having a deceased parent can be very alienating. The subject embarrasses other people and the children are seen as somehow defective. "I felt really strange when I went back to school the week after my father died," Melody recalled. "People treated me like I was the one with the disease."

No one ever knows what to say to a bereaved person. People are especially concerned about saying the wrong thing to children, and are sure they could not handle the situation if the child started to cry. Even though his father died ten years ago, if Michael mentions to a new friend that his father is deceased, the friend usually offers his condolences. This is, in turn, rather embarrassing for Michael. He is long past the sadness, but he doesn't want to look as if he didn't care that his father died. Michael finds himself reassuring the friend that it's all right his father died! Michael told me,

> "I have close college friends I've never mentioned my father to. It's as if I'm afraid they'll think I'm defective. I don't want them feeling sorry for me. I like to compete. I don't want them thinking I have any less than they do. Most of my friends come from two-parent families and I want them to feel like I'm their equal."

Often, even family members have difficulty talking about the deceased. Because they may also be losing someone close to them, they find it hard to talk without crying. I remember that at my own father's wake the relatives talked about everything but my father. The O'Rourkes have certainly experienced this reluctance in the father's family. At Christmas when the O'Rourkes visit his family, no one mentions the deceased father. Occasionally, on the grandfather's Saturday visits, he will talk about what a hell-raiser the father was when he was younger, but the grandfather's stories go up to the father's college years and stop there. Michael commented,

> "I guess I've talked to my grandfather the most about my father, though I think it's hard for him. He answers what I ask, but he doesn't elaborate on it. He doesn't tell stories about my father on his own. He seems so uncomfortable that I have to ask myself whether it's that important for me to find out something about my dad. Most of the time I'd rather not upset him."

Melody has also experienced this resistance in her father's family.

"My uncle and my father were really close growing up, but my uncle never came around when my father was dying and we never saw him much after that.

"Last Christmas my uncle said to me, 'Melody, I'm really sorry but when your dad was sick I just couldn't come around. You never think your brother is going to die. I was so upset with my own loss that I just couldn't be there for anyone else, but I want to be there for you now.' "

Michael did have a wonderful opportunity a few years ago to learn a lot about his father from someone who thoroughly enjoys talking about him.

"When I was eighteen I met my father's college roommate who lives near my college. I got in touch with him when I came up to school. I didn't have a spot in the dorm yet and he invited me to stay with him.

"He talked about my father's college days. My father would rather read war books than study. He flunked out and had to go to a junior college. Anyway, Mr. Deaton loved to talk about my father and if we were sitting down to dinner he would do things like pick up his wine glass and say, 'A toast to Mickey!' "

Though Michael clearly feels the difference it has made for him to have this man to talk to, he doesn't really understand the need his other family members may have to talk about their father. He stated judgmentally, "I don't think Katy is old enough to talk about it yet. Maybe when I'm thirty and she's twenty-five." Because I had already spoken to Katy and was aware of her very vulnerable feelings about her father I was flabbergasted when Michael commented to me, "I don't think my dad's death affected Katy much because she was so young. Maybe she feels a loss at father-daughter events, but I doubt she actually misses him."

I shared with Michael that Katy knows very little about their father and has very strong feelings about his death. It seems to me that she needs to have people sitting around talking about him. It's a shame that she missed hearing about her father when the Deatons talked about him. That was a really important opportunity for Michael. Melody can remember all the way back to happy family times when she and Michael went camping with their mother and father, but Katy doesn't even have memories—just a blank space. Though the grandfather has told Katy about the father in his youth, she needs to have family memories, to see through family stories how her father was in the *family*.

Though the Hadleys (whose father committed suicide) had deeper problems in other areas, they seem to take a very healthy approach to talking about Dad. They all seem comfortable talking about him, and are very aware of each other's feelings and struggles. The daughter Sylvie told me,

> "Now my mom tells me stories about when my dad was little. She was in the same class as his sister so she knew them all when she was growing up. She would tell me about things she and my dad did in high school.
>
> "And my grandmother really likes to talk about my dad. She lives right near here so I see her about once a week. She's given both me and my brother pictures. And she's going to give me his high school yearbook. She thinks we should have those things.
>
> "I think sometimes people are afraid to talk to me about my dad or his death because they don't know how I'll react. When people ask me about my dad and I tell them he died, they look a little embarrassed like they think they shouldn't have said anything. But it doesn't bother me to talk about it. My friends were all really there for me when he died. They said anytime I wanted to talk or come to their house and do something with their family I was welcome."

Her brother Mark also found comfort with his friends,

> "I still have all my friends from when I was little. My best friend Jason has talked to me about my dad. We've always been able to talk to each other."

This family has been talking about Dad's death ever since it happened. Perhaps because suicide is such a psychological danger signal, the entire family rushed into counseling and began talking.

Though the children initially put up a great deal of resistance, it was certainly clear to them that it's okay to talk about Dad and his death. This ease has come across to their friends, who in turn feel no embarrassment talking to Mark and Sylvie.

In the O'Rourke family, on the other hand, Melody was the only one having problems at the time of the father's death, so Melody was the only one who went into counseling with the mother. The family has never discussed the death as a group, and their friends no doubt sense the anxious energy surrounding talk of the father. Until the O'Rourkes are at ease with the father's death themselves, and can convey that comfort to others, their friends are likely to steer clear of the subject.

There are a number of approaches that can be used to open a comfortable conversation about Dad. As Sylvie illustrates, many children find comfort in the belongings of their deceased father, and are particularly helped by looking at family photos. Fortunately, the O'Rourkes do have a family album they've kept. Shirley told me. "Mickey was a big picture taker. He took most of them, but on each occasion I'd try to take one picture with him in it. So the kids can see what he looked like throughout their childhood. We, as a family, don't ever get out the picture albums and look at them together. The kids look at them alone or with their friends."

Pictures should be readily accessible, and it is good for each child to have some object of Dad's for his or her own. Looking at family photos together provides a good opportunity to talk about Dad, but the photos should be left around so each child may have a chance to cart them off to his or her room in case he or she needs a good private cry.

If the mother can stand it, it also helps the kids to do activities they used to do with their father or to visit old favorite places where they went with him. Though these familiar settings may be painful reminders of the family's grief, they also show that, through memory, Dad will always be with them.

Michael, who now lives away at college, decided he would begin a series of letters to his sister to share some of his memories with her. Letters are a great avenue for exploring uncomfortable feelings. One thing that is really nice about a letter is that if you feel sad reading it, you can stop until you feel ready to go on. You can reread the letter as many times as you want. The person writing the letter can carefully choose his words. Letters also open up opportunities for the recipient (in this case, Katy) to ask questions without feeling too self-conscious. This would help her work through her sensitivity. She could read the answers to her questions in private, and take as long as she needs to think about her father's death or to cry about it. This would be a start for the O'Rourkes toward breaking the taboo.

IRREPLACEABLE LOSSES?

When she tries to take the father's place, Shirley feels at a particular loss with her son Michael. Shirley explained,

> "Mickey had been a boy so he had those interests and they could share them. I've always been closer to the girls because I like to talk about the things that interest them. I like to hear all about the girls' dates, where they went and how the guy treated them. But there are a lot of things Michael and I can't talk about. I would never ask him who he is dating. If Mickey were alive, he would know what to ask him. If Michael doesn't volunteer it, I don't know how to draw him out. His father would."

Michael also feels that his father would have possessed the knowledge he needs about girls.

> "A few years ago I would have liked advice on when you should ask a girl out, or how you should go about it. I didn't ask many girls out in high school because I just didn't feel comfortable with that. I still tend to go out with girls as part of a group rather than individually. And I don't know how to tell what girls are thinking. I probably have one of the worst records for not realizing when a girl likes me. At least four times in college I've found out too late that someone liked me. By the time a friend lets it slip the girl is already going with someone else. I think if my father were around he might help me pick up on some of the clues and tell me when I should ask a girl out. It's definitely a game that has rules, and I never had anyone to teach me those rules."

I was rather astonished that Michael believes his dad would be better at telling him what girls think or like than his mom would. I was even more surprised when Katy told me, "My mom has had to tell me about boys and I think that was awkward for her. I think my Dad would have told me about stuff like that. My mom had to explain to me how some guys act and what to watch out for. And if my dad was alive I could see how he was with my mom and that would help me know more about relationships."

For a sense of perspective, I interviewed the young adults in an intact family about their father's part in their dating education. What sort of advice had they sought or gotten from their fathers? Brent Carson recalled an incident when he was in junior high school.

> "One time my dad said to us we could ask any girl out on a date, and he would pay for it. He suggested we take out these girls that lived up the street. I think we were in junior high. We weren't interested, and we thought it was kind of weird. We do more things in groups anyway."

On the other hand, Brent and Garrett told me tales that reveal their father's intense curiosity and interest in their heterosexual development. Brent related,

> "If I'm going out, he'll ask me, 'Who are you going out with?' And I'll say, 'I'm going out with Leila, and Rene and Terry.' And he'll say, 'Oh! a date!' And I'll say, 'No, Dad, it's not a date when you go out with three girls.' And he'll ask, 'Is one of them your girlfriend?' And I'll say, 'No, Dad. You'll know when one of them is my girlfriend because I'll take her out alone.' "

Unlike Michael, Brent and his brother Garrett feel confident that they can let girls know when they are interested and sense when the feeling is mutual. "You can just feel it if they are interested in you," Brent stated. "There is a lot of non-verbal communication." Garrett added, "It's always been real gradual with me. I've just taken things slowly and I don't force it. I've dropped hints to see how someone is going to react. If I get a good reaction, I pursue it further." Brent stated, not arrogantly, but confidently, "Most of the time if I find I am really attracted to a girl, chances are she is also attracted to me."

Their comfort in their attractiveness is striking, particularly in contrast to Michael, who seems so unsure of himself, even though he is equally attractive. I asked if they think their father believes they are attractive to girls. Brent jumped in, "Oh, absolutely. I remember one time we were walking around the mall and my dad was walking about twenty feet behind us. After awhile he came up with us and said, 'You should have heard what all the girls said as they passed by you two. They really think you're good-looking.' He thinks any girl would be nuts to refuse us if we wanted to take her out."

As they describe these behaviors of their father, it's obvious he's been checking on their developing sexuality. He keeps an eye on it, and encourages it. As I explained this theory to the boys, Brent nodded in agreement, "My dad once told us that we both like blondes and I said, 'How do you know that?' And he said that whenever a blonde goes by we both turn our heads."

How about their sister Nadine? Did she discuss boys with her father? Nadine was careful to let me know that she dearly loves her father and thinks he is the best dad in the world, *but* she would never go to him to talk about matters of the heart. She sees her mother as her best friend, and her mother has been able to give her all the advice she needed about boys and dating. Nadine talks to her father about gardening.

This fantasy of Dad as dating expert does seem peculiar to the O'Rourkes. I think what the O'Rourkes truly reflect is their mother's discomfort and difficulty at re-entering the dating field. Shirley is attractive and vivacious. She is economically independent and would not be a financial burden on anyone. Though Shirley states that she doesn't want to have to compete for men, she would certainly come out as a top contender if she ever decided to enter the competition. Perhaps the O'Rourke children really wish Dad were there to show that men and women need each other. They want a *whole* living relationship to observe, not specific advice on who and how to date.

At the same time, Shirley's experience makes it clear that re-placement dads are not always so easy to find. A few years after her husband died, Shirley did try to meet men. She joined Parents Without Partners and attended several functions across a two-year period. However, there were ten women to every man, and she didn't like the tremendous competition to get a man's attention. Shirley explained, "One man invited me to go out to his car and listen to the radio, but I said no. I mean, who needs that?" In ten years, Shirley has had one blind date arranged by a friend, but the man never called again, which was fine with Shirley. There was no attraction between them.

> "I know I've been a little afraid to get involved. I didn't want to go through all that sickness and death again. I felt like nobody would ever be as good to the kids as their dad had been. I didn't want to put them through having to adjust to a new person, who maybe wouldn't love them. So I haven't looked very seriously for a man. I felt like losing a father was so much to go through; I didn't want to put them through anything else."

Betsy, widowed five years ago, has been dating a man and is thinking of marrying him, but she also senses the conflict this would create between her and her children. As Betsy explained,

> "Sylvie said she wanted me to go out but I don't think she wants me to get attached to one man. On Mother's Day my boyfriend took me and the kids out to dinner. Sylvie didn't even say thank you. When he left she said to me, 'He has a mother. Why wasn't he with her?' He's very supportive of me and I think that irritates her.
>
> "At first I thought I would never date. I have seen so many situations that don't work out for the kids. But then I started to think that they need to see adults in a relationship."

Probably the best thing Betsy can do for Sylvie right now is to continue dating this man or men who are good to her. Despite Sylvie's protests, the example of Betsy dating someone who is considerate and kind will have more impact on Sylvie's dating pattern or choice of mate than a thousand words.

THE MALE CHILD

Despite the fact that her brother Michael is only four years older than she is, Katy accepts him as an emotional guardian. "I think I'm turning out pretty well now," Katy stated. "I used to be a trouble-maker, but I've gotten over that. My brother talks to me about doing well in school. He really believes that I'm smart and I can do well.

I got a 4.0 last marking period. I sort of think of my brother as my father."

Katy's brother, indeed, sounds like an ideal supportive father. He has serious talks with her about how to do well in school and her future plans. He checks up on how she is doing and encourages her. As we will see in Chapter 8, Michael is clearly patterning himself after his father here.

Katy also likes to make sure Michael meets all her boyfriends. "Believe me, he knows whether they're good for me or not. Once he told my mother he didn't know why I was with this one guy because he was so dumb. Michael thought I was much smarter than my boyfriend, and it just couldn't last. He was right! He really knows about guys. He wants me to date guys who treat me well."

Someday when Katy gets married, she wants Michael to give her away. She would never consider marrying anyone that Michael hadn't met, because she trusts his judgment. Indeed, it is quite an advantage to have a "father figure" so close to her age. He can remember much more easily what boys are like since he was that age just five years ago.

Michael expresses mostly positive feelings about his leadership role in the family. However, even though Michael described his mother as a sturdy disciplinarian, he often feels responsible to be "the man in the family." Michael told me,

> "I sometimes feel like a father to Katy and she often takes my advice. I don't just talk to Katy when my mom asks me to. I think Katy listens to me more than she does my mom because I'm not around all the time, so what I say has more impact.
>
> "I try to help her put things in perspective. If she is upset or too excited about a particular boy I tell her, 'You'll have a lot of different boyfriends in the next few years so try to take the long view.'
>
> "My older sister Melody just graduated college and she doesn't have a job yet and I feel like I should be sending her some money or something. I've always been very mature and level-headed for my age. I feel like the one who will be responsible to give my mom financial help when she is older. I just assume I'll do that."

For the most part, Michael's role as the "man in the family" is comfortable and pleasant. He takes some pride in his ability to guide his younger sister Katy. But when we hear Michael express his concern about Melody and his Mom's finances, we realize how easily this role can become a burden. Giving his mother financial help when she is older is an unusual concern for a young man of Michael's age to have. Most college students are not thinking beyond their own financial security. If Michael's father were alive and his parents together, Michael would probably assume that his father was taking care of his parents' old age. Michael is where the buck stops now.

SEEKING MALE ROLE MODELS

Shirley has always been aware of her son's strong need to be with males and learn from them. Sometimes the smallest things can leave her at a loss. "I never knew how to tie a man's tie, so whenever Michael had to get dressed up he would go next door so the neighbor could show him how to tie the tie." I recalled for Shirley an incident last year with my son, when his father had already moved East, ahead of us, and I was the only resident parent for a few months. My son got the idea that he needed to wear a protective cup over his penis when he played soccer. He had seen one a boy had at school.

So my son and I went to a sporting goods store. He was too embarrassed to ask about it, and I had to discuss this gadget with the teenage salesboy, trying to describe something I had never seen and didn't know the name of. The salesboy didn't know what I was talking about, but thought my son might have seen something a catcher wears in baseball. We gave up and decided to talk it over with my husband on the phone.

It turned out that this gadget (I still don't know the name of it) was not necessary for soccer and what was really happening with my son was that he was beginning to have anxiety about his body, about protecting his penis. His dad's reassurance that he didn't need to wear a protective cup during soccer was enough to end the issue. But he wouldn't have taken my word for it.

Shirley commented, "I'm sure there were things like that that Michael worried about, but he didn't even bring them up to me. He played sports. If he needed one of those, he just had to do without it. Who was I going to ask? You don't just ask anybody's husband about something he wears over his penis!"

On a more somber note Shirley added, "I know Michael really misses having a man to talk to. He's called me many times and he's said, 'Other kids have their dads to talk to about girls and stuff like that. Who do I have to talk to? I can't talk to you or Melody and Grandpa is too old. I need somebody that could give me good advice. Guys my own age just get raunchy about all that stuff.' I think it's really hard for him sometimes."

Michael does have a strong drive to find male role models and has looked beyond his grandfather to seek relationships with men. In high school two young priests at the rectory where Michael worked part-time spent many hours in conversation with him. One friend's older brothers provided male comraderie as they let Michael and their little brother tag along and play basketball. Michael also felt that the Scoutmasters he knew were wonderful role models.

Michael fondly remembers his last summer job as a special time of male bonding. He told me, "The best part was that they were all guys my age and the one boss who was older was just like a father to me. I could really talk with him."

TIME HEALS

Father's Day has always been hardest for Katy. She told me, "Other kids say, 'What are you going to do with your father on Father's Day?' and I have to say, 'I don't have a father.' " So she takes a card to her grandfather on Father's Day. Father-daughter events are hard for her, too. "This group I'm in has a father-daughter dinner every year but I just don't want to go to it." She knows she could bring her grandfather or go with a friends' family, but she cannot bear the thought of walking into a room full of girls with their dads. When she was about fourteen she began to feel more relaxed about her father's death. Katy feels the grief does get more bearable as she gets older.

Five years seemed to be a turning point for the bereaved families I interviewed. Each of the O'Rourke children talked about a trip the family had taken to Europe five years after the father's death. Though the trip was not consciously planned as a means to compensate for the father's death or to celebrate an end to mourning, it did seem to mark the beginning of family life without Dad. The trip was a large project. They planned it together (as a family of four—three kids and

Mom), they travelled together to startling new places, and they created a set of shared memories that did not include the father. They toured with a group and were the only children on the trip, so the O'Rourke children gained the attention of all the "would-be" fathers in the group.

It has now been five years since Rich Hadley killed himself and we see evidence of the family healing as Sylvie talks about their growing ability to be close again. As Sylvie looks back she realizes the stages of grief her family has been through and can see the progress they've made.

> "Though Mark and I used to be pretty close when we were younger, when my dad died, we all sort of went our separate ways. Mark was always hiding out in the basement.
>
> Recently I think we've been getting closer. We all talk about my dad now, not about the way he died, but about the things we used to do together. We just talk about *him*.
>
> Before, Mark and I used to just yell at each other. Now when I come home he says, 'Hi! How was your day?' We're planning to go up to Cleveland some weekend soon and spend some time with our cousins. We haven't done things like that together for a long time."

MOVING ON

We know we are ready to move on from a tragic time or event in our lives when we can find something positive in the experience. This is also a sign of good mental health. Even so, it is surprising to learn that the O'Rourke children can find something positive in the death of their kind beloved father. Melody told me,

> "If my dad were still alive today I don't think I would be as mature as I am. A lot of kids, even in graduate school, still think a good time is going out and getting drunk and I just don't think that way. I'm less self-centered. I'm definitely more concerned about people than I would be if my dad were still alive. My mom said something to me just after my dad died that I always think

about. She said 'You'll never spend enough time with people you love.' You'll spend plenty of time with the people at work and others who aren't that important to you. But the ones you love the most, who you mean to spend the most time with, are the ones you'll see the least of. That's always stuck with me.'"

Michael can also find some good in his father's death.

"I've tried to live up to my father's hopes for me. I think I've done better than he ever dreamed I would. I've actually put more pressure on myself than he ever would have put on me. My mom says I'm an over-achiever, but I have a lot of inner drive.

"I used to really push myself to study. I spent a whole summer studying for the SATs. I didn't have to do that, and most kids don't do that. But I had no safety net. I felt like I better be able to do it on my own. I've felt like that ever since I was little.

"For some reason, with my dad deceased, I felt more like I should reach for the sky."

SUMMARY POINTS

- Most children who have lost a parent show strong symptoms of bereavement during the first month after the death, and on up until about a year has passed. Though more than half recover fully in the first year, many do not really return to normal for about five years.
- It is common for bereaved children to be clingy, uncooperative, or aggressive. Unfortunately, their behavior makes Mom's adjustment all the more difficult, and they alienate other sources of support such as teachers and relatives.
- It is important for the family to talk about the father after he has died. Younger children will have no memories, and they can only gain a sense of who Dad was in the family if mother, brother, sister, aunts, and uncles are willing to talk about Dad.
- Children need to be reassured that they are not the cause of Dad's death. Boys in the oedipal stage and rebellious adolescents are particularly vulnerable to feeling guilty for causing Dad's death, as if their anger at him had killed him.

- Parents need to model that it is okay to show one's grief, for when Dad is not talked about half of the child's hereditary history is lost.
- Psychologists recommend that mothers tell children the facts of the father's death, create a stable environment where children feel safe to let go emotionally, and remember that they each have their own ways of grieving.

7

The Closed Door

"My dad's worst point was that he had too much pride. He could have avoided his death if he just would have got help but he was too proud for that. That's the way I look at it."

—MARK, A BEREAVED SON

W hen a father dies it seems apparent that the opportunity to talk with him, to gain comfort from him, or to grow to know him better ends. However, anyone who has lost a parent knows this is not strictly true. We have our memories. We may also have a very good idea of what father might have advised us to do in response to a problem. Sometimes our fantasies take the form of internal conversations, looking for closure. How we fill in Dad's side of the conversation depends in part on how well we knew him before he died, how much his friends or relatives can tell us about him, and the flights or limitations of our own imaginations. We can also use investigative and introspective means to get to know him better, but the result is still part conjecture and can become distorted.

Unlike the divorced dad or the long lost "real father" of an adopted child, we cannot track down a deceased dad to confirm or destroy the image of him that we have formed. When we have no real live fallible human being to scrutinize, we can get lost in the fantasies of what Dad could have done for us, to the destructive end of failing to do for ourselves. How does a son live up to an idealized image? How does a daughter find a mate that is "good enough" when she compares her mortal boyfriends to an inflated vision of Dad? But these are often the final questions. In the beginning there is just grief and pain.

HADLEYS AND SUDDEN DEATH

Mark remembered the day his father died:

> "I was sleeping on the couch and I heard this noise and I thought, 'What is going on?' My dad ran up the stairs, grabbed this gun at the top of the stairs and then he ran back down. I figured he was going hunting and I fell back to sleep. When I woke up my mom and my sister were looking for my dad.
> "There were a lot of people here and we were worried. Then I was outside and my buddy Jason came up to me and said, 'You'd better go up to the house.' I found out that my dad did that out behind the shed. I was in shock. For awhile after that I would wake up and think I had dreamed it, then I'd realize it was true."

Sylvie, Mark's older sister, told me,

> "My mom became hysterical. She was crying and uncontrollable. Of course, we were all crying, but Mom was really really upset. My dad had turned on the air compressor in the basement to make a lot of noise, so Mark wouldn't hear him. Later we saw signs that he had planned it. It was getting cold and it would have snowed soon. I found windshield scrapers set out on the stairs so that we could find them.
> "I was just in shock at first. I remember sitting through the funeral but I don't remember a thing they were saying. I was just sitting there thinking, 'Why did he do it?' We went to the cemetery and since he'd been in the service they shot off these guns. It really upset me to hear that."

Their mother, Betsy, looks on her husband's death with more knowledge than she had at the time, knowledge that would have helped her to see it coming, though not necessarily head it off.

> "He'd always had highs and lows which I now realize were a sign of manic-depression, but I didn't think anything of it. He

worked construction and naturally he would be depressed when
the weather was bad and he had no work. He also drank—there's
a history of drinking in the family. It was during one of those long
lay-offs that he killed himself.

"He had started saying crazy things. First he'd tell me I ought
to divorce him and then he'd tell me if I did it he'd poison our well
or turn on the gas and kill us all. In the same breath he'd told me
that he had prayed to God—and he wasn't the kind to go to
church—to watch over us and protect us.

"The morning he did it he had actually seemed better. The
night before he was in a real cheerful mood. It's been five years
now and I keep thinking about what I could have done. I should
have committed him, but when he got out he might have killed me
for doing it. His pride could not have stood what others thought."

Sylvie spoke very highly of the experience her family had with
their counselor, though her mother reported that both Sylvie and her
brother complained vehemently at the time.

"My brother and I didn't want to go so we were real mad at my
mom because she insisted. When the lady would ask us questions, we were just real real short with her. But actually, she did
help. Even though you're sitting there acting like you're not
paying attention, you really hear what she's saying. When I
thought about what she said some more I knew it wasn't any of
our faults."

The Hadleys have experienced the most traumatic circumstances
of death. Suicide leaves behind a wake of guilt and anxiety. Mark was
home alone when his father killed himself. Though Mark reports that
he did not know what was going on, his mother worries that Mark has
suffered the greatest trauma of all:

"I've often worried that Mark found his father. I remember I
started to go into the shed and Mark said, 'What are you doing?' I
said, 'I'm going to look and see if he's in the building.' And Mark
pulled me away and said, 'I've already looked.' My husband was
actually behind the building.

"Mark never cried when he found out about his father. I think
that's locked up inside of him. He won't mow or trim out there

behind the shed. (She shows me the shed out back, and surrounding the shed is an island of tall grass and weeds that stands out in
contrast to the neatly mowed lawn.)

"Mark seemed scared a lot after my husband died. I would go
in his room and he would have all these knives there. I asked him
what they were for and he said he was afraid somebody would
break in, but I think he was afraid of ghosts."

Rich Hadley's story seems to be a classic, and tragic, case of
manic-depression. His widow and children mostly remember the
"up" times. Rich had many friends because he was such an outgoing,
helpful person. As Mark related, "I always went places with him to
see his friends—he had a lot of friends. My dad used to do projects
for his friends when he wasn't working. He'd work on cars and he
helped one friend start a junkyard." Sylvie Hadley told me,

"I really miss my dad's sense of humor. When we get together
with the whole family now it's boring to me because
my dad's not there. Everybody else might be having a good time
because their dad and mom are still there, but it's different
for me."

Betsy is still very aware of what her late-husband's more endear-
ing traits were. She confirmed his gregariousness. "When Rich was
not depressed he was very energetic and outgoing. He was always
ready to help a friend, and many of them came the day he died."

There is some denial and some residual need to protect their
father—especially since he died because he could not see his own
strengths. For the most part, we see the Hadleys using selective
memory to embrace what was best in the father. As the Hadley
children emphasize the father's better qualities, they symbolically
build a reason for him to go on living. We all wonder if we will do as
our parents have done. When the Hadleys line up evidence that the
father had reason to live, they are preparing to fight the possibility of
their own darkest thoughts.

One could argue that Rich Hadley's death was as much of a
desertion as if he had gotten into his truck and just driven off. In some
ways his family has the emotional landscape of a deserted family.
They are sinking into poverty, and the stress has been so great at

times that the mother cannot marshall her strength to look for employment.

Suicide is the outer limits of the desire to run away. Because of Rich's emotional handicap, we see the exaggerated reaction of a man who is deeply disturbed by his inability to be a "good provider." How many men who desert their families are responding to that same point of shame? When men feel the only important thing they give to children is money, what is the point in sticking around when the money runs out? If Rich had been able to understand how much his children needed other parts of him, would he have chosen to kill himself?

THE DARKENED PARENTAL MIRROR

As bereaved children assemble their memories of their fathers, they are making choices about who they want to be, what kind of mate they want to marry, and what pitfalls they want to avoid. Unfortunately, Mark's memories work against him. Though he praises the memory of his father, he never sees himself as measuring up to his dad's level of competence. Mark was twelve when his father died, and he is now seventeen. He has very full memories, but he has regrets about what he didn't have time to learn from his dad before he died. His father worked construction and drove machines like a backhoe. Mark went with him a few times and remembers that his father enjoyed his work. "One time my dad was messing around on a Bobcat doing wheelies." But Mark was not old enough to learn these skills from his father. Mark told me,

> "I would hang out with him when he was working on things around the house. I was little and I didn't really pay attention. I wish I had paid more attention, but I have a really short attention span. I didn't learn much."

Mark is very proud of his father and wanted to show me some wood carvings his father did. His father had whittled a chain, each link cleanly away from the next, but connected. "He did this all out of one piece. He didn't put it together later."

Mark thinks he is not at all like his father. He explained,

"He was pretty smart about everything and I don't know much about anything. He could figure out how to make anything. He'd just sit there and think about it and then he would do it. He had a helluva lot more talent than I have."

Mark is embarrassed about his poor school performance. However, as far as Mark knows his father did not do well in school either. I pointed out that Mark's father's "smarts" may have come from living. I asked Mark if his father ever reflected to him what Mark was good at and not so good at. Mark has no memories of anything his father told him about his strengths and weaknesses. Apparently, Mark's father was not much of a parental mirror.

When asked about his weaknesses, Mark was very specific. "I don't do work around the house unless my mom pushes me. I don't have much energy. I don't treat my mom or my sister as well as I should. I went to this Search Program where they teach you to look at things from a different point of view and that's when I realized I don't treat them very well and I've been trying to do better. I used to get into a lot of arguments with my sister and my mom and now I try to back out of it. I've been trying to get home at the time my mom expects me."

When I asked Mark what his good points are he falls silent. He is very down on himself at this time in his life. "I just don't think I have any good points." Mark desperately needs other people to mirror his better traits. I reflected to Mark that as he speaks I hear evidence of three good traits:

"You're very easygoing—that's the positive side of 'lazy.' You do care about people because when you realized that what you were doing hurt your mother and sister, and learned what you could do differently, you wanted to change. Also, you *can learn.* You are good at learning about people. Many kids who go to a program like Search don't even learn from it. They come out just the same as they went in. All these things are connected to people and it sounds like your father was a people-person, so that's one way you are like him. He may have been more outgoing so it isn't obvious to you, but *inside* you both like people."

Mark smiled and nodded.

Mark made me think of all the positive-thinking movements popular now, and the millions of people who get up every morning and look into their mirrors to read their affirmations for the day to themselves: "I am a worthwhile person." I also thought of how many times a day my son seems to look toward me, waiting for me to notice and *comment on* something he is doing well. Kids need this so much. At best, Mark's father failed to affirm him before he died. At worst, he supplied him with many negative images which will haunt Mark for years. It will take many many affirmations to overcome this unintentional negative programming.

The father is gone. Mark's mother needs to concentrate her efforts on being a positive parental mirror by constantly commenting on Mark's strengths.

WHO AM I LIKE?

As we discussed in earlier chapters, children are driven to compare themselves to their parents as part of their identity formation. When a parent is no longer present for us to observe, we must rely on memories to form an image for us to imitate. Good memories can be pulled up for comfort, in trying times as well as times when we just need a positive role model. Bad memories can help us avoid our parents' mistakes. Most of us spend a lifetime negotiating our relationships with our parents and working through our feelings to a place of understanding and connection. When a parent has died, we must rely solely on memories and fantasies to help us complete this developmental task. If used correctly, these can be powerful tools.

Children need lots of information about their deceased father, particularly if he died when they were very young, so that they can begin to look at how they are like their father, and how they are not. It is especially helpful if aunts, uncles, or grandparents can supply details about Dad in his younger years. A ten-year-old child will be fascinated and reassured by tales of what Dad did when he was ten. This provides concrete details through which the child can know his or her father at a level he or she can understand. A boy struggling with his school grades will find it very reassuring to hear about an F his Dad once got in school. We have all seen teenagers dig out their parents' every fault as they strive to find something they can do "better." This can be difficult since finding fault with a deceased person is taboo in our culture, but, as common wisdom states, "Nobody's perfect!"

When we listen to the memories of the O'Rourke children, whose father died of a long-term illness when they were all rather young, we see a portrait of a father who knew how to make children feel important and useful. They have fond memories of his appreciation for the small things they could do for him, and are able to realistically measure themselves against his accomplishments and traits. Melody reflected on what she has inherited from her father:

> "My mom says she sees a lot of my dad in me. I didn't get very good grades in college and I know I could have done better. My mom said that my dad did only what he had to do when he was in college, but he didn't put extra effort in just to get good grades. He had other things he was interested in. He loved people and he became a social worker. I'm more people-oriented too, and I have fun along the way.
>
> "My dad worked for child protective services. I asked him once why he did that and he told me, 'I always think that if you three kids were ever in trouble I would want someone to look out for you.' I majored in Sociology and Psychology and I've decided to become a teacher. I've always felt like a piece of my dad lives in me. I'd like to do something that helps other people."

Michael told me,

> "I have my father's good moral values that I consider a strength. I am willing to make sacrifices. I'm a good friend and a kind person like he was. But I'm more of a hard worker and a leader. I do the most I can with my abilities. I don't think my dad did that. I learned to do my best at all times when I was in Boy Scouts.
>
> My father was really well liked. I don't think he had any enemies. All these people came to his funeral. I probably won't ever have as many friends, but that's not as important to me as it was to him. He was a cooperative-type person, but I think he compromised too much at times. I'm not the teamwork-type and I think I should be a little more like that."

Michael has a good balanced view of his father. His father wasn't perfect or the greatest man on earth, but Michael has a healthy, warm regard for him. Michael's description of himself has the same objective quality as his description of his father. We see obvious good points in each of them, which are tempered by the acknowledgement of weaknesses or failings. Not only does Michael's awareness of his father's faults allow him to acknowledge his own faults and still respect himself, Michael's image of his father also leaves Michael space to do better.

The contrast between Michael and Mark is heartrending. Mark over-idealizes his father, and until he can allow himself to admit his father's faults, Mark can never "measure up." Betsy needs to help Mark see his father's weaknesses, but this will not be easy. Betsy will have to proceed cautiously and gently if she hopes to break through Mark's defensiveness and denial. This is so delicate because to name the father's weaknesses can be seen as justifying the suicide. Betsy must strike a balance. For example, she can say that the father never did well academically, but was a good worker, and his unemployment was due to a lack of work in the area, not a judgment on the husband's skills. Or she can mention the father's unreasonable criticisms while admitting that he could be warm and fun when he was more relaxed.

FANTASIES OF WHAT'S MISSING

Once Dad is gone we can only imagine what life would be like had he survived. The grief itself causes difficulty that goes beyond coping with the extra work and trying to get by on less income. Many problems can be traced back to the father's death, but sometimes the death can become an excuse for never really dealing with life's challenges. When our fantasies of what Dad would have provided stretch beyond the capabilities or habits of most men, we deceive ourselves and "sell our souls" to unrealistic expectations.

The Hadleys often long for the financial security that a man can provide, and both Betsy and Mark feel helpless because Rich is not here to find a job for Mark. Betsy told me,

> "A lot of the parents around here get their kids jobs. But I don't have any contacts. If Mark's dad were alive he might have been able to help him find a job."

Mark seemed contaminated by this wishful thinking also.

> "I don't think I'd a worked with him because he didn't want me to do construction. He never told me what he thought I should be instead, but I figure if he was still alive I'd be working somewhere right now."

Since Rich killed himself over the uncertain seasonal nature of his work and his fears that he couldn't provide money for his family, it is doubtful that their fantasies about his helping Mark find a job are realistic. Instead Mark is left with a paralyzing legacy. He is expected to do something "better" than construction, yet his job skills are even less than his father's, and he will grow up without a father to teach him things. "It seems like when he was alive I had more energy and more motivation," Mark stated wearily. "If he was still alive I'd still know all his friends and maybe one of them would have a job for me." Mark has no idea what kind of work he would like to do. He doesn't even know if he'd rather work indoors or out.

How do living involved fathers help their sons discover their talents? Garrett and Brent Carson are very aware of their father's contribution to their strong belief in their own talents and capabilities. When I asked these young men how they feel their father has affected their achievement, Brent told me, "My dad's got a Ph.D. in chemical engineering, and I'll never achieve that, but he wants us to achieve in our own areas. He wants us to be happy."

As we talked about their father's expectations for them Brent stated,

> "I think he expects us to do our best at whatever we choose to do, whether it's schoolwork or something we volunteer for. For example, schoolwork is not my main focus in college. I'm very involved with music, with directing musical productions, more than classwork. My father isn't worried about me focusing my energy there, even though he's not at all musically inclined himself. He does tell us to buckle down on our schoolwork, but he would never say we should stop doing our musical activities because he knows that's what makes us happy."

Garrett added,

"I remember him saying that he would much rather I be a B student who is involved in other things, having a good time, than killing myself to make straight A's. He wrote us each a letter right before we went to college. I had written a lot of short stories in high school and in his letter to me he said he was really proud of me but he was disappointed that I'd never tried to write a novel. He felt I had the talent to do that. I know I wouldn't have the patience for it. But what came across was that he wanted me to do my best at whatever I was doing, and he had a lot of faith in me.

"Once we had been on a weekend with our youth group and about five minutes before we were going to make a presentation to the congregation the leader asked me to give a brief summary. I got up and gave a good summary and my dad said that my ability to give such an organized presentation on such short notice was the moment when he knew that I would be successful."

Brent recalled his own moment.

"I worked on this Camp Hope project and I had to do a slide show for our church. I opened it up for questions and I had to defend why they should give money to my project instead of Habitat for Humanity. They were both good programs. After I got done, my father said I would do really well in politics. Now I've been asked to do a slide show for some senators in Washington, D.C. My supervisor at the camp would be the natural one to do it, but she said I'm a better presenter and I thought, 'My dad said that one time.' "

Their father's praise made their early experiences with public speaking positive. They see themselves through his eyes as accomplished, competent speakers. He has empowered them to find their own jobs someday. Mark, on the other hand, can only remember the many things his father said he couldn't do, so he feels helpless about finding his own job.

CONSISTENCY AND BOUNDARIES

Mark knows what kids need when a Dad dies, because he has suffered from a lack of it. He advised, "After a father dies, the mom should get strict real quick. My mom wasn't strict at all. Now she's starting to get strict, but it's kind of too late."

Sylvie, five years older than Mark, also sees him as being the one who suffered most from a lack of discipline. "My brother has been really rebellious. I think my dad's death really affected him the most. He smarts off to my mom and doesn't come home by the curfew. If my dad were around Mark wouldn't talk to my mom like that, and he would be home on time. My dad never hit us or grounded us or anything, but we just took him more seriously. I tried telling Mark what to do but he's not going to take orders from his sister. He told me, 'I've already got a mom.' "

Discipline is not just crime and punishment. To be disciplined means to have boundaries and limits. The chaos of life and one's internal chaos are controlled. Children look to their parents to tell them when their behavior has strayed too far. When Mom is not up to the task, either because she is too emotionally weakened, or because she has no experience with being a disciplinarian, the family has no center. Until the family heals from their grief and reorganizes, the hole left by Dad keeps everyone on edge.

Sylvie advised, "The mom should be strict and not let the kids overrule her. It's better to be too strict than too weak. They might think you're mean at first, but they'll know in the end that you're only doing it because you love them."

A lack of discipline leaves a feeling that problems cannot be *contained*. If Mom doesn't do anything about a child's coming home at 11 P.M., then she probably won't do anything about him coming home after midnight, or 1 A.M., and so on. Adolescents particularly need their parents to set limits and create uncomfortable consequences that they will have to face if they go beyond those limits. They are under tremendous pressure from their peers to try out all sorts of potentially self-destructive behavior. The consequences for breaking the rules have to create more discomfort than the teen feels when he must tell his friends he's got to call it a night and go home. Not only did Mark become painfully rebellious, he began failing his school subjects. Eventually, he caught mononucleosis from running himself ragged at such a stressful time.

The role of disciplinarian did not come easily to Betsy. She had never had to fill those shoes before. Though she is beginning to learn to demand more of her kids, she is still floundering.

Shirley O'Rourke had a great advantage over Betsy in that her husband's decline to death had been slow. Shirley had gradually taken over more of the discipline as Mickey got sicker. He was just too weak and would often go directly to bed when he came home from work. Shirley commented, "When they needed a swatting, he was too sick to give it to them. He could still talk to them, like that special time with Michael when he had been doing poorly in school, but he was too tired to do that unless we especially requested it." Day to day, Shirley was already the disciplinarian.

Michael gave some details about the simple but important ways his mother provided a sense of *containment* after the father's death:

"My mom always made us do stuff. Like she didn't let us drop out of piano. I'm really glad my mother pushed us. My mom would say, 'No TV until you practice your piano.'

"The more the mom can keep things the way they were, the better it is for the kids. Church was important to me and so was Scouts. There were people there I could count on and my mom helped me keep my connection with them.

"Also, I think the best thing my mom ever did was to stay home. I really needed my mom around. We could have had a lot more materially if she had worked, but she was willing to do without in order to be there for us."

When a parent dies it's a big shock to a family, and the kids are going to have a lot of needs. It is a time when that one parent almost needs to be *more* than two parents. Though Mom needs to show her willingness to go on being involved in normal activities, this is not a time to sign up for a lot of extra responsibilities to keep herself so busy that she cannot think of her loss. Kids need the surviving parent to be available, to reassure them that the family will remain together, and to let them know their needs will be considered. In short, they need stability, predictability, and consistency. Children find it easiest to give in to their own feelings of sadness and work through them when they feel safe in their environment.

Through Michael, we get a picture of Shirley as a sturdy family leader. Mrs. O'Rourke humorously admitted, "Sometimes I'll say what I think their father would think or say about a family decision. I must admit that I always say their father would agree with me. But, really, Mickey and I always used to agree on things. We both always wanted them to do well in school and to be good to each other. He was more of a neatnik than I am, and he would have had them clean their rooms more, but otherwise I think the rules are the same as they would be if he were still here."

The careful research of Elliot Kranzler, assistant professor of clinical psychiatry at Columbia University, shows that the children whose surviving parents were able to carry on with family life much as it was before, suffered the least long-term damage from a parent's death.[1] If the emotional shock was too great, these mothers sought outside help. If finances meant the family would have to change their habits, mothers made these accommodations with as little fanfare as possible. They took jobs, moved into lower-income housing, or bought at discount stores.

In a sense, Betsy had lost her limit-setter when the family lost Rich. Though Rich was out of work for extended periods of time, there was an overall feeling of financial security in the family. However, after Rich died, Betsy quickly spent the insurance money, instead of looking toward the years ahead and budgeting or investing the money more carefully. As we will see in the next chapter, Betsy's money has run out, and she is not yet ready to be employed.

SUPPORTIVE OTHERS

Blood may be thicker than water, but sometimes family and friends cannot even be counted on to take an interest in the children. It is a bit sticky for a single woman to find men to be involved with her children. Shirley explained,

"As a single woman you have to be careful what you ask men, and you have to be careful around other women's husbands. Even though you're not after them, the women might think you are. My brother-in-law is right here in the city and he's never tried to do anything with the kids. He never came by when my husband was sick and he's never bothered to stop since. If I approached him, what would it look like?

"I have some real good lady friends whose husbands are great with kids, and I have thought that it would be wonderful if their husbands would take an interest in Michael, but I can't initiate it because I don't want to lose a good friend."

Betsy corroborated this uncomfortable feeling around her husband's former friends. "I thought I had lots of friends and Rich had lots of friends, but once something like this happens they don't seem to come around anymore. Once, I needed to go look for cars and one of my husband's friends was going to come with me, but his wife got jealous. I don't want to make trouble."

Mark never looks up any of his father's old friends. He told me, "I'm not sure any of them would even remember me." None have thought to call Mark to see how he is doing. However, there have been a few times men have reached out to Mark. He told me, "My one uncle is a plumber, and I helped him once at his job. I was the go-getter. He paid me, but I mostly went just to be along. Now if that uncle told me what to do, I'd probably do it. I respect him."

But other family members nearby have been disturbingly unsupportive. Betsy told me:

"It's been really hard. My sister decided Mark was a bad influence on her boys and wouldn't come over anymore. My parents had never been good around the kids. My parents say they love the kids but they feel kids should be seen and not heard. They didn't like me and my brothers much, so I can't expect them to like my kids any better. I contacted Rich's brother who lives near here and offered to have Mark come over and help him bale the hay because he's had a heart by-pass, but he didn't want Mark around."

Fortunately, Betsy has become involved with a kind, supportive man. Though Mark will not permit this man to father him directly, the boyfriend can be an important source of support for Betsy and, indirectly, her children. Mark commented,

"I don't mind my mother dating but I told her that no guy better start treating me like I'm his son. He can be around here but he can never replace my dad. If he doesn't interfere with me, I won't interfere with him."

Some children are ready and willing to welcome a new man into their lives, particularly if Dad died when they were very small. But teenagers, in particular, have a great deal of difficulty accepting Mom's new partner. They feel disloyal if they like the man, and they don't want anyone stepping in to father them at this late date. In addition, seeing a man escorting their mother, or acting in a fatherly way towards them, is a painful stimulant of old memories. But these are not reasons for the mother to refuse to date or get seriously involved with a new man.

Though it would not be wise for Betsy's boyfriend to discipline Mark directly, next time she gets in a bind with one of her kids she may be able to get on the phone and talk the situation over with the boyfriend. He might be able to encourage her to stand firm in her position or to go back in for another round. She would feel as if there were someone on her side when she is trying to be the disciplinarian her children need, instead of feeling alone in the situation all the time.

Having another adult to talk things over with increases our stability and ability to respond appropriately to our children. I remember that when my husband was out of town for long periods, I would sometimes call other parents and talk over situations with them. They would help me calm down, verify my judgement, or help me see a new angle. Once I had a car accident when my husband was out of town, and I felt really upset. I just needed someone to talk to, and I didn't want to scare my son. Betsy's adult ally can lend her strength so she can become increasingly firm and consistent.

OPENING NEW DOORS

It might seem particularly callous to bring up this possibility in this chapter, but sometimes a father is so abusive and gives so little to his children that the children are better off when he dies. As Maryanne put it, "I was about fifteen when my father died and I was happy because he could no longer hurt me. My only regret was that as long as he was alive, there was the possibility that he could change, but he never did. He died the nasty man that I had always known."

Maryanne, whose father died of cancer, has no delusions about his character.

"My father was very prejudiced, he drank a lot, and was a very angry man who took that anger out on anyone who got in his way. I can't think of anything good to say about him. I remember when he died one of the neighbors commenting what a poor child I was because my father had died and I felt like singing 'Ding-dong the witch is dead.' "

Maryanne remembers her mother crying and grieving and drinking when her father died, though the mother had spent much of the last ten years of her husband's life trying to get away from him. Maryanne's father had always been violent, and though he'd never beaten her mother, he was always like a bomb ready to go off. Her mother avoided being with the father as much as possible. To that end she had taken a night job that required her to leave the house before her husband returned from work each day. She would get home in the middle of the night, when he was already asleep, and stay in bed until he left in the morning. "I never remember my mother being around before my father died. I would come home from school and she would be getting ready for work. When I got up in the morning she would be sleeping and I would get yelled at if I woke her up. I never saw her." This left Maryanne and her older brother to cope with the father's sour moods at night.

Fortunately, the father went out drinking most evenings, and all Maryanne and her brother had to cope with were feelings of abandonment, but when her father was diagnosed as having terminal cancer, her really hellish life began. He had always been an extremely irritable person, and her relief had come when he would take off for the bar. But now he was too sick to leave the house. "He was here all the time and I couldn't talk on the phone, I couldn't watch TV, I couldn't play music, I couldn't even have friends over." Her formerly hyperactive alcoholic father was like a caged animal when he was laid off from work for his medical problems. He would harangue her, beat her, and chase her friends from the house.

"If I made a noise while he was watching TV he would come after me with his belt. Finally, toward the end he came after me once and I turned around and saw that I was as big as him. I said to him, 'Don't you touch me!' but he grabbed me and I pushed him. He fell down and then got up and walked off. He didn't hit me after that but he used to say awful things to me. He'd say, 'When I go, I'm taking you with me.' They were death threats and I wondered if he might poison me or something."

The family was ill-prepared financially for the father's death. Maryanne's older brother had married by then, and Maryanne and her mother had only Social Security to live on. The money from the sale of the house went to pay the staggering medical bills from her father's two years of treatment. "My life was turned upside down when my father finally died. We had to move because we couldn't afford the house anymore, and I had to go to a new school where they put me back a year."

Still, after a brief period of recovery, it was clear that Maryanne and her mother were much better off. The family had always been relatively poor and the Social Security checks that she and her mother received went a long way in their new, smaller home. The mother was able to quit her night job and take some brush-up course work in typing and bookkeeping. She got a daytime job, and for the first time in nearly ten years Maryanne had a parent at home in the evenings.

While Maryanne was growing up she had longed for a father like her best friend had.

"I always wished I could have a dad like Betty Lou's. He would take her out shopping with him every Saturday and sometimes they would take me along. They took me along on family trips to festivals in New York and to see the Rockettes. When I was in their house I could see how their family acted and it wasn't anything like my home life.

"But I know it would have been worse if my dad had stayed alive. I had wanted to be Daddy's little girl and that never would have happened. I miss being loved by a father but his dying had nothing to do with that, because he'd never acted loving anyway. I didn't feel damaged by his death, I felt damaged by who he was alive."

Once Maryanne's father was dead, her mother was free to date, and after a few very brief bad relationships, she began dating a very nice man. Maryanne comments on this boyfriend, "I always liked Walter. He didn't treat my mother like dirt. He was good to her. He would be here sometimes when I came home from school because he worked nights, and he would always ask me how school went. He would take us out to dinner and to fairs and buy me balloons."

After so many years of living with an abusive man, both Mary-anne and her mother had very little understanding of healthy relationships. Maryanne became pregnant during her senior year of high school and married the father, who turned out to be a wife-beater. One night he hit her until she bled and then stormed out of the house. Maryanne called her mother in hysterical desperation. The mother's callous comment was, "You made your bed, now lie in it." Luckily the boyfriend Walter was there, and he asked Maryanne's mother what the call was about. When she explained Maryanne's predicament, he insisted that she call Maryanne back and assure her that he was on his way to pick her up.

"Later, when I had divorced my first husband and had moved back in with my mother, my car broke down and I couldn't get to work. Walter lent me the money to get a new car. I wrote him a thank you note later and told him how grateful I was and how he was the closest thing I've ever had to a real father.

Walter has always been thoughtful. He's bought nice gifts for me and my son, and now at Christmas he always gets a gift for my new husband. He gave me away at both of my weddings. I asked him and he did it."

As we can see, ending the relationship with an abusive father not only ends the child's humiliation and pain, it clears the way for new more positive relationships. Maryanne's story makes us aware of the difference between fathers by biology and fathers in deed. She had longed for the father she never had years before her biological father died. It took his death to open the way for a "real father" to come into her life.

Death, divorce, or desertion may not be the end to the father-child relationship; it may open the door to a more caring relationship with a new father, or at least a less stressed relationship with Mom. After Maryanne's father died, she not only got back her mother, she ultimately got the considerate father she had longed for during her early childhood. As we will see in Part II, stepfathers, and other men who open themselves to relationships with unrelated children, can have a tremendously positive impact on children whose biological fathers are absent, for whatever reason.

SUMMARY POINTS

- It is important for children to have a realistic idea of their deceased father — to know not only his strengths but also his weaknesses — so that they will have an attainable role model and manageable expectations for themselves.
- If the children over-idealize Dad, the boys are left feeling like failures, and the girls can never find a mate that matches up to dear old Dad. Though it is difficult to find fault with a deceased person, kids need to know Dad's failings.
- Children have a tremendous need for approval and encouragement from their parents. When Dad has died Mom is burdened with trying to make up for his lost praise. It helps to bring kids in contact with other positive supportive males.
- There is no doubt that the death of a father creates many hardships for his bereaved family, but it is a mistake to dwell on all Dad could have provided. It is healthier for the family to accept the loss and learn to do for themselves.
- Since men have traditionally been the disciplinarians, Moms must be on the alert to be firm and set limits on their children's behavior when they are the only available parent. Though friends or boyfriends should not be called in to discipline the children directly, their behind-the-scenes emotional support can be a great help to Mom.

PART II

8

What's Missing When Dad's Missing?

"My dad was my teacher. He taught me about loyalty and friendship and doing your best. I wanted so much to please him. I still do."

— KEVIN COSTNER, *Parade Magazine* [1]

What do we seek from our fathers? What special traits, characteristics, or responses do men provide in a relationship with a child? Could they be replaced by a female roommate? Can the androgynous woman make up for the loss? The new men's movement has made us sorely aware that boys, in particular, need the attention of men. As we dissect all the functions of fathers in the home, we can better analyze what mothers can and cannot do on their own to make up for an absent father. Many of these questions have been answered through the stories of families with absent fathers presented in this book. Now we will take a more objective look by reviewing research on the father's impact on childhood development.

At birth the father has already had a major impact on his child; he has contributed half the gene pool that has created that new person. Every time we fill out a medical family history we realize our inexorable link to the past and the people who created us. Problems such as diabetes, mood disorders, or alcoholism can be inherited, as well as talents like musical ability and a high math aptitude. Even if Dad never sets eyes on the child, he has had a profound and long-lasting influence.

There is also an undeniable emotional connection that children feel towards their biological father. We are all familiar with the stories of difficult searches adopted children have made to find their biological parents. Children of unwed unions and children of divorce whose fathers have not visited them for years have just as much curiosity about their fathers as adopted children do. So even when the father has had little contact with his children, his offspring will have emotional and practical needs to know about their father.

A number of studies have been done to explore how fathers and mothers interact differently with their children. Researchers have discovered that mothers have a rather low-key approach to their children compared to fathers who favor rough-and-tumble play, tossing the children into the air, or stimulating them with loud bursts of noise. Mothers typically touch their children in caretaking and nurturing ways, and generally spend more time talking to them than dads do. Renowned pediatrician T. Berry Brazleton comments, "Most fathers seem to present a more playful, jazzing up approach. As one watches this interaction, it seems that a father is expecting a more heightened, playful response from the baby. And he gets it!"[2]

Infants not only get more active stimulation from their fathers than their mothers, but the character of that stimulation is also different. For example, fathers expect more independent behavior from their children. In one study that asked parents at what ages they felt their children could handle various tasks such as going next door alone, using a hammer, crossing the street, playing with scissors, or taking a bath without help, fathers consistently expected more at younger ages. This trend continues as the child grows older, with fathers expecting more at every stage. And the earlier that fathers expected these independence skills to emerge, the higher the children were in cognitive development. Other studies show that while mothers cautiously put stricter limits on children's explorations, fathers encourage more open exploring. Dad will only step in and guide or instruct his children after they have encountered difficulties or when they have asked for information.[3] Dads typically discuss current events with their children, introducing them to ideas and environments of the outside world, and they have traditionally prepared children for their ultimate journey into the work world.

BOYS AND FATHERS

Comparisons between boys whose fathers were involved with them and boys whose fathers were absent help define what it is a father gives to his son. For example, studies show that boys with involved fathers could handle strange situations more smoothly and balk less at being left with a babysitter. This comparative boldness was even evident in five-month-old infant boys. This social adaptability continued to be influenced by the boy's relationship with his father as the boy grew older, and these more adaptable boys were more popular with their peers. As we noted earlier, young boys with active fathers were more physical in their play and played more contact sports. Studies show that father-absence generally affected boys who lost their father before age six more than those who lost their fathers in adolescence. Teen boys who lost their fathers had fewer adjustment problems because their masculine identities had already been formed by the time Dad left.[4]

BOYS WITH INVOLVED FATHERS

are

Bold and confident

Popular with other boys

Physical in their play

Boys who lost their fathers while young often showed little understanding of "male" behaviors. They have missed that important early period of rough-and-tumble play that dads usually provide. However, mothers who encouraged aggression, independence, and other typically masculine behaviors raised boys with a well-developed masculine self-concept.[5] Research shows boys grew into masculine behaviors most easily (despite the lack of a father in the home) when mothers had a positive attitude toward the father and encouraged traditionally masculine behaviors such as independence and exploration. Unfortunately many women parenting alone tended to be overprotective and discouraged adventurous or boisterous behavior. The sons of these mothers were more timid.[6] It is important that boys not feel shamed when naturally occurring masculine behaviors emerge.

What is crucial is that a son still feels loved when he bounds through the house or wants to compete at sports.

When boys have little contact with fathers early in life the symptoms of distress can appear at any time in the first six years. Deprived of their father's attention, they are often depressed, socially inept, or exhibit aggressive acting out behaviors. Also, boys respond to Dad's absence with antisocial behavior more often than girls. Boys frequently exhibit poor self-control and have sleep disturbances, as well as other signs of stress. By contrast, boys whose fathers have custody of them do as well as boys in intact homes with very involved fathers. Amicable joint custody arrangements also provide boys with enough fathering to give them the role model they need to grow up into well-adjusted men.[7]

Robert Bly, renowned poet and leader of men's consciousness workshops, talks about male initiation rites as important to the forming of a boy's identity as a man. In many primitive cultures there is a marked passage, a ceremony or ritual, that brings the boy to manhood. Bly describes the custom in New Guinea where the boy lives with the mother exclusively in his early years. The men come in a group, armed with spears, to get the boy and take him away to become a man. In a ritualized drama, the boy calls to his mother to save him, and she and the other mothers wield spears against the men but are driven back. The men drag the boy off for his "initiation." He will spend a year with the men before he will see his mother again.[8]

Interestingly, this follows the logic and best advice of modern psychologists who recognize that children bond first to the mother, and that boys, in particular, must later break that bond and become closer to the father in order to become healthy and independent. It is a playing out of the oedipal conflict. While many professionals debate who should get custody following a divorce, they might gain from considering such primitive rituals. Perhaps boys should remain in custody of the mother until age twelve and then be sent to live with their fathers. (Of course, this presumes a willing father.)

A study of children of divorce involving 144 school psychologists from thirty-eight different states provided further evidence that shows the importance of the father's involvement in the child's life. By comparing children of divorce with children in intact families, these psychologists discovered that boys of divorce are most strongly negatively affected by the absence of a father-figure. Children of divorce consistently perform more poorly on a wide variety of social, academic, and physical health criteria. The NASP-Kent State University Impact of Divorce Project shows this negative impact of divorce to be greater for boys. However, in most cases, boys who had good relationships with their non-custodial fathers scored higher on intelligence tests, were more socially adept, and showed a higher degree of originality and independent thinking than those with little father contact.[9]

Robert Moore, another writer and speaker who explores mythological male images such as the king and the warrior, has also considered the impact of role models on burgeoning young men. He observed, "The only warriors we have in the United States are the negative versions of it, the shadow versions, who are the druglords." This is a far cry from the badly needed "positive warrior" who does not go out to harm or damage others, but rather defends the boundaries and acts as protector.[10] Perhaps Moore's dismal vision explains, in part, the recent growing popularity of "gangs" in cities large and small across the United States. How do these warlords compare to heroes of old like George Washington or Abraham Lincoln? Unfortunately, our heroes reflect America's current values. Rambo was our first contemporary hero of violence, and toymakers have capitalized on the theme since then. Without enough live "whole" men around to provide a contrast to these violent fantasy figures, our boys are left to idealize some very dangerous caricatures of masculinity.

GIRLS AND FATHERS

Dad's effect on his daughter is often a "win some/lose some" prospect. Available fathers who talked to, praised, and responded to their daughters boosted their girls' social responsiveness and positive feelings about self beyond the level of those girls whose fathers were uninvolved.[11] On the other hand, involved fathers who were more locked into promoting stereotyped behavior, discouraged their daughters, intellectual explorations and had a negative effect on their cognitive development.

As a matter of fact, studies show that fathers, more often than mothers, strongly promote sexual stereotypes. When a parent and child were placed in a room full of toys, fathers selected traditionally

feminine toys for girls (such as dolls) and traditionally masculine
toys for boys (such as trucks), whereas mothers usually did not.
Fathers even discouraged the child from playing with the "wrong
sex" toy.[12] These fathers also encouraged dependence in their daughters and often gave little support to the daughter's achievements.
Therefore, many girls without fathers may be freer from these
limiting stereotypical gender roles.

GIRLS WITH INVOLVED FATHERS

are

Socially adept

High in self-esteem

More traditionally female in behavior

Confident about attractiveness

   The rare fathers who were able to break out of these stereotypical
ways of thinking often had profound positive effects on their daughters' achievements and aspirations.[13] As girl children approach age
two, that first great leap toward autonomy, they begin to try to make
and do things on their own. If a father shares projects with his
daughter, praises her accomplishments, and compliments her capabilities, the girl will have a positive attitude toward achievement.
One study of self-directed, high-achieving young adult women
showed this kind of relationship with a father early in their lives. The
fathers of the successful women in this study had encouraged or
stimulated their curiosity, exploration, and independent judgment
and had worked with the daughters on their projects. Interestingly
enough, one of the most successful women had a father who was a
pilot and was absent a great deal during her childhood. Though he
had spent a relatively small amount of time with her and had died
while she was in college, his approval of her when he had been
present was so strong and enthusiastic that she still hears his voice
encouraging her, even beyond the grave. A control group of less-
motivated women described their fathers as having discouraged their
curiosity or exploration and as being uninvolved and uninterested in
their academic achievement.[14]

   Fortunately, after the crucial early years, the girl's connection with
her mother becomes a more important factor and can often make up

for a disinterested father. If she has missed out on affirmation from Dad, identification with a well-adjusted mother and mother's strong support and approval can often make up for the loss. However, other researchers note that many girls never get over the loss of Dad's attentiveness during the preschool years and continue to have difficulty forming long-lasting heterosexual relationships throughout their lives.[15]

Fathers seem to have the most importance for daughters in forming their sexual identity and in helping them relate to the opposite sex. Around age four, when little girls begin to flirt with their fathers, his positive response to her appeals will affirm her femininity and her expressiveness. A vivacious, thirty-year-old, married urban planner who took part in the study of successful women, reported, "Once when I was little, I remember asking my father why he never won the Nobel Prize and his answer was, 'because I wanted to have dinner with you every night.' "[16] She felt wonderfully valued and important! Girls who had little contact with their fathers, especially during adolescence, had great difficulty forming lasting relationships with men. Sadly, the girls often either shied away from males altogether or went after them like sirens, being sexually used in the bargain. Girls with involved fathers learned how to interact with males by using the father-daughter relationship as a model. They not only had a warm, male adult to talk to, they also had the feeling of being accepted and loved by at least one man, whereas girls without fathers often became desperate for male attention.

Shirley O'Rourke, widowed when her oldest daughter, Melody, was eleven, explained the problems she sees for her daughters and dating, since the girls have basically had no men in their lives other than their grandfather and brother. The brother Michael is about five years older than Katy, the youngest daughter, so that Katy had opportunities to watch older boys together and learned how to talk with them without the awkwardness of seriously considering dating any of them. She could be nearby in the background, a sort of cute little mascot. Unfortunately, Melody is almost three years older than her brother, so she had not been able to look up to him. Her role in the family as the caretaker probably made him seem all the more like "little brother." Shirley explained:

"That's another way Melody has had the hardest position as the oldest. She didn't have parents to model how couples interact.

Even when Mickey was alive we didn't have a normal relationship. Then she didn't even have any older siblings. Katy had a chance to see how her sister handled boys and then she got to spend time with boys because of her brother. Katy has always been comfortable around boys. Katy has had several boyfriends who have lasted for months and months but Melody's relationships have been very short-lived."

Melody added her perspective:

"Dating is really hard without a father. I'm the oldest child and I didn't have a father to ask questions about boys. My mother thinks she sheltered me too much and I've been slow about dating. I'm not a shy person and I have a lot of close male friends. But I never know how to make the relationship romantic. Guys have said to me, 'We're such good friends I don't want to mess it up.' My mom thinks it's because I haven't had a father. When I was really little I used to go up and introduce myself to everybody, even strangers. I was actually too friendly. But my mom says I really withdrew when my dad died."

Now that her brother Michael is a man, Melody can see his strong developing character. Recently, he has become a model for her of what to look for in a mate.

"For the last few years I've been going out with a lot of needy guys, but the guy I like now reminds me of my brother. They're both very goal-oriented, loving, kind, and they each have a great sense of humor. They value family and all that. And my brother reminds me of my grandfather. They believe in doing what's fair and just. They don't believe in trampling over other people to get what you want."

One important study compared daughters of widows, daughters of divorcées, and daughters of intact families. There was no noticeable difference in the girls' behavior before adolescence, but then daughters of divorce sought much more attention from men and more physical contact with boys their age than did girls from intact homes. Daughters of widows, on the other hand, avoided any contact with males. The adolescent girls of divorce had the most contact with boys their age while the daughters of widows had the least. However, the daughters of divorce were the most critical of their fathers, while the girls whose fathers had died had the most positive concept of their fathers and also felt the saddest about the loss of their fathers.

Those affected most strongly were girls who had lost fathers before age five, whether through divorce or death. The daughters of divorce had more aggressive behavior, constantly sought attention from adults, and were physically aggressive to both male and female peers. The girls whose fathers had died before age five were extremely reticent around male adults, shied away from physical contact with them, and rarely smiled.

This study also polled the attitudes of the mothers and revealed that the divorced mothers had the most negative attitude about the fathers, themselves, and life in general. They saw their lives and their marriages as having been very unfulfilling and worried about being poor mothers. Despite this, their relationships with their daughters were very positive. At the same time, both widows and divorcées were overprotective of their daughters. As might be expected, the widows expressed concern about their daughters' lack of ease with and interest in boys, while the divorcées complained about their daughters' promiscuous behavior.[17]

DAD'S CONTRIBUTION TO INTELLIGENCE

Unfortunately, studies show that children with absent fathers often have diminished cognitive development and poor school performance. The earlier the father is missing, the greater the damage. In a study done with infants only five and six months old, the boy babies who lived in homes with fathers scored significantly higher on the Bayley Scales of Infant Development than did boys without fathers. (Father's absence made little difference for girls at this stage, perhaps because mothers unconsciously focus on verbal interaction with young children, and females specialize in verbal interchange, so girls are getting the kind of stimulation they need.) The boy babies who had spent more time with their fathers also showed greater curiosity and interest in new objects. This developmental delay was not simply the result of fewer adults living in the home, for investigation showed that there were just as many adults living in the homes of the babies without fathers. Surprisingly, it was the father's specific presence that made the difference.[18]

But the father's influence on cognitive development doesn't end at six months, and an especially active father can have a significant effect on his child's achievement at any age. One study done on boys whose parents were still married showed that boys whose fathers spent six hours or less per week with them were functioning below grade level while boys whose fathers spent fourteen hours or more per week with them were superior in academic performance.[19] Sometimes Dad's expectations alone can have a significant long-term influence.

Michael O'Rourke had had school problems the year before his father died (shortly after his mother, Shirley, had told the kids that Daddy wasn't going to get better). The teacher advised Shirley to have her husband talk to Michael about his schoolwork. "I don't know what Mickey said to him," Shirley told me, "but that talk has lasted Michael all his life. From that time, and right on up to today, Michael has always done well in school." Michael told me:

> "I felt really close to my dad, so I still felt he was a part of me when he died. I remember before he was that sick, when he could still get around, I wasn't doing too well in school for some reason. He took me to this book fair and he bought me this little ceramic frog. He told me that even though he was sick he wanted me to do well in school. I think this had a really deep effect on me because I have always done well in school since then.
>
> "I kept that ceramic frog for a long time. I used to sit it on my desk where I would do my homework. It seems like a minor thing—buying me this little ceramic frog. But I think I have done well because I wanted to live up to his hopes for me. I think I had lost my will to do well in school and that talk gave it back to me. When I looked at the frog I would think of his words to me."

Other studies have shown that children who spend more time with their fathers not only get better grades, but also do better on achievement and IQ tests. Of course, to grasp the whole picture we must also take a peek at the side issues. Children with very involved fathers have mothers who are not too exhausted to pay lots of rewarding attention to their children, whereas single mothers who work all day and come home to prepare a meal for the family without help may be too worn out at dinner even to make conversation.

Dad's Ongoing Influence

1. *Dads encourage independence.* Dads are generally less protective, promote exploration and risk taking, and model aggressive or assertive behaviors.
2. *Dads expand the child's horizons.* They are a link to the "outside world" through their jobs.
3. *Dads serve as "alternative parent."* Dad can improve the quality of Mom's parenting by reducing her stress and stepping in to give Mom a break during crises.
4. *Dads are strict disciplinarians.* Dads accept fewer "excuses" and demand more of kids at each stage.
5. *Dads are men.* When a Dad treats his child respectfully and can put the child at ease with him, the child is likely to have positive relationships with other men throughout his or her life.

DAD AS ALTERNATIVE PARENT

One of the most essential roles a dad can play is that of the "alternative" parent. There are days when moms can endure constant resistance from their children, hours of endless noise, and even concerted efforts of total defiance, but everyone has her limit. Sometimes the kids go one step too far when Mom has already had a bad day at the office, or she has a splitting headache. Then moms lose it. When parents blow their cool, they need a fresh adult to step in and bring things back to order. Dad is his most precious when he is there to fulfill that function.

Pamela's family has been through a lot of changes. Her parents actually divorced and later remarried. Pamela has lived alone with each parent at one time or another. When Pamela's parents first split up, she was six. I interviewed Pamela when she was in her early teens. Her parents had just been through a second, though brief, stormy separation. This was an especially hard time for Pamela.

"My brother was really out of control and my mom couldn't work because she couldn't afford to pay for his daycare. She said she was better off just getting support from my dad. I get away with a lot more when my dad isn't there, but I have a lot of fights with my mom. I start swearing at her and she hits me. One time my mom was so mad that she went in and ripped up all my tapes and then later she said, 'They're only tapes. At least I didn't kill you.' This doesn't happen when my dad is there. He controls my brother much better and I just like him being there."

However, having Dad back at home isn't all a bed of roses. According to Pamela,

> "Now that they're together again it's harder. They have to agree on everything. Like if I want to go skating, they both have to say yes, or when I wanted to get my ears pierced, they had to agree on it."

Like any child, Pamela appreciates her father being there to calm down Mom and set limits on the brother, but she doesn't really want him to set limits on her!

In most homes times are generally tensest at the end of the day when everyone is tired and hungry. Single parents, working wives, and even stay-at-home moms (whose husbands stay at the office until all hours) know they are more likely to say or do something they regret when they are stressed and have no means of escaping a provocative situation. Father's absence makes us aware of the important role he could play as moderator, mitigator, or pure fresh energy to be used in the eternal struggle to outlast the kids.

But the father is not just a reinforcement sent in to continue the battle. Fathers have traditionally been the disciplinarians, and although they may not have seen their own fathers model nurturing behavior, most of today's fathers have some memories of a dad's discipline to model in crisis. The gentlest image of father as "disciplinarian" emphasizes father's role as limit-setter. He helps the child channel his or her energy constructively toward work or cooperative play. Father is at his best when he is coaching soccer or organizing the children to rake up leaves. He often steps in when the children are getting so wound up that they may get hurt or hurt each other, and he frequently keeps things on an even keel. Many women parenting alone cite the role of disciplinarian as their most difficult challenge.

When a stepfather arrives on the scene, these mothers are astonished and relieved by the instant obedience a man can usually command with little more than his deep voice.

In calmer moments, Dad can also add significantly to the smoothness of the household. The male's more rigid scheduling in the work world inspires him to bring structure into the home, thus providing the consistency children crave. Even Dad's much criticized flaw of not forming close bonds with his children works to his advantage in calming a family crisis or setting limits on over-stimulating activities. Because he is less emotionally invested in the children, he finds it easier to step back and mete out discipline. He doesn't care if the child gets angry. He may actually have a healthy distance from the situation that an overinvolved mother might lack.

ENMESHMENT WITH MOM

When fathers are very uninvolved with their children there is a great deal of pressure for the children to become overly close to the mother. Children need a lot of love and attention. If there is no Dad to provide his share, they will naturally seek more from Mom. Mom, who is often lonely herself and wishing she were getting more attention, empathizes with the children. As she tries to make up for their lost attention from Dad, she is rewarded with the children's grateful attention, and her own unmet needs for closeness are fed.

When children begin to fill the void Dad left in Mom's life, there are two potentially destructive outcomes. Mom may begin to lean on one of the children to become her co-parent, or she may become so emotionally close to her child that she blocks that child's natural healthy movements toward independence.

Shortly after Mickey's death, Shirley went into counseling with Melody.

"Melody had always been the most sensitive and I had been the hardest on her because she was the oldest. I knew I had depended on her too much and expected an awful lot from her. Michael is tougher. But when you criticize Melody she starts to cry. Michael had been free to go his own way, but I had really relied on Melody to take care of Katy. Because Melody was there all the time when I was feeling exhausted and at my wit's end, I would take it out on her."

Melody, who has now graduated college and is living in an apartment two hundred miles away from her mother, added her long-range perspective.

"If I had to give advice to widowed moms I would say, 'Be supportive but not smothering.' I think my mom leaned on me a little too much because I was the oldest. I've always been family-oriented. But I'm glad I didn't lose my mom, because I needed her more.

"Actually, it wasn't so much my mom leaning on me, as me letting her. I wanted her close to me. So it's been hard for both of us to separate. I don't want to go back and live in the same town as my mom because it would be too hard to be independent. I feel like she's pushing and pulling at the same time. She likes to hear every minute of my dates and I'm beginning to want more privacy. But sometimes I want to just call her up and tell her all about a date. Separating is really hard for me."

Both mother and daughter are aware of the problem, and they have taken steps all along to correct the imbalance that existed at the time of the father's death. But we can see how easily a cycle of unhealthy closeness that is hard to break can begin. Mom finds it easier to get her emotional needs met through the children instead of her peers because the children are right there every day. The children, whose self-esteem is often weakened by Dad's inattentiveness, find it easier to seek affirmation from Mom rather than neighborhood adults or teachers because there is less risk involved in reaching out to Mom. The mother-child unit becomes self-reinforcing as mother and child withdraw further from society and sources of outside support. Like the alcoholic who would rather drink than face her problems, the enmeshed mother uses her closeness with her children to soothe herself and avoid changing her sad circumstances or taking risks. Meanwhile, the children learn this pattern of coping, and their motivation to try new solutions atrophies.

Enmeshment is almost a natural outcome that mothers must consciously struggle against. It is an excessive and prolonged form of the healthy symbiotic tie between mothers and infants. As we discussed earlier, it is the father's task to initiate and inspire the child's separation from mother. He does this by offering himself as another source of love. Picture a baby taking his first steps. He clings to mother's outstretched arm for support and looks toward his father crouched four feet away with his arms held out to receive him. The child lets go of mother and reaches and steps toward Dad. This is how it should be.

But what if Dad is too busy or disinterested to be the other side of the bridge? The image becomes Mother detaching the child's hand and giving him a shove. With no one to receive him, he will either fall or drift off into space. That is, if Mom can even get him to let go. Is there a more humane way to do this? Yes. Mom can help the child form connections with others – siblings, grandparents, neighbors, teachers – and, at the same time, encourage the child's independence by engendering a "you can do it!" attitude. Of course, Moms need to stop depending on the children at the same time. Those who have built up their own support systems can generally find the strength and confidence to do this.

DAD AND THE CHILD'S IDENTITY

Children will have a great need to talk about their fathers as they look toward their fathers to discover more about themselves. While sorting out their identities, children will naturally make comparisons between themselves and their parents. In fact, most children are confronted with these comparisons constantly as relatives and friends comment on how alike or different they are from Mom or Dad. The subject cannot be avoided and children must know as much as they can about Dad, so they can judge for themselves how well these comparisons stand up.

What sort of things do children need to know? They like to get an objective view of what Dad's strengths and weaknesses were. What special talents did their father have? What did his friends like best about him? What did he do that irritated others? Are there ways that Dad has changed? What changed him? What are they likely to inherit from Dad? Does he have any physical or emotional handicaps that they should know about? They need as much information as they can get about what their Dad was like in order to be able to answer the question: Am I like Dad?

If Mom can be neutral, she may be a good listener and informant. However, it is good for children to get some other opinions. The mother should try to help the children link up with Dad's friends or relatives so that the children can get a broader picture of Dad. This is especially true for children who were very young at the time of divorce and have had little contact with the father since. Sometimes families mistakenly believe that the young child is unaffected by the loss since she "never knew Dad anyway." However, the youngest child often has the vaguest sense of who Dad is since he or she will have so few memories. Older siblings frequently do not even think to fill in the younger child and may even believe they are protecting the youngest child by not talking about Dad too much. Mom needs to let everyone know that Dad can and should be talked about. The best way she can do this is to model that herself, telling stories about Dad at appropriate times in a family setting.

Talking about Dad can also help develop the sense of roots that is important to each of us. As my interviews with bereaved children revealed, children love to hear about Mom's and Dad's early romance. What was Dad like when he was much younger? How did Mom and Dad meet, and what attracted Mom to Dad? Children in intact families ask these questions, too. Children in divorced families are no less curious about these details of their parents' lives, but they are sometimes afraid to ask. They may sense that Dad is a sore subject, and they do not want to hurt their mothers by bringing him up. Indeed, in some homes of divorce Dad seems to be a taboo subject.

Deborah Anna Luepnitz, a psychologist on the staff of the Philadelphia Child Guidance Clinic, tells a moving story of Leroy, a teenaged boy who longed to know his father, though publicly he feigned hatred and disinterest:

> . . . This led to talk about his father, at whose name his face immediately contorted with anger. I asked Leroy what he knew about his father and he said, 'Enough.' It turned out that 'enough' actually meant nothing at all. He knew that his father's name was Leroy, but he did not know what state he lived in, or who else was in his family. He couldn't name a single good quality of his father's or say what job or what interests he had. He had never seen a photograph of him.

[Dr. Luepnitz then commented,] 'So you don't even know if you look like him or not.'

[And Leroy replied,] 'Don't want to know. I told you—if he ever came near me, I'd mess him up.'[20]

As Dr. Luepnitz explained, Leroy had been in trouble since kindergarten when he had ruined his classmates' art projects during recess. He had hit a teacher in third grade and had been suspended five times in fourth grade. When he was sixteen, he was arrested for breaking into a store and was in a correctional school when Dr. Luepnitz met him. The mother had never spoken of the father except to say that he had beaten her when Leroy was younger and this is what prompted her to leave him. During family-therapy sessions, Dr. Luepnitz encouraged the mother to share some information about Leroy, Sr., with Leroy. The mother told Leroy that he did look like his father and that his father was handsome and tall like Leroy. She admitted that the father had a good sense of humor and added other details, like the fact that Leroy's father had played saxophone in a jazz band. Dr. Luepnitz asked the mother to describe some of Leroy's father's good qualities and to show Leroy a picture of his father.

Before this, although Leroy's mother had often told him he was like his father, she mentioned nothing about the father but his violent behavior. Now Leroy began to respond very positively to this talk of his father. When Dr. Luepnitz asked Leroy if he would like to meet his father, Leroy replied that he wanted to get his life together first. He wanted to finish his detention sentence and get back in school, so that his father could be proud of him. How remarkable that Leroy could suddenly care so much what his absent father thought of him!

Unfortunately, when Leroy was ready to contact his father, he and his mother learned that the father had died in a car accident three years earlier. However, Leroy was able to meet his father's family and learn more about him. Dr. Luepnitz sees Leroy's discovery of his father as key to his recovery:

. . . Leroy started therapy with a history of antisocial behavior, and ended therapy with no further trouble with the law. He started therapy with no idea of who his father was, and ended with the ability to talk about his father, to describe him and ask questions about him, to understand how he was like his father and how he was different from him. Because of therapy, he learned of his father's death and was able to mourn the fact that he never knew him. It is reasonable to hope that this acknowledged loss of the father will contribute to the importance Leroy will one day give to taking care of his own children.[21]

Just as the bereaved child needs to mourn the loss of his father, a divorced child in the mother's custody needs to mourn the loss of his dad, whether or not the father has disappeared completely from the scene. Together, the mother and child may find it easy to grieve the loss of their material comforts, but the mother may have trouble sympathizing with the child's grief for his or her father's companionship. Nonetheless, children are better off if they can talk to someone about these feelings and perhaps cry over the loss. Mother should arrange opportunities for this by linking her children up with the father's relatives, therapists who specialize in divorce grief, or clergy trained to talk to children about such losses. Children are especially helped by sharing in groups of their peers who are having similar experiences. Many schools and community counseling centers offer such programs for divorced children.

As we can see, Dad does have an important impact on a child's life. If we can get Dad involved with his son or daughter, that child will grow up to be confident, competent, and secure. When it is impossible to bring Dad back into the child's life, we need to keep Dad's special contributions in mind so that we can systematically try to meet the child's special needs for Dad in other ways.

SUMMARY POINTS

- Even if Dad never sets eyes on the child, he has a profound and long-lasting effect because so many traits and talents are hereditary. Therefore, it is essential for children to know as much as they can about their fathers.
- Mothers are very verbal and have a more low-key approach to children than fathers do. Dads are more physical and favor rough-and-tumble play.
- Though boys who lose their fathers young typically show little understanding of "male" behaviors, mothers who encouraged

aggression and independence produced boys with a well-developed masculine self-concept.

- A father's effect on his daughter is often a mixed blessing. Involved fathers who praised their daughters produced more socially responsive girls than uninvolved fathers. However, at the same time, most fathers discouraged their daughters' intellectual explorations and pushed them toward more stereotypical female roles.

- Many girls without attentive fathers had problems with the opposite sex when they reached adolescence. Daughters of divorce tended to be promiscuous, while bereaved daughters tended to be overly shy around males.

- Studies show proof that fathers have a significant effect on children's cognitive development. The children of absent fathers often had poorer school performance, lower achievement test scores, and lower IQ scores.

- One of the father's most important roles was that of "alternative parent"—someone Mom could turn to as disciplinarian when her energy ran out. More importantly, Dad offered an alternate relationship to the children so they were not so emotionally dependent on Mom.

- Children need to have an unbiased well-rounded picture of who Dad was so that they can sort out their own identities in relation to each of their parents.

9

Dad Is Money

*American divorce law in practice seems to be saying to
parents, especially mothers, that it is not safe to devote
oneself primarily or exclusively to children.*

— MARY ANN GLENDON
Abortion and Divorce in Western Law[1]

*We are all one man away from welfare until we develop our
earning power.*
— GLORIA STEINEM

I hate to be cynical, but after talking to families of all kinds
with uninvolved fathers one important very unromantic point keeps
emerging—when Dad is missing but his money is not, the families do
much better. Wives of workaholics and men who travel excessively
or are transferred away with their jobs feel some financial strain.
Sometimes the family must pay for a separate apartment for Dad,
and usually the family must hire handymen to do many jobs Dad
could do if he were home. But large corporations generally pay
enough to compensate families for these hardships. With that extra
money and health benefits Mom can even "hire a psychologist" to
take the place of Dad in supporting her and helping the children work
through the emotional hardship of being without a father.

The kids in these families feel the loss of Dad, even an aching for
that special relationship they hoped and expected to have with the
man who fathered them. But often the financial means the family has
available can go a long way to help them heal and come out of

childhood relatively undamaged, and the women are free to work full-time or not, based on the needs of their families at that time. Though most mothers work now and women's self-reliance has many side benefits, the loss of flexibility on this issue for the widowed, divorced, or unwed mother can have a significant negative impact.

During each decade, the mothers of younger and younger children have gone back to work so that, as of 1986, half of the mothers of children age one or younger now work outside the home. On the bright side, studies by the National Academy of Sciences panel found that maternal employment had no consistent negative effects on the children (although boys in middle-class families seem to suffer some harm while the girls seem to benefit from mother working).[2] Furthermore, working mothers avoid becoming "overinvolved mothers"—the most frequently discussed family problem situation cited by psychologists in my research. Studies showed that married women who worked outside the home were healthier both physically and psychologically than married women who confined themselves to being homemakers. The homemakers suffered more from migraine headaches, insomnia, nervous breakdowns, and depression, as well as other ailments.[3] So there are potential benefits to both mother and child when the mother works at an absorbing job.

On the other hand, full-time demanding jobs do not allow parents to be available when their children need them, and childcare in the United States is so underfunded that many children must spend vast amounts of time in groups with too few caretakers per child to give any one child the special attention each needs. Sturdy children can learn to "postpone gratification," to hang in there until Mom can get home or make herself available to really listen. However, there are many small children and sensitive children who are not ready or suited to do well in daycare. They may feel emotionally abandoned and carry that fear and emptiness into adulthood.

Mothers of sensitive children who must work are bound to develop defense mechanisms that block out their knowledge of their children's needs. Arlie Hochschild, author of *The Second Shift*, discovered that, as women grow weary from playing "Supermom" and find they must pull back on some of their mothering duties, they soothe themselves with the new image of the "superkid." Her research showed that the more uninvolved parents of any sex are, the more "independent" they perceive their children to be. The caretakers often see the children differently, noticing their neediness, but they never have time to broach the subject with a parent who dashes in and sweeps the child away without asking about the child's day. Hochschild finds that many working parents are in denial about their children's needs. Children are perceived to need only as much as their parents have time to give them.[4]

In most intact families both parents must work to provide a good standard of living for the family. Therefore, there is little chance that the single mother can avoid working without the children suffering greatly from economic hardship. Even if an absent father faithfully contributes his court-ordered child support, the standard of living for children will drop substantially. The available money must now cover two residences (and, in many cases, expensive lawyer bills, for a divorce must be paid for). So even in best-scenario divorces, children usually suffer the loss of many creature comforts as well as the loss of Dad. When Dad does not contribute any money, the children's standard of living often drops to poverty level.

Most mothers, especially of small children, have tried to balance their lives so that career does not make them abandon their offspring. They have usually chosen to work part-time so that they can be available to their children, and even mothers of older children often lean toward low-powered, low-stress, (and consequently low-pay) jobs, so that they can be emotionally accessible to their children.

In an article in *Ms.* magazine feminist writer Jane Lazone ruefully admitted that, when she considered returning to work when her child was three years old, she avoided "mother's guilt" by vowing:

> I will take no job which will prevent me from being home by, say, three o'clock. And this "three o'clock" turns immediately into another rigid commandment, engraved in solid rock; coming home a minute after three means my baby will be a "latchkey kid," a lonely, deviant neurotic. . . . [5]

Because all mothers have felt this pressure to limit their work commitment, many women who are widowed or divorcing with children are already holding lower-paying jobs. Dad's missing salary is not half the family income, because men earn far more money on the average than women. The oft-quoted figure of women earning sixty-five cents to each man's dollar is still an optimistic picture compared to the true financial plight of a recently divorced or widowed mother with children in the home. If the children must depend on Mom's income alone, the financial impact is so great that it is psychologically trauma-tic. When a sharp drop in funds means a move to a lower-income neighborhood, the children often experience the loss of friends, the loss of enrichment activities, and the loss of familiar comforts.

Money and father-absence are so intertwined it is hard to sepa-rate them. First of all, most children who show ill effects of being without a father (the typical acting-out behavior that may eventually lead to delinquency) are also those children living at or below the poverty level. Dr. Deborah Luepnitz raises the question: Are we looking at the effect of absent fathers or are we looking at the effect of being without money and hope for better economic opportunity? [6]

This dilemma is not solely the father's fault. The problem also lies in the lack of good childcare, adequate tax deductions, reason-able health care and parent-support systems that can help make up for the network lost to the modern isolated nuclear family. Our society has got to make it a little less stressful to care for children if we want to raise a healthy generation of future citizens.

FINANCIAL SECURITY

Betsy and Shirley, both widows, make us sadly aware of the difference financial security can make. As we have seen, whether the mother works or not, most two-parent families depend heavily on the father's income because men earn much more per hour than women. When Dad's income is eliminated through his death, few families have enough insurance and pension money to continue living at the same standard. Mom must go back to work, work longer hours, or somehow manage on less money. In most cases, the family's stan-dard of living will drop.

Unfortunately, for many mothers the strain of having to develop a serious career while grieving for their spouse is more than they can bear. They may find it difficult to give their children basic care, and emotional support, let alone seek employment. Many need profes-sional help or the support of a widows' group to get them over that first great hurdle.

Money has certainly been a difficult issue for Betsy Hadley. She got Social Security payments for herself and Mark until Mark turned sixteen. The payment for Mark alone, which will end when he turns eighteen, is only half of what she had been receiving. There was some insurance, but because her husband, Rich, committed suicide, the insurance company paid a lot less. Luckily, the mortgage insurance on the house was still valid, and so Betsy has no house payments. However, because she owns her own home, she could not qualify for Aid to Families with Dependent Children (AFDC), which would have been an important source of income.

Rich had been drafted during the Vietnam War. While in the service, he had a "nervous breakdown" and was given an honorable discharge. Although it would seem she should qualify for veteran's benefits, the military denied her claim. Betsy's resources are limited.

"Until I marry again my husband's work insurance pays me a little bit. I got a lump sum from his retirement but I spent that right away on cars and home improvements.

"I'm just now learning to manage money. At first I really overspent. Whatever the kids wanted, I got it for them. I felt sorry for them.

"Even though the kids are almost adults they seem so much younger and dependent. My daughter has a good job as a secretary but she doesn't pay anything to me. She bought me a nice gas grill for my birthday and she is making payments on her car. I bought her last car for her out of the insurance money, but I just don't have it anymore. Mark feels bad because I can't buy him a car when I'd bought one for his sister. I've got a part-time job now but that doesn't go very far."

Shirley O'Rourke's circumstances are strikingly different. Not only was the financial strain less after her husband's death, her work load lightened. During the last years of her husband's illness, his medicines had become so expensive that Shirley had begun doing daycare in her home to raise money. Then nine months before her husband died a "miracle" lifted this burden off her shoulders.

"I was reading a news magazine and saw an article about a new experimental drug. We decided it might help Mickey. The doctor who verified that Mickey would be a good candidate for Rocatrol discovered that Mickey had had a medical discharge from the service for a condition related to his disease. Eighteen years earlier, Mickey had been told he was not eligible for disability, but Doctor Kayakawa, at U.C.L.A. Medical Center, assured Mickey that he would now be eligible for 100 percent disability."

This had an incredible long-range impact on the family's financial situation. Mickey qualified for veteran's benefits for only three months before he died, but the eligibility meant that his children would have stipends and full base privileges until they completed school. The children get a monthly stipend of $400 each throughout college for forty-five months. Melody, the oldest, earned a Bachelor of Arts degree and a teaching certificate and still has a little VA funding remaining.

In addition to this, Shirley had been getting Social Security benefits. Up until 1985, the children would continue to get Social Security benefits until they graduated college or turned age twenty-two, whichever came first. Now children stop receiving benefits when they graduate high school or when they turn nineteen. Mothers still receive stipends from Social Security until the child turns sixteen. Unfortunately, budget cuts to Social Security benefits have, in effect, decided that some children won't go to college.

Shirley will continue to get checks from the Veterans' Administration as long as she lives unless she remarries. She also gets money from the Welfare Department where her husband had worked. It is considered his retirement, but in this case it is widows' benefits. Between the VA benefits, Welfare Department benefits, and Social Security she has had a steady income. They also had life insurance, which they had purchased before they knew Mickey was ill. Shirley invested most of the insurance money and uses only the interest.

The difference between Betsy's and Shirley's financial predicaments is not a simple story of squandering versus prudence. They each made wise moves and mistakes in the early years following their husbands' deaths. They each wisely decided to spend some of the immediate cash on counseling for themselves and their children. However, they each also spent disproportional amounts on the oldest child and did not leave enough to treat the younger children equally. Shirley allowed Melody to go to a very expensive college that she now cannot afford for Melody's younger brother and sister, and Betsy bought her daughter a new car but has no money to buy even a used car for her son.

In the first five years Shirley probably spent three times as much money as Betsy, but Shirley is financially secure. Betsy has learned her lesson, and would be more careful with money, but there is no more money. Ironically, Betsy also has few work skills because she did not need to work while her husband was alive, while Shirley, who had an established childcare business in her home at the time of her husband's death, no longer needs to earn any money.

As a nation, we have long recognized that widows need financial assistance to raise their children. These children now receive the same amount of money from the government whether or not the mother works or the father left the family well provided for by investing in life insurance. Our laws guarantee a measure of financial security to these children.

If a father who was earning $50,000 dies at the age of thirty-five, his first child will receive $892 a month, and his second child will receive $300 a month. Hence, a two-child family with a deceased parent who had earned more than $48,300 is believed to need $596 per month, per child.[7] There is no distinction made by Social Security for the age of the child. I'll add the figures for other levels of income:

Parent's income	$ per month / one child	$ per month / two children
$20,000	$545 per month	$396 per child/month
$30,000	$715	$476
$40,000	$805	$537

Social Security also provides figures for family units with stay-at-home moms. The parent's income in these two tables is the deceased parent's income at the time of death. The benefits in the table below assume the mother earns no money. The maximum in the last column is the most she would get even if she had six children.

Parent's income	Spouse and one child	Spouse and two or more children (maximum benefit)
$20,000	$1,090 per month	$1,338 per month
$30,000	$1,430	$1,668

$40,000	$1,610	$1,879
$50,000	$1,784	$2,082
$51,300 & up	$1,790	$2,088

As we can see, Social Security is willing to pay mothers $545 per month ($1090 – $545) or more to stay home and take care of the children until they are sixteen years old.

We guarantee a strikingly lower measure of financial security to the children of unwed mothers whose fathers "cannot be found." When children have been totally abandoned by their fathers, they too can collect AFDC (Aid to Families with Dependent Children). However, many children in homes where the fathers contribute what little they can and the mothers work at minimum wage are still very poor, but not eligible for benefits. By the time these mothers get done paying for daycare, they may be worse off financially than stay-at-home welfare moms. It is no wonder that many mothers feel they are better off not working. At least they can be there more often for their children.

In the state of West Virginia, for example, where the cost of living is low and the wages are generally even lower, a parent (usually the mother) who has been abandoned by the non-custodial parent (usually the father) would receive the following from public assistance:

Beneficiary	Base amount	Maximum food stamps	Total
one child alone	$145		
parent + 1 child	$201	$193	$394
parent + 2	$249	$247	$526
parent + 3	$312	$352	$664

Financial assistance for housing is also available through HUD, but the amount of eligibility for food stamps is then lower. (By the way, our standard federal income-tax deduction of $2,000 per child assumes each child costs $166 a month, while other developed nations' standard yearly deduction would be the equivalent of $5,000, or $600 per month.) Even with the help of food through the WIC (Women, Infants, and Children) program, it is unlikely that the mother can provide enough on her own to keep her children healthy.

Megan is grateful for the WIC help she gets. At this time, WIC provides thirty-one cans of formula a month, sixteen cans of juice, and two boxes of cereal, but the amount of food increases as the child grows older. Megan also has a medical card.

"Welfare is not a pleasant place to go. People are not very polite and I don't like to have to do it. I'm eighteen and my parent's income doesn't count, so I'm eligible. But the way we work it is my parents support me and I support the baby."

Megan's parents provide her a roof and food, and Megan provides for all the baby's needs with her WIC supplements and money from her part-time job. Megan's parents have been watching her baby while she works. The state would have paid for childcare in licensed homes, but Megan felt the homes were overcrowded and dismal. She has put her name on the waiting list for the YMCA childcare program and will be able to put her baby there when she begins her radiology training.

Many families see the AFDC as an intrusive government agency that robs them of what is rightfully theirs, and the unwed mothers from these homes become very evasive. When an unwed mother applies for funds from the AFDC with a claim that the father does not pay support, the agency asks for information on the father. If the agency successfully tracks him down it can mandate automatic wage withholding and have both back child support and current child support sent to the agency. But this money is not passed directly on to the mother. Instead, the mother receives an additional $50 a month, maximum. The rest of the support money goes into the AFDC funds and helps pay for collection services as well as awards to other mothers.

For mothers who had been receiving money "under the table" from the child's father, this would actually mean *less* money at the end of the month. Many unwed fathers do give the mothers of their children what they can. Even $25 a week, passed "under the table" to the mom, would give her an extra $100 a month if she could keep this secret from the AFDC. Further, the father, who has been receiving wages "under the table" himself, has more cash available because he avoids paying income taxes. If the mother "turns the father in" and his illegal wages are discovered, they may all end up with a great deal less. So the mothers often tell the AFDC that they just don't know where the father is. Statistically, this shows up as another deadbeat dad.[8]

DIVORCE, CHILDREN, AND THE LAW

Mary Ann Mason, assistant professor of Law and Social Welfare at the School of Social Welfare at the University of California–Berkeley, writes about our shameful lack of consistency in public policies for children. Our laws require children to attend school until a certain age; we remove them from homes where they may be abused; we set limits on the employment they may accept and the number of hours they may work; and we provide financial support through AFDC and Social Security. But although divorce can have a serious impact on their ability to learn, the likelihood that they will be neglected by an overburdened parent, the age at which they will seek employment, and their financial situation, we consider the matter private and do little to regulate the destruction caused by divorce. Mason maintains that when we changed to the no-fault system (where neither partner is blamed for the divorce), children lost many of their protections. Because 90 percent of mothers are the custodial parents, when alimony was eliminated and property division became more "equal," children's financial circumstances became harsher.[9]

Author and lawyer Mary Ann Glendon agrees that our nation's family policies are very poorly thought out. In her book *Abortion and Divorce in Western Law*, Glendon tells us:

> The American story about marriage, as told in the law and in much popular literature, goes something like this: Marriage is a relationship that exists primarily for the fulfillment of the individual spouses. If it ceases to perform this function, no one is to blame and either spouse may terminate it at will. After divorce, each spouse is expected to be self-sufficient. If this is not possible with the aid of property division, some rehabilitative maintenance may be in order for a temporary period. Children hardly appear in the story; at most they are rather shadowy characters in the background.[10]

A professor of law at the Harvard Law School, Glendon specializes in comparing American family law with family laws in other countries. She finds that our divorce laws as well as our public policies are much less protective of children. The high tax rates in

Sweden help provide funds for all Swedish children, who then receive generous subsidies from the government whether their parents are married or single. In some countries the government will pay out the expected amount of child support to the custodial parent when the non-custodial parent fails to pay. This money is considered a "loan" that will be paid back by the non-custodial parent when the government agents find him. This avoids delays in funding that can make children suffer. In 1975 the Swedes established child-support enforcement legislation similar to our 1984 laws (which will be discussed in Chapter 10), and 60 percent of the child-support debtors paid 90 percent of what they owed. Wage withholding was used in only 25 percent of these cases. The other 35 percent were scared into complying when the men realized they would be held accountable. So these measures can be successful.

At the same time, children in Sweden and Germany are also eligible for free health care and tax benefits. As a result of child-friendly laws in France, Sweden, and West Germany, single mothers in these countries live on 67 percent to 94 percent of what an average production worker earns, while the average U.S. counterpart must try to get by on only 50 percent.[11] Glendon's comparisons help us realize that we, as a nation, must give our children's needs higher priority.

NONPAYMENT OF CHILD SUPPORT

The most unfortunate families are those who are without father's financial support through divorce. There are men from all social and economic classes that have failed to pay child support. According to a *Denver Law Journal* study, many men pay more for monthly car payments than they do toward monthly child support. Men offer a variety of rationalizations. They feel the mother doesn't really need the money, or they complain she doesn't really spend it on the kids. Some men feel that once the ex-wife remarries it's up to the new husband to pay the bills, and likewise, when they take a new wife, they believe their financial responsibility is to the new family. Others withhold money as "revenge" over bad feelings about the way their ex-wives handle visitation. Some of these complaints are valid, but nonetheless they become a self-protective denial of the children's harsh reality.

Varying statistics have been collected to try to determine how many children are not receiving financial support from their fathers. The most recent information available is provided in a report entitled *Child Support and Alimony: 1989*, which was prepared by the U.S. Department of Commerce and the Bureau of the Census. Of the 9.9 million women raising children without a father in the home, about 60 percent were awarded child-support payments by the courts. Half of these women actually received the full amount due, one quarter received partial payment, and one-quarter were receiving no support despite a valid court order. Nearly 40 percent were not even awarded any child support, though half of these mothers had hoped for court-ordered financial help from the father.

Those not awarded support included never-married mothers, joint-custody cases where no support was awarded, divorces where the mothers waived the right to child support, couples who had come to a voluntary support agreement without involving the courts, and cases where the father was deemed unable to pay support. All in all 75 percent of absent fathers paid some child support in 1989, while 25 percent contributed nothing. It is not surprising that 32 percent of these families with absent fathers had incomes below the poverty line.[12] Representative Nancy L. Johnson (R-Conn.), who sponsored a bill to help states establish paternity and enforce mandatory wage withholding, stated, "The failure to collect child support is one of the major reasons so many female-headed families are on welfare."[13] (Child support will be discussed at length in the next chapter.)

Our entire social structure assumes that the father is giving money in the form of child support. When he is not, the whole system falls apart. These families have been falling "through the cracks." Does a child whose father has abandoned the family and sends no money deserve any less than a child whose father has died? Yet, Social Security payments from the government far exceed the welfare checks unemployed, divorced mothers receive when child support is not paid. Why is it that we take pity on widows and their children and see ourselves as responsible to help support them, but we turn our back on divorcées and their children?

Obviously our attitudes and our laws need to change so that we offer more compassion and protection to the children of divorce. All across America these changes are starting to take place. Men are being forced to pay child support. States are cooperating with each other to prevent men from running out on their obligations to their children. Groups are organizing to help women obtain money for the care of their children. We'll be looking at this more closely in Chapter 10.

HOW MUCH IS ENOUGH?

At one extreme, an article in *Money* Magazine by Andrea Rock claims the average family with an income of $50,000 will spend $265,249 just for the basics to raise a child through college to the age of twenty-two. This figure includes housing ($84,880), food ($61,007), transportation ($39,787), clothing ($18,567), and medical bills not covered by insurance ($18,567). However, this does not include college tuition at a private university ($300,134), live-in-nanny costs for the preschool years ($63,432), tuition at private elementary schools ($143,271), piano lessons ($5,145), or summer camp (which she estimates at an incredible $27,606 for eight years or $3,450 per summer), and other items that parents are being told their children will absolutely need. The *real* cost of a child according to the article is somewhere between $342,000 (a "poor" couple with one income) and $748,000, depending on how frugal a family manages to be.[14]

I include *Money*'s estimates because I think they help form one end of the expectations that are out there. I have heard divorcing parents complain that they will no longer be able to send their kids to private school, when there are good public schools (often with better programs for the "special child," both gifted and handicapped) in their area. But the "gourmet baby" syndrome has raised our expectations of what we must provide for our children to such an impossibly high level that even intact families feel guilty about what they cannot provide.

To get a sense of scale we need to get hold of some economic realities for this generation. Due to inflation most of us will not achieve our parents' standard of living, and divorce deals a blow on top of this. Families that break up and must support two households on the money that once supported one will have a lower standard of living. It's just simple math. Yet, many parents waste lots of emotional energy and prolong conflict over economic hardships that cannot be avoided.

What is a realistic amount to spend on your children? The U.S. Department of Agriculture Family Economics Research Group publishes a booklet that shows what two-parent families of various income levels spend on their children. Their information comes from extensive surveys of families raising children now. I think this information is easiest to grasp and absorb when given in terms of monthly expenditures. The yearly incomes provided are before taxes, and the three income levels each represent a third of the population. The families studied were two-child families. The figures given are national averages.[15]

| | Cost per child per month at | | |
Family yearly income	Age 2	Age 10	Age 16
Less than $29,900	$360	$373	$457
$29,000 to $48,300	$511	$527	$624
More than $48,300	$730	$745	$855

FEELINGS AND MONEY

National statistics tell us what the average family spends per child. Social Security has come up with a figure that it thinks is fair for children whose fathers have died, and we have estimates for what children "cost" when families must depend on welfare and food stamps. All these statistics and figures give us a more realistic context that should help us be more objective. However, we may also have a personal and emotional definition of what our children need that defies the logic of economics and grows out of our unrealistic expectations.

Sometimes our expectations have no relation to our own financial capability. In some cases we assume we must give our children what our parents gave us. Yet few parents, even in intact families, can afford to send kids to college without taking out loans or expecting their kids to take part-time jobs. Other parents, whose own parents could not or would not give them much materially, may be dealing with the pressure of the internal vows they made never to make their children suffer materially as they once did. But because of inflation and the soaring cost of housing, even many parents in intact families must make their children forgo Nintendos and $100 sports shoes.

We need to keep all these economic realities and attitudes in mind as we talk to our children about money. A child who feels he should be getting more materially than he is will feel undervalued and unloved. He will be filled with resentment. If he has been taught to believe he should go to an Ivy League college and his parents have only enough money to send him to a state school, he will feel deprived.

On the other hand, a child with realistic expectations, who feels she is no worse off than her peers who are suffering from the economic difficulties of an absent father, can face the challenge with courage and feel good when she overcomes these handicaps. She will feel fortunate to be able to continue living at home while she works her way through the local junior college. It is easy to see that in these cases the child who actually has more will be unhappier and feel more deprived than the child who has less. We, as parents, help determine which attitude our children will have.

SUMMARY POINTS

- When fathers do not live in the home there is a significant drop in the standard of living, and mothers must work outside the home whether or not their children are developmentally ready to give up Mom's care.
- Our government programs seem very arbitrary and inconsistent in their determinations of what children need. While the cost of living has risen considerably, Social Security benefits to bereaved children have been slashed, and the amount the government deems these children need far exceeds what children on welfare are awarded.
- Because our nation does not provide support for families in the form of decent subsidized childcare, a reasonable tax deduction for dependent children, national health care, or reasonable financial aid to non-working mothers, children with absent fathers often suffer economic hardship as well as a lack of feeling safe, secure, and loved.
- AFDC practices and procedures often encourage noncompliance. Unwed mothers are much better off if they refuse to expose a father who can contribute any small amount "under the table."

- Until the new child-support legislature of 1984, divorced children were the most seriously neglected group. There was little protection or assistance for children who had been awarded child support but whose fathers did not pay it.
- In these difficult economic times it is important to encourage realistic financial expectations. Even many intact families must deny their children much they would like to give them. We need to teach our children that money does not equal love.

10

Child Support: How to Get It

"My mom would have me call him up and ask for more money. I would yell at my mother and say that since she wanted the money, she should call him, but she would say that she wanted the money for me so I should call."

— Debbie, a child of divorce

Glenna went in to ask her boss for a raise. Somewhat tongue-in-cheek, she explained, "My husband's ex-wife's husband's ex-wife is suing him for more child support. The lawyer's costs are being a real hardship on my stepchildren's family, so my husband's ex-wife has asked us to send her extra money. I don't have an ex-husband so you're the only person I can turn to."

This chain of money-grabbing began with Glenna's husband's ex-wife's stepchild needing braces for her teeth. Glenna worries how she will have enough money for her own son's braces if they spend the next five years helping finance braces and college for the seven teenagers in her husband's "supra-extended family." Anger, threats, and guilt-trips often pass all the way down the line along with the requests for money. Many professionals were raised with the expectation that they and their children would be able to afford a middle-class lifestyle, but a weakened economy as well as divorce has frustrated these ambitions.

I discovered a more benign chain in a group of working-class parents (many of whom were often not working at all). Their harsher reality seemed to make them more tolerant of each other's problems. Marlene, whom we met in Chapter 2, calmly accepts Lenny's father's inability to pay her child support and does the best she can with the wages she and her boyfriend bring in (when they can find work). She knows her ex-husband has it hard enough trying to pay for the three children of his third wife with whom he now lives. Lenny's father's wife receives no child support from her ex-husband Tom because Tom has been out of work for more than a year. To relieve the pressure on this family unit, Marlene is allowing Tom, her ex's wife's ex, to live in the RV in her backyard, rent-free. Watching the growing number of homeless who populate the streets of southern California, the members of this loosely related group all peacefully co-exist with a "there but for the grace of God go I" spirit of cooperation. At any moment, any one of them could be out of work for a year, and their cooperative habit of covering for each other is the only "insurance" they have against future hard times.

THE SUPRA-EXTENDED BLENDED FAMILY

As we can see, life goes on after divorce. People remarry, and the new spouse may already have children. The non-custodial parent of those children may or may not be paying child support. The new couple may decide they want to have a child of their own. Who pays what for these children is no simple matter. When two adults are living with a group of children, how can they really be financially objective and follow the letter of the law? If Mary's ex-husband Frank makes a great deal of money and pays his child support, but her new husband John either earns a low salary or has large child support payments of his own that make him a "financial handicap," is it fair for Mary and John to spend some of the money from Mary's ex-husband on their new baby? Is it fair for John's children by his first marriage to have a much lower standard of living than Mary's children who are living with *their* father? When a blended family goes out to dinner should we expect the parents to hash over the bill to decide who will pay for each meal based on who is receiving child support for which children?

These families represent common dilemmas that boggle the mind and confuse lawyers and judges. A child-support decision meant to lessen the hardship on one set of children may serve to create financial hardship for another set of children in the supra-extended blended family. But this is just a fraction of the complications that should be considered in setting a child-support award that is fair to all parties involved. The judge's task is not an easy one. Often no matter what the judge decides, someone will leave the courtroom feeling wronged.

GUIDELINES FOR CHILD SUPPORT

Prior to 1987 many states had no guidelines, and support awards were totally unpredictable. Now federal mandates have pressured the states to create objective formulas for judges to use in all cases so that there is some fairness and consistency in these judgments. Hopefully this will lead to less conflict and greater compliance.

However, even though every state now has child-support guidelines, the stipulations of these guidelines vary widely. Some states provide a simple formula of what the non-custodial parent should pay based on percentages of that parent's income. Typical figures would be 20 percent of income after taxes for the first child, 10 percent for the second, 8 percent for the third, and 5 percent for the fourth, up to a maximum of 50 percent of income. (Our information from the Family Economics Research Group presented in Chapter 9 shows us that the average intact family with two children spends about 17 percent of its net income per child. However, splitting a home and supporting two residences, as in the case of divorce, should cause these percentages to be lowered.)

Generally these figures are written into the divorce contract as dollar amounts, and they rarely include increases as the children grow older and cost more, or as the non-custodial parent's salary increases. This works in favor of the non-custodial parent if he or she gets raises and does not remarry. It works in favor of the custodial parent if he or she gets a better-paying job or marries someone with a good-paying job and low debt load. But it is an oversimplified formula that can become very unfair. It is neither flexible nor complex enough to apply to the complicated blended family situations that inevitably occur within five years after divorce.

At the other extreme, many states have adopted a very inclusive and complex formula for calculating support that was first created in

Maryland. The Maryland formula considers the incomes and needs of all the adults and children in the supra-extended blended family.

For a copy of the child-support guidelines
in your state contact your state Child
Advocate Office or the Family Law Master

DEADBEAT DADS

For the protection of the next generation, states need to develop better policies and procedures to deal with child-support evasion. On the upside, a lot of good legislation in support of the payment of child support has been passed in recent years. In the state of California a divorcing mother may now request that the child support be deducted from the father's paycheck and sent to a collecting bureau which will then mail her a check. The court-ordered child support is apparently seen as legitimate and binding, not just a "suggestion." The man has no choice but to pay, and the woman doesn't need to spend money on lawyers to get her court-ordered child support. In 1984 the federal government mandated that all states wishing to continue receiving AFDC funding must institute child-support guidelines and collection procedures by 1987. These laws have now been in force for seven years, and their effects are beginning to be felt. On the downside, state and federal governments have not chosen to fund the personnel needed to carry out this legislation.

Lawyer Dennis Cohen founded the Center for Enforcement of Family Support in Los Angeles to help mothers go after "deadbeat dads," as the press popularly calls men who pay no support for their children. Since Cohen started his center in the late seventies, Cohen and his staff of lawyers have collected more than $8 million in overdue child-support payments. His clients pay him a $35 fee to open a case and one-third of all back child support he successfully collects. Parents have the option of having the Los Angeles District Attorney's office collect the back support free of charge, but the process is hopelessly backlogged. According to Cohen, the D.A.'s office had about 250,000 cases and only about 600 people to work on them, and the D.A.'s office had to give priority to the cases costing the state money—women collecting welfare monies due to lack of child support.[1] (However, other analysts and state child-support agencies assert that they now go after the more collectible cases first—and those are usually the middle-class, steady-wage-earner ex-spouses.)

Elaine Fromm of the Organization for Enforcement of Child Support does not advocate getting a lawyer. She is strongly opposed to money being taken away from children and given to lawyers for collection fees. Fromm feels that the new mandatory wage-withholding and tax-intercept measures authorized and implemented through the 1984 Social Security Act will significantly simplify the process and cut down on the need for lawyers.[2] These programs do seem to be succeeding. In 1990, of the three million mothers who had contacted a government agency for help collecting child support at some time, one million women received aid in locating the father, establishing paternity, or establishing support obligations, while another one million received assistance in enforcing an existing support order or obtaining collection. Only one-third of the women who had sought assistance received no help from the agency.[3]

Obviously, paying a lawyer one-third of the collected child support is a loss to the children's standard of living, and better government protection and regulations, as well as increased staff to carry out the new legislation, are needed to get more of this money straight into the pockets of the mothers who pay the children's expenses.

HOW TO GET IT

The Child Support Enforcement Amendment of 1984 has had an important impact. On the deepest level it reinforces the notion that parents are financially responsible for their children until they are eighteen years old. We no longer think of women as having "gotten *themselves* knocked-up." The male impregnator is now in the picture. There are still fathers who manage to avoid paying child support, but the new laws are tougher on them, and many of their freedoms are lost by making that choice. New statutes and collection procedures make it increasingly difficult for a father to avoid paying support.

Custodial parents can collect support that is not being paid and past support that has not been paid through any and all of the following means:

Means Available for Collecting Support

- Up to 50 percent of the non-custodial parent's wages can be garnished, even from non-custodial parents employed in another state.
- Up to 50 percent of unemployment compensation can be garnished.
- All money in bank accounts can be seized.
- A lien can be placed on houses, cars, or other personal or real property so that back child support will be paid out of the equity.
- A lien can be placed on a self-owned business, and money may be collected directly from the business's debtors and given to the custodial parent.
- Federal or state income tax refunds can be intercepted.
- Property may be seized and sold (or held "hostage" until support is paid).
- Non-paying parents can be put in jail for contempt of court.
- The statute of limitations on collection of child support is ten years in most states, so that up to ten years of arrearages can be collected.

These methods are all readily available to state child-support enforcement teams. If your ex has a steady job and you know where he lives, his employer, and his social security number, the task of enforcing payment is easy and can be accomplished in less than a month. Any complication or lack of information causes delays. Collections that must cross state lines are much more complicated and take much more time than in-state claims. If your ex-spouse moved out of state, many methods of collection can still be used. Federal income tax refunds can be intercepted across state lines; any federal government employee or employee of a company that has a branch in your state is subject to wage-withholding without going through the other state's child advocacy department; and accounts in banks with branches in your state are easy to access.

Child Advocate Robert Riffle of Parkersburg, West Virginia, who has been in the business of helping women get the child support due them for more than ten years, has seen the effects of this new legislation. "Those who work on a cash basis won't ever have to pay," he commented, recounting the impossibility of tracking such a man's finances and proving his worth. "But people who have good jobs are paying a lot more than they used to."[4]

Before the Child Support Enforcement Amendment of 1984, many judges were free to pick any figure out of the air when deciding on the amount of child support to be paid. And since most judges are male, many of them had no idea what children actually cost. The lack of a standard meant that in most cases the award was too low. Consequently, those who were required to pay a realistic amount often felt persecuted. If they knew other parents who were paying far less, they began to question why they were paying so much. They were certainly not moved to hand over money bonuses when their children had special needs, such as school trips or soccer uniforms. Riffle, himself the father of two children, feels the present guidelines, which require non-custodial fathers to pay much more than they had been, are fair. "Even under the new laws, they are not paying what most people in intact families usually spend on their kids."[5]

Although we will see the concrete aggressive steps a mother can take to obtain child support when the father will not cooperate, it is important to first proceed in a "spirit of goodwill" and consider negotiation strategies that mothers can employ; for a peaceful resolution of the child-support problem not only saves lawyers' costs, it stands as an inspiring example of good conflict resolution that will always be remembered by the children.

KNOW YOUR OPPONENT

After much experience dealing with the men and women in child-support struggles, Cohen has concluded that there are three basic types of men who do not pay child-support:[6]

1. *The Angry Ex-spouse*. This father is often feeling vindictive about the divorce and is using the withholding of child support as a punishment of the ex-wife. He has lost sight of the kids in this.

2. *The Earnest Ex-spouse.* This father may be truly strapped financially and cannot come across with the full support at this time. He is the easiest to work with because he generally cares about the welfare of his kids.
3. *The Game-Playing Ex-spouse.* This father is not a father at all. It's all a power trip to him. He would rather pay thousands of dollars to a lawyer than send his ex-wife $100 for the kids.

Each of these types needs to be dealt with differently. The peace-promoting strategies discussed later in this chapter should help diffuse the hostility and resistance of the Angry Ex-spouse. When the gentle approach fails, state child-advocate officers can step in to try to turn the father's attention back to the kids. If the child-advocate officer cannot reach the Angry Ex-spouse with persuasion, there are many means for getting the child support by force.

With the Earnest Ex-spouse low-conflict personal approaches should be tried first. If the non-custodial parent believes in financially supporting his children but simply does not have the means right now, he may agree to sign a contract delaying the payments. This can also be negotiated with the help of a child advocate, but there may be no need to "turn him in" to the state. Having the Earnest Ex-spouse's pay garnished when he is barely surviving financially creates hard feelings and may drive him to flee out of state.

Sadly, the Game-Playing Ex-spouse may be a total loss financially. If he is unaware of the new child-support legislation and means of collection, the mother may get some funds from him temporarily. But chances are, as soon as he learns how the game is played, he'll do whatever he needs to beat the system. All the tracking methods are slow, and if men change jobs frequently or move often, the system cannot catch up with them. Those low on the income scale will move from state to state or work on a cash-only basis. Interstate enforcement takes the longest because the request has to work its way through the child advocacy departments of both states. If men never put their money in a bank or they put their money in accounts in the names of friends or relatives, bank accounts cannot be seized. Some men even choose to live far below their means and hide or hoard the money.

The wealthier Game-Playing Ex-spouse will probably go into business for himself and hide his assets by claiming huge business expenses. He may even move his business out of the country to make sure he wins. All the mother can do is provide the state with all the information she can gather and then let it go.

MOTIVATIONS

Cohen believes the basic underlying reason why so many men avoid paying their child-support payments is that the laws have been too lax. It has been so easy to get away with not paying that men put child support on the bottom of the list of their bills. "Men think they have a choice," Cohen fumes. "If we had a choice about paying taxes, how many people do you think would pay?"[7] We need laws that not only effectively and efficiently enforce the payment of child support, but also assess penalties on those who are behind. Our laws need to convey a serious belief in men's financial responsibility for their offspring. Cohen often sees mothers who come to him torn over their loyalties to their children. They feel the money is rightfully owed their children, but fear that going after the support aggressively will damage the children's relationship with the father. Though many men threaten to cut off contact with the kids, Cohen often finds that the reverse is true. "When a delinquent dad starts paying," Cohen says, "the relationship with the kids is often normalized."

One delinquent dad, who hadn't seen his child in three years, drew close to his child after the sheriff had seized the father's Corvette in lieu of past-due child-support payments. The father felt that if he was going to pay for the kid he might as well see him.[8] Generally, we don't value what we have gotten for free. Once we have to pay money for something, it is suddenly worth more to us. In Chapter 3 we saw how Jesse's father made an effort to get in touch with his son (after a seven-year silence) when the mother sued him for arrearages to help finance Jesse's college education.

Of course, the mother's attitude throughout the process of the suit will greatly influence how the suit affects the father-child relationship. The more neutral and businesslike the mother can be, the more she focuses on the objective needs of the child, the more she acts appreciative of getting what is rightfully hers when she finally gets it, the easier it will be for the father to have a relationship with his children. Hostility and power trips should always be avoided.

Parents of either sex who no longer live with their children or see them on a daily basis experience a weakening of emotional bonds, and this can translate into a weakening of financial commitment. Bureau of the Census statistics show that the amount of contact and power a father has over his children's lives correlates with his willingness to pay child support: while 90.2 percent of fathers with joint custody pay their child support, and 79.1 percent of fathers with visitation privileges pay, only 44.5 percent of fathers without visitation or custody rights pay any support.[9]

FOR THE SAKE OF THE CHILDREN

There are two main goals that should take precedence at the time of divorce when children are involved:

1. Every effort should be made to reduce the conflict between the parents prior to divorce.
2. Future benefits for the children should all be spelled out clearly in the contract, including how they will be carried out.

Many states are realizing the need for arbitration and mediation at the time of divorce. California has been a leader in this area. It is the divorce mediator's job to sit with the parents and try to help them work through their differences until they reach a point where they share a common goal: to put the best interests of their children as their highest priority. This is an ideal, but it is achievable if both parents can call upon their most mature instincts. It means give and take on both sides. If the father is truly interested in being actively involved in the children's lives on a daily basis, it may mean a decision for joint custody. If the children are young and need their mother it may mean that the father will have to pay the lion's share of financial support. The parents need to get past their anger and their need to be in control of the situation. It works best if they can each accept the guidance of the mediator and let him or her be the final objective authority on what is best for the children.

If divorce mediation is not available in your state, I strongly urge you to seek family counseling or some other substitute to help you come to a "spirit of goodwill" in your dealings with your children's co-parent. Try to be sympathetic to the needs and fears of the other side. If you are granted custody, be generous about visitation rights. Give wherever it is within your power to give. Keep in mind that your children will suffer tremendously if you have ongoing conflict with your ex-spouse. If you can achieve an atmosphere of true cooperation, the rest of the negotiations will be a piece of cake.

Your state child-support guidelines should help you reach an agreement on a fair amount of child support. Keep in mind that there will be no increases in child support unless the parties renegotiate. If at all possible, try to have a clause written into the decree that states that child-support benefits will increase as the children grow older. Experience shows that whatever is written into the contract is probably the most the mother will ever receive without going back to court. If child-advocate agencies must be called in later, they can only collect the amount stated in the decree.

The written child-support agreement should also include medical and dental benefits which can be maintained through the father's employer. In addition, mothers should try to bargain for some college fund for the children. Mothers might want to give up rights to some property on which they cannot make payments in lieu of a monthly sum to be paid into a special account in the children's names that can be used for post–high school training or education. If your ex cannot afford this, suggest that it be written into the contract that some property you jointly held be sold at the time of your first child's graduation from high school to provide money for further education.

In the division of property strive to remain in the family home if you will be the custodial parent. Your state may require that this asset be divided equally between the spouses, but you can negotiate to postpone the sale of the house. If the children can remain in their old neighborhood, among their friends, where they may attend the same school, their adjustment will be less traumatic. You may not be capable of buying out your spouse, nor he you. But he might buy out your share with monthly payments to you while you and the children continue to live in the house. This is ideal if the ownership of the house then passes to the non-custodial spouse when the last child graduates high school.

Throughout your negotiations remain neutral and business-like. If possible choose an automatic deduction plan. Some states allow the child support to be deducted from the non-custodial spouse's check from the outset of divorce. If, early on, you can both form the attitude that child-support is a deduction, an obligation that simply must be paid like income taxes or Social Security, it will neutralize some of the bad feelings. Explain that you will have a lot of new challenges to deal with in the wake of the divorce, and it would reduce your anxiety if the matter of payment was routinized. Be firm, calm, and pleasant.

PEACE-PROMOTING STRATEGIES

Most parents have a great deal of post-divorce conflict over money. At the time of divorce, in the majority of cases involving children, everyone — Mom, Dad, and the children — will experience a drop in their standard of living. Mom often gets the house (at least to live in, if not to own), and Dad must move to an apartment and find furniture. The money the family has been living on simply does not go as far. This is a terrible shock to everyone at first, and each party inevitably feels they are worse off than the other. To lower the intensity of these conflictive feelings it is best to make as objective a financial assessment as possible. Such objectivity can help everyone accept the new realities and move on.

How can custodial mothers help dads work through their resentment about child support? One of the most common complaints of fathers who do not want to pay support is that the money is not spent on the kids. Whether this is true or not, there are ways to simultaneously relieve such fathers' anxiety and teach your children some valuable economic lessons.

Keep track of all your expenses for the child. For younger children (under twelve) you need to keep a record of everything that is spent on clothes, lessons, childcare, medical expenses, and toys. You have a right to expect remuneration for food and housing, too, but be scrupulous about calculating the charges. For example, if you and three children are sharing a home, do not simply split the cost of the home four ways and decide that the children's portion is three-quarters of the whole. Begin instead by deciding what you would have to pay for comparable housing if you were single and childless.

If you are the type who would be happy in an efficiency apartment, then open up the paper and see how much efficiency apartments are renting for. If you know that you would be willing to spend a large part of your income on housing because you just can't live without a yard, then calculate how much it would cost you to rent or own a small house. Deduct whichever of these amounts you decide is most realistic for you from the total housing you pay for the place you share with your children. Likewise, when figuring your food bill, keep in mind how much it would cost to feed yourself. Remember, many adults living alone eat expensive TV dinners because they don't want to cook for one, and children often eat far less than adults. Add up these figures and find the true expense of the children by carefully separating out what it would cost you to support yourself.

Now consider how much your ex-husband earns compared to you. If he earns twice as much as you do, he should pay twice as much as you do for the *children's* expenses. In other words, you should contribute one-third of the money needed and he should be paying the other two-thirds. If you cannot afford to contribute your fair portion, your children are probably living "too high." The two-thirds share will be a burden on your husband, also, and everyone may need to readjust their expectations for a fair and reasonable standard of living. Explain this to your children. They are much better off facing these realities than being left on their own to figure out why they have less than other kids their ages. Without guidance many children will mistakenly believe that their parents don't love them as much as the parents of their "better-off" peers love their children.

Share these calculations and decisions with your ex-husband, in writing, so that he can look them over calmly. Acknowledge that it may be hard on him to pay such a large portion of his salary. Talk the budget over with the kids and see what they might like to give up. Let your husband know what will have to go if you cut back on expenses and then accept his decision to help out "more than his fair share" or to choose to limit spending on the children to be comfortably within his means.

With older children, it is even more effective to give them a budget and let them learn how to work out their own expenses. You needn't hand them the money in cash. Record the amounts in a book. Deduct food and rent and show them what is left for discretionary spending. If they want designer jeans that would break the budget, show them how much is available and help them devise a means to earn the rest. Let them make some mistakes, and let them live with the consequences.

If your ex is especially paranoid, another way to go about this is to say that your one-third will go for rent. Ask your ex-husband how much he would like you to set aside for food (and you could suggest an amount, reminding him to consider what his food expenses are) and have him make out a check for that amount to you. Let him pay the discretionary amounts to each child by check. This gives him a sense of control, a feeling that money is actually being spent on the kids, and the feeling that the children are aware of what he contributes.

Another peace-making economic arrangement would be to allow your ex-husband to deposit a certain amount of the support in a secured account for the children's future education. This account can be set up so that it requires the signature of both you and your ex-husband (and possibly your child) to withdraw any money. Then the money will be there when your child is ready to go to college or continue his or her education after high school.

This is a "simplest-scenario" approach. It assumes that the mother is still single, is working and earning an income above poverty level, and that the father has a moderate income. But it is an approach based on a certain attitude or mindset about sharing financial responsibility that allows each parent who contributes money to have some sense of control over where the money goes. It opens negotiations with a more neutral attitude.

Perhaps this approach can alert the father with a very high income to differences between what he wears and eats and what his children can afford. If he cannot see his way clear to let them have a current standard of living more comparable to his, he may be able to take satisfaction in providing for their future education. Then this will be a battle you won't have to fight later. Money in the bank for education can also be reassuring and inspiring to children, and once Dad has been convinced to invest in their college education he may more easily see the wisdom in helping them go to a better school now or get tutoring that will make them eligible for college.

It might be a pain to keep track of all the kids' expenses, but it is good discipline for everyone, and it defuses money suspicions and the resultant conflict. The better you become at this type of negotiating, the more money will be available for your children. Remember, the alternative to peace-promoting strategies is for you and your ex to give vast amounts of money to lawyers to settle support conflicts for you.

AGGRESSIVE ACTION

When a father has been dodging his child-support responsibilities and has refused to respond to reasonable steps by the mother, aggressive action may be necessary. Whether parents choose to use their local Child Advocacy Office or hire a lawyer, it's wise to consider some of Cohen's advice on how to start the information gathering that can lead to the collection of delinquent child-support payments. Cohen advises that you begin immediately to keep detailed records of any non-payments.[10]

Steps for Obtaining Support

1. *Document.* Keep dated records of all payments received and those not received.
2. *List his assets.* Houses, cars, motorcycles, boats, stocks, bank accounts, and property are all vulnerable assets.
3. *Know his place of business.* Keep track of the address and name of your ex-husband's employer.
4. *Know where he lives.* Keep your address for him current.

When you keep records, the more specific you can be about each time the support was not paid, the better. This would ideally be done by keeping photocopies or records of payments that were received. Look back through your bank books for deposits. Establish, in as objective a way as possible, exactly what payments were not made, and when you received only partial payment. If you have no previous record, begin this moment to keep records of all future failures of payments. However, don't give up if you can't assemble this information. Since the 1987 reforms, the non-custodial parent, usually the father, has the burden of proof. If there is no record, it is assumed that he did *not* pay.

When your claim to back support is established, all his assets are vulnerable—houses, cars, motorcycles, boats, stocks, bank accounts. Photocopy his check so you know where his bank accounts are. Think back over his financial habits when you were married. What has become of the property he obtained in the divorce? Consider hiring a private detective on a contingency basis (but don't set your kids up as private investigators).

If your ex works for a company or government agency it is often very easy to have his wages garnished. In California it is as simple as filling out two court forms, and the child support will be mailed directly to you by his employer. If your ex is being coy about his place of employment, try asking for a daytime emergency phone number for your child's school. Then simply call the number and see who answers. Also, your lawyer can learn a great deal about the father's worth using his Social Security number. Any previous income tax form will contain it, and if your ex-husband took your joint forms with him at the time of divorce, you can request a copy from the IRS. If he is self-employed, send a friend to his place of business to make a transaction and have him or her pay by check. When the check is cashed, you will have the name of the bank where your ex's business account is located.

Be vigilant about keeping track of where your ex-husband is living. If your ex has "skipped town" try contacting old friends and relatives who may have heard from him. In some states you can obtain his address from the Division of Motor Vehicles. The Federal Parent Locator Service, a government agency set up to locate absent parents, charges about $15 to locate your ex. Try your local district attorney's office to contact this service.[11]

WHEN THE BUCK STOPS

Judith Wallerstein, the noted psychologist who has followed families of divorce for the last fifteen years, writes that she is saddened by the way the children of even upper middle-class fathers are financially abandoned when they turn eighteen and the support contract abruptly runs out. This is symptomatic of a loss of feeling she saw in many of the fathers. Once these fathers no longer lived with their children, they put up walls of denial and preferred to think of their children in abstract terms. This was true of even those fathers who had been very attentive and involved with their children prior to the divorce. They had lost that altruistic bond of generativity that Erik Erikson describes as the urge to guide the next generation. As we discussed in Chapter 2, the loss of connection is in part a defense mechanism—a way that men emotionally distance themselves to avoid feeling the pain of separation.

Many fathers with advanced degrees and high-paying jobs, who can well afford to send their children to college, do not. To make matters worse, the incomes of these disinterested fathers must be listed on applications for scholarships. When the father can afford to pay for college tuition, but refuses to, the child may be ineligible for scholarships or government loans. Among the fathers in Wallerstein's study, only one-third of the fathers who could easily afford to pay their child's tuition were willing to make any contribution,[12] and only one child in ten was receiving full financial support for college.

As a result, many children of divorce are discouraged about their futures. Some give up plans for college because they cannot recover from their disappointment over the schools they had hoped they would attend—schools that their high school peers from intact families were able to go to—and feel overwhelmed by the specter of putting themselves through college. Many of those who do work their way through undergraduate school give up hope of advanced degrees because they are too worn out from the long haul to the B.A. Wallerstein found that 60 percent of the children over eighteen, whom she interviewed ten years after her initial study at the time of each family's divorce, seemed fated to get poorer educations than their fathers had, and 45 percent would not achieve the level of education held by their mothers.

Wallerstein relates,

> One-quarter of these men hold advanced degrees in medicine, law, or business administration, and the majority have college educations. But when I ask about college for their children, they don't want to discuss it. They don't plead poverty. Rather, they tend to say, "I paid my child support through the years. I met all my obligations. I've given my wife thousands of dollars, and now it's up to her."[13]

I hear the underlying resentment here. I think it is significant that these men perceive that they have paid these monies to their ex-wives, not to their children. Since the child-support checks are written to the mother the men do not feel a financial connection to their children. It is ironic that at this point the fathers could finally write checks directly to these children and at last be recognized for their financial contributions.

This refusal to support the child through college seems to be a last angry act or is symbolic of the father's need to finally assert his free will. Can this need be turned toward a more constructive end? Surprisingly, in one of the families whom Wallerstein studied, the father only needed to be asked. The oldest son, who saw his support checks stop at age eighteen, assumed that was the last word on Dad's financial assistance. But a few years later when his youngest brother graduated from high school the brother simply called up Dad to ask for money. The result? Dad sent it.

By current laws the father's financial obligation ends when the child reaches age eighteen. (Indeed one of Wallerstein's interviewees reported that his father had prorated the support check to end on the tenth of the month to coincide with his eighteenth birthday.) To many emerging young adults this carries a message that is often interpreted as "Good riddance!"

Though it has been the norm in most middle-class families for the parents to want their children to go farther—to get a better education than they had—we must remember it is not against the law to fail to finance your child's college education. In today's financial climate, many parents can do little more than help, and they expect the kids to pitch in with part-time jobs. What children most need is the feeling that their parents are behind them. If the child has kept in touch with Dad, and it is *her* idea to do it, she may succeed at getting some help by using a direct approach.

You can help by discussing the possibility of financial help from Dad in the same tone of voice you would use in talking about grants or loans. Consider it one more option she has and teach her assertiveness skills to use in all her pursuits for college money. If she objectively tells Dad the costs and shows that she has taken other steps to obtain funds (applied for loans, work-study funds, etc.), this will alert Dad that she is serious and responsible and deserving of whatever help he can give.

TALKING ABOUT CHILD SUPPORT

When dads fail to pay child support or continually shortchange the custodial mother, moms feel a great temptation to expose the father's failings. Moms struggle to bite back comments like, "Your father doesn't even care enough to pay this piddling amount for you!" or "How are we supposed to eat this month?" And the struggle is all the harder when children idealize their irresponsible dads. Although there is no simple formula for discussing money shortages with children, psychologists agree that one should honor two basic principles:

1. Keep the child's self-esteem intact.
2. Don't burden the child with adult problems that the child has no power to solve.

We may feel that Dad's failure to pay support is a pretty strong message that he doesn't really care about his children, but it will do them no good to hear it. For though we mean for the children to see the truth about their father, all they will hear is that he doesn't care about them. Children always interpret that to be a true reflection of something lacking in them. They think, "If only I were smarter, quieter, louder, more affectionate, more reserved, more polite, etc., then Dad would care about me!"

Usually the reality is that Dad is still very angry at Mom, and this anger prevents him from being completely rational about the money issue and from realizing it is the kids who will suffer from his financial neglect. Dads rarely hold back money to punish the children. So why should children be burdened with the feeling that they have done something wrong?

When it becomes necessary to tell a child that there is no money from Dad, it is better to make it clear that this is a problem between Mom and Dad. The child needs to know that Dad is really still angry at Mom because of the divorce. It's not something the child has caused and it is not something he or she can fix.

How do we know when we should mention the matter of money at all, and what are the best ways to bring it up? First, don't jump the gun. Even children in wealthy, intact families will whine for toys they don't have or ask why they can't eat out more often. Just because you can't give your child everything they tell you every other child in the neighborhood has (and take this with a grain of salt!), there is no reason to sit them down and give them a talk on the hard financial facts of life. As when talking about sex and other delicate matters, it is best to let the child guide you. Answer what they ask and avoid going into more detail unless they seem to seek it. Be as matter of fact about money shortages as possible. When you need to moan and worry over the issue, call a friend. Children can't solve the problem, and children shouldn't be burdened with it.

As the children grow older, the rules governing these decisions vary slightly. When pre-adolescents are able to figure out for themselves that money is a problem, don't deny their reality. If you pretend that money is not a problem, when the child can clearly see that it is, it will only leave the child wondering if he or she is crazy. At this stage it's okay to admit that money is short, but assure them that you are taking care of it. If they want to help out, encourage them to look for appropriate ways to earn money (such as babysitting or lawn work for neighbors) for the special things they want that you cannot afford. Avoid blaming the situation on Dad. This tactic could seriously backfire if they need to idealize Dad. Just because a child can see the reality that money is short does not necessarily mean that he or she connects any family problems to Dad. If *you* do, *you* become the bad guy. For the child will see Dad's faults only when he or she is ready to.

For awhile your child needs to believe that Dad loves him or her. At the same time the child needs to feel safe and cared for. You can keep your children feeling safe with or without their dad's money. It has more to do with your ability to remain calm than it has to do with any amount of money you have available. Keeping a tight budget and living within your means (so the electricity doesn't get turned off) will also help your children feel secure and cared for.

At the same time, you are not obligated to "make excuses" for Daddy, nor do you need to refrain from taking whatever measures are necessary to get the child support due you. It's okay if the children know you have gone to the state child advocate or a lawyer to force the father to comply with his child-support obligation. This can be done without harming the children as long as you keep the emotional tone neutral and refrain from expressing your anger. You can calmly explain that Daddy has failed to pay and the law says he must. Just like a witness to an accident, it is your duty to give the child advocate as much information as you can to help straighten out this matter. Explain that the state wants to see moms get more money for children and sometimes they need to step in when dads are still mad at moms. Tell them you hope the child advocate can help Daddy understand that you really need his money and that you plan to spend it on them when you get it.

If Dad stops sending money this is no time to deny or discourage visitation. Encourage the children to call and chat with Dad about things that have nothing to do with money. In their normal chatter stories may come up about things they have missed because they didn't have enough money. *If you have not coached them*, Dad may recognize a need they have and get some gratification from offering to pay for something of his own free will—a gift that they will know came from him. Make the phone available and keep a "hands-off" attitude. If the children can maintain an emotional connection with Dad, they may later have success getting some financial support from him when their adolescent hopes and dreams exceed the budget.

SUMMARY POINTS

- The child-support issue is more complex than initially meets the eye. New blended families of former spouses place many financial demands on the parents. Child-support guidelines need to be flexible enough to cover many extenuating circumstances.

- Like income tax and Social Security, child support should be regarded as a compulsory deduction. We need to back our strong belief in the father's financial responsibility with legislation that includes unpleasant consequences when the father does not pay.

- The Child Support Enforcement Act of 1984 has made it much more difficult for dads to evade child support and has forced states to develop guidelines so awards are not so arbitrary.

- Since conflict between the parents is always damaging to the child, everyone should approach the child-support issue with an attitude of goodwill. Divorce mediators can be invaluable in not only setting child-support awards, but also in resolving the peripheral conflicts that cause divorcing parents to quibble over everything.

- Both parents need to gain objectivity on the issue of child support. When the custodial parent keeps a clear budget and record of the children's expenses, it can relieve a lot of the father's anxiety about how the money is spent.

- If the father does not respond to the mother's humane and reasonable attempts at collecting child support, it is time to turn to the Child Advocate Office or a lawyer. Experience shows that in most cases pushing for child support will not damage the father's relationship with the children, especially if the mother can be emotionally objective.

11

Two Dads

"A lot of times I would feel really funny talking to my father about Aaron. Aaron could give us a lot of things that my father couldn't afford. I thought he must feel bad about that."

—DEBBIE, A CHILD OF DIVORCE

D espite the potential problems in the stepparenting situation, many stepdads fill an important place for those children whose fathers have abandoned them. Even men who have little to do with their blood-children may show an unusual willingness to father the children of their girlfriends or second wives. Frank F. Furstenberg, Jr., professor of Sociology at the University of Pennsylvania, who has specialized in new father trends, acknowledges this growing tendency. Interestingly, Furstenberg relates that a substantial number of men who lose contact with their own biological children often become very involved with stepchildren in a subsequent marriage. Writes Furstenberg, "This picture of men migrating from one family to the next modifies to some extent the proposition that a growing number of men are retreating from fatherhood."[1] In his studies, children living with such stepdads report as much involvement with these new dads as children in intact families have with their fathers. Furstenberg describes fatherhood as a transient status, dictated largely by the man's place of residence.

Julie, who was only briefly married to her daughter's father nine years ago, now lives with Steve and two of his natural children. This arrangement has been very healing for her daughter, Leila. Leila's contact with her natural father has been so minimal that she cannot even describe him. When I spoke to Leila she was very excited about her mother's upcoming marriage and her impending legal adoption as Steve's daughter. Leila has not seen her father since she was three years old and often pretends that her mother's boyfriend, Steve, is her real father. When she wants to join in on the conversations of her peers, "Dad" is a label that fits Steve far more easily than it would apply to her "real" dad. Julie explained:

> "Steve is a great Dad to both his kids and mine. When it's time to work he really puts his foot down, but he can get down on the floor and play with them, too. Leila really likes him and I know she really wants to be his 'real daughter.' She's had to put up with putdowns from Steve's kids sometimes when they brag that he's their real father, but not hers. We've explained that when Steve adopts her legally, he'll be her real father, with all the rights a real father has, and she wants that. She wants to be able to call him her dad instead of her stepdad."

Leila would basically like to just forget about her natural father and be free of the obligation to acknowledge that link. On the playground, she'd like to be able to simply say, "My mom and dad." Julie, too, is looking forward to being able to give Leila a dad. Julie sees Steve as the kind of father who listens to his kids' stories, disciplines them, and provides some structure. Julie told me:

> "He's also a very loving man, he plays frisbee and goes bike riding with the kids. But he's better at discipline than I am. He's got rules about the chores like I always wanted to have. I wasn't organized enough to follow through on it. Steve does all the things that my dad did. I used to think that my dad was really mean, but when I look back on it now I think he did exactly the right thing. I was a terrible rebel and he was so patient."

PLAYING MUSICAL KIDS

Ironically, Steve, Leila's dream stepdad, has a daughter whom the courts took away from him and who now refuses to see him. His oldest daughter, who was very upset by the breakup of his first marriage, had lived with Julie and Steve when she was in junior high. Jealous of Julie, jealous of the new "sister," Kristen had been a constant problem and rebelliously looked for ways to upset Julie and Steve. One day she took a bad tumble on her bike and was bruised from head to foot. At school the next day, when the teacher asked her what had happened, she stated that her dad had beaten her.

Julie, a respected professional, who had seen the fall and knew full well that Steve had not hit Kristen, tried to explain the real story to the social worker. But child-protective services, afraid to err on the side of parents—when children's testimonies have too often been wrongly discounted in the past—refused to believe this version of the events. Julie and Steve looked all the more wrong for "trying to lie," and Kristen, embarrassed to admit the truth, was shipped off to her mother. The father is still too angry to speak to her.

This is unfortunate. Now that Kristen is with her mother a thousand miles away, the father and daughter have no easy opportunity to resolve this conflict. When a father does not live with his child it cannot help but affect the quality of their relationship, and geographical distance is sure to interfere with developing closeness. There are few opportunities to share daily events or to work through bad feelings that may come up. A man living in a different household from his children is more like an uncle—how distant an uncle depends on many factors including how close he was to the children before he moved out, how far away he lives from his children, and how easy it is to see them when he feels in the mood to be with them.

When we realize that most men have great difficulty being ready for intimacy or relaxing with children, we can understand why it would be easier for them to become close to the stepchildren who are readily available. Debbie's reflections on her feelings for her father versus her mother's long-term boyfriend help us see more of the difference between living with a child and trying to keep up a relationship from a distance. Debbie told me,

> "It's weird because my dad and Aaron are very much alike. I might have liked Aaron more just because Aaron is much more affectionate than my father and he's more responsible. I feel like my father doesn't really try to get to know us very well. Like my father always sends me a check for my birthday, but Aaron tries

to figure out what I would like, and he shops until he finds something really special for me."

Debbie is not conscious of how much easier it is to buy an appropriate gift for someone you see often. When we buy someone a special gift that they will like, we have usually listened to them talk about their needs and desires when they least suspected we were listening, or we have been out shopping with them and seen them admire something they couldn't buy for themselves. Debbie's father does not have that opportunity. Add to this the difficulty of mailing a bicycle, and one can picture the problem the distant father faces.

We can see why many men steel their hearts to their own children and opt to shower their attention on the kids with whom they live. It is so much more gratifying to give to someone when you can see their appreciative reaction. Whether there are two sets of kids or just two dads, these differences are bound to create some competitive and hard feelings.

WHO IS MY DADDY?

Megan (from Chapters 4 and 5) has worried about her son Keith growing up without a father. She knows that her own father will always be interested in him. "And I have lots of male friends," Megan tells me. "Keith has two godfathers." But the question of whom the child should call "Daddy" is often truly murky in the case of the teenage mother. Is Daddy the man whose name appears on the birth certificate who never pays any attention to me? Or is Daddy the man Mommy calls "Daddy" – that nice man who takes me places and bounces me on his knee? Or is Daddy that man who is always with me and Mom when we go places? The children of teenage mothers may be fathered by the mother's former boyfriend (the child's actual father); the mother's present boyfriend or husband; or by the mother's father or stepfather. Often the fathering is done by a number of these men either simultaneously or serially.

Megan has had a new boyfriend since two months before the baby was born. Rusty was a high school friend in Megan's class who stood by her and later fell in love with her. A year later, this boy is still very involved with Megan and has taken a strong interest in the baby.

Rusty comes to pick up the baby and takes him back home to keep him for awhile so that Megan can do other things. According to Megan, "He changes him, and feeds him and everything. He said to me, 'You tell that writer that Keith's father isn't absent. I'm around all the time.' "

Rusty and Megan's father have been the fathers in Keith's life. Megan coached Rusty in how to handle Keith: "I told him, 'Just come in and let him check you out first. Let him see you while I'm holding him so he can feel secure and then you can hold him.' Rusty likes to take off and have Keith all to himself, too. Rusty tries so hard and he has so much patience with him."

Rusty is very willing to take over the role of father to Keith if he becomes Megan's husband. In fact, Rusty is so involved with Keith, it would be difficult for Keith's birth father, Donny, to compete with him for Keith's attention. Right now Donny's interest in his baby is low. His name does not even appear on the birth certificate.

Megan told me that Rusty wants to have his name put on the birth certificate. At first glance this may look like the easy solution to Keith's "father question." However, Donny, who has just turned eighteen and is not yet very mature, still has rights as a father and could later challenge Rusty's paternity by insisting they both take a genetic blood test (which are 95 percent accurate, unlike earlier blood tests that only narrowed down the paternity to a blood type). So Rusty's offer to name himself as father does not provide any security from Megan's fears that Donny may later decide to demand his son.

At the same time, psychologists often warn against letting children get too attached to any of Mom's boyfriends. Many children have lived through repeated losses as they attach to the new adults Mom brings into their lives. If men come and go too much, and the partings are painful, the child will soon take up the defense of not getting attached to anyone. It is hard to decide if Megan is doing the right thing in allowing Keith to get so attached to Rusty.

MOM'S BOYFRIENDS

Normal, well-adjusted teenagers try out many relationships before they commit to one permanently. Many of these relationships are deep and look as if they will last, but the "fit" is just not right, and the couple parts. Though Megan shows a remarkable amount of maturity for one so young, if she had followed her intended life course (college after high school, and marriage sometime in the distant future), she would still be trying out relationships. Unfortunately, she may be less inclined to "date around" because her situation makes her feel more pressed to be married and establish a permanent home for herself and Keith. On the other hand, she and Rusty are planning to postpone marriage for a few years because Megan knows that she can provide much more easily for her baby while living in her parents' home.

Kim, although the same age as Megan, has been a mother for five years and has had more time to explore her options. She dated a few different boys casually in the first few years after Brian was born and now has a very steady boyfriend. Kim is now in a relationship with Jeffrey, a twenty-one-year-old boy she has been dating for about two years.

> "Jeffrey is really good with Brian. He works forty hours a week and then he coaches baseball after work with his dad. I've learned a lot from Jeffrey because he has taken a lot of child development classes and he works with kids in a daycare center. Jeffrey tells Brian that he wants him to learn to behave so that he'll have friends and everybody will like him—not just think he's a horrible kid. Brian really knows better, so he accepts Jeffrey's discipline pretty well.
>
> "Jeffrey comes over a lot and has taught Brian to play baseball and soccer and all that. When Brian went to Bible school a few weeks ago he told them that Jeffrey was his daddy. We all posed for a family picture together. Eventually Jeffrey and I hope to get married, once we're done with school and we have good jobs. Brian has told me he'd like me to marry Jeffrey so we can all live in a house of our own."

The relationship has a look of permanence. Jeffrey is an undeniably positive influence in both Brian's and Kim's lives. Indeed, he is such a plus that we would have to wonder if Brian would be missing out on far too much if Kim had kept her relationship with Jeffrey separate. It will be sad if they part, but divorce is sad too, and if Kim and Jeffrey were not so level-headed and cautious at this time in their lives, they would probably be married. If we argue that Brian should not become attached to Jeffrey, we may find ourselves advocating that children never become attached to men under any circumstances because it is just too risky!

However, Kim is either fortunate or an excellent judge of character. As they try to pull their lives together and soothe their bruised egos, many moms date a bewildering number of men following a divorce, separation, or unwed pregnancy. If they are not careful, they can expose their children to hurtful relationships, both because they may date men who are not good with children, and because they may date men who attract children but can't hold Mom's interest. Then the child must "break up" with the newfound "Dad."

Debbie had lived with her mother and her mother's boyfriend, Aaron, from the time she was eight until she was sixteen years old. When the relationship between Aaron and her mother soured, and he finally decided to leave, she had lived with him almost as long as she had lived with her natural father before her parents' divorce.

> "I was upset at first that Aaron was leaving us. It was like another divorce. I saw it coming just like the last one. He had moved out of the room he shared with my mother and was sleeping in a bed by himself. He started drinking a lot. I was kind of glad he left, though he was never a mean drunk. But I could tell he was really really unhappy. When he was leaving he told my mother that he had never wanted to be married and have kids and he felt trapped.
>
> "I didn't see him for about a year, and then I realized how much I missed him. I tracked him down and wrote him a letter. We're back in touch again, and we have a really good relationship. He's not at all judgmental. He's just a really good friend.
>
> "My mother said that he'd gotten all the best parts of us and then he wasn't there when we needed him. But he has been there for us. My car broke down and he gave me the money to fix it. My sister got sick once when my mom was out of the country. I called him because I didn't know what to do and he came over and took care of her. I feel comfortable calling him if I have a problem."

Though Debbie has experienced loss twice, she is now in touch with both of her dads and so has ended up richer than many in father-love.

Mothers need to proceed with caution. It is not wise for a mother to build a relationship between the children and every man she dates, and certainly a mother should think of her children's vulnerability when she is considering moving in with a man. On the other hand, mature relationships that are likely to survive for an extended period of time can enrich the children's lives.

UNBEARABLE PRESSURES

The most devastating conflict for a child happens when the newly formed parental unit pressures the child to give up his love for the father—by either pushing for a legal adoption or discouraging visitation. When Mom has been toughing it out as a single mother for quite awhile and finally finds the security of a good marriage, there is an urge to make everything new and whole again—to be like an ordinary family. As we saw with Leila above, even the children are drawn toward this idea. The question of adopting the stepchild ultimately comes up, and it is not always easy to foresee what is the best response for all involved.

Vanessa Riley, our older unwed mother from Chapter 4, believed her son, his father Larry, and his new stepfather Jack had all reached an amicable agreement about Kirk's adoption by Jack. However, when Larry signed the papers to allow Jack to adopt Kirk, he was suddenly saddened by the symbolic meaning and went out and got roaring drunk. He went over to Vanessa and Jack's house and loudly complained to them that Jack was trying to steal his child from him. Larry and Jack had been friendly co-fathers, and now they no longer speak to each other. Although Larry has been reassured and has kept in touch with Kirk, Jack has since drawn back from Kirk. "After that, it was like Jack shut Kirk out," Vanessa related. By keeping his distance from Kirk now, Jack seems to be saying to Larry, "See! I'm not trying to steal your kid!"

How did this adoption plan get started? Kirk's specific desire had been to have the same name as the rest of his family, but the legal adoption seems to have caused more harm than good. Going through a simple legal name-change procedure without a legal adoption would have been a less threatening way of solving the problem. This might be one way to give kids a sense of belonging to the new blended family without making the natural father feel shut out, or making the new stepfather feel a sense of obligation for which he is not ready.

Larry has actually shown surprising fortitude in this situation. Because Vanessa had previously refused to marry him, his hold on his son is quite tenuous. He has shown much courage and devotion to his son by recovering from his threatened feelings and reestablishing his relationship with Kirk, despite the now added pressure of Jack's coldness. Vanessa has also negotiated her way through this situation well. She has always been committed to Kirk knowing his real father, and she has managed to go on conveying this.

For the sake of the child, when Mom remarries, she must be willing to tell even a very jealous new husband that she will not cut off contact with the child's father just because it makes the new husband uncomfortable. (Obviously, this should be settled before the marriage takes place.) Everyone should try to keep the best interests of the child in mind and not manipulate the situation to soothe adult egos. Subtle hurt feelings expressed by the new stepfather when the child prefers not to call him "Daddy" will also put the child under painful pressure. Ross D. Parke, professor of Psychology at the University of Illinois and the author of *Fathers*, emphasizes that both the mother and the new stepfather should encourage the child's love for the biological father, and both fathers should be willing to share the child generously with one another.

Of course, the stepfather's attitude is even more important when the child's father has died. No matter what the father was like, most children have a need to idealize the father after his death. Children also often feel as if their mothers should be in mourning forever. It can be very hard for them to accept a new man in Mom's life. When Betsy Hadley started dating again after her husband's death, her son Mark accepted it, but Betsy's daughter Sylvie, who had always been close to her father, was outraged by her mother's dating and refuses to like the boyfriend. Betsy explained to me:

> "Sylvie told me, 'Nobody better ever say anything bad about my dad or they'll be sorry.' She was real upset when I went to Florida with my boyfriend to see his kids last October. It was the anniversary of her dad's death and she said, 'I was at the grave, where were you? Do you know what day that was?' Mark has always said that he didn't want me to be alone for the rest of my

life because he would worry about me. But Sylvie has said that she doesn't think that I should ever marry again."

Here we see where the mother's and daughter's needs clash. Sylvie is angry that her mother was with another man on the anniversary of her father's death. Part of Sylvie's anger might be that she needed her mother with her to share her grief. Meanwhile, it has been five years since the father's death, and Betsy is anxious to leave the hurt behind and get on with her life. In Betsy's mind, the opportunity to get out of town and meet her boyfriend's children just happened to come up the same month in which her husband died. However, there is probably a part of Betsy that jumped at the chance to do something new and distracting during that "anniversary" month. What Sylvie is striving to remember, Betsy is struggling to forget.

If Sylvie had been younger, it would have been wiser for Betsy to "tough out" the anniversary of her husband's death at home so that she could provide support for her children. But Sylvie is twenty-one years old. She is an adult and has little need for a new father in her life. It is natural and appropriate for her to want to hold the memory of her father sacred. She is old enough to separate psychologically from her mother and have her own feelings toward her deceased father. It is time for her to seek the comfort of friends, or perhaps her paternal grandmother, so that her mother is free to end her mourning and make a new connection.

LOYALTY CONFLICTS

We need to realize that once a stepfather or long-term boyfriend becomes involved with our children, we have created another potential barrier to the birth father's involvement. Anyone who has tried to carry on affairs with two lovers can well imagine what a balancing act two dads can become for the children. Debbie told me about her conflict over her father and her mother's boyfriend Aaron.

"While Aaron was living with us, I was still attached to my father and I used to feel bad about loving Aaron. Sometimes I would play this game with myself and try to imagine how I would feel if they each died. Would I be more upset if Aaron died or if my father died? When I was about thirteen I began to feel for the first time that I would be more upset if Aaron died.

"A lot of times I would feel really funny talking to my father about Aaron. Aaron could give us a lot of things that my father couldn't afford. I thought he must feel bad about that. My father never said anything that made me feel bad about liking Aaron, but I felt embarrassed about liking Aaron so much anyway. I think my father was probably feeling okay about Aaron, but ever since Aaron won the 'death test' I felt really guilty."

Fortunately, Debbie's dad has never demanded her undying loyalty. He seems to gracefully accept her attachment to Aaron.

Still, most children feel compelled to protect their natural father from knowing how much they care for their stepfather. Ben, the son of David, our super-loyal, long-distance dad, had obviously never talked to his father much about his feelings for his stepfather. David's ex-wife remarried when Ben was three years old, and David acknowledges that he has been jealous of the stepfather at times, but he feels the stepfather has been good to Ben and a stable influence in his life. The stepfather has occasionally been able to drive Ben halfway at visitation time to help David out.

Since I had interviewed David first, and he had indicated that Ben's stepfather was cordial and helpful, but didn't seem to be very close to Ben, I was very surprised by Ben's glowing report of his stepdad. Ralph started dating Ben's mother shortly after Ben's parents separated.

"When my stepfather was dating my mom he would come over to eat just about every night, so I knew him really well by the time they got married. He always used to go places with us on the weekends. I've known Ralph for as long as I can remember."

Ralph had two daughters in a previous marriage, but they were much older than Ben. Ben is Ralph's first boy, and Ben feels somewhat treasured by his stepfather. With Ralph the main activity has been travel. Ralph used to work for the railroad so, when Ben was small, Ralph used to take him to see the trains. Ralph was also part-owner of a plane and took Ben on occasional plane rides. This interest has evolved into traveling as a family pastime.

Ralph is an "older father" and isn't interested in playing sports, but he frequently takes Ben and his friends to nearby professional games. One of the things that helped keep Ben from feeling disturbing loyalty conflicts between his father and his stepfather is the difference in the two men's interests. Scouts was what Ben did with his father, David, and that worked out fine since "roughing it" is not exactly Ralph's cup of tea.

TWO × TWO = FOUR

Ben now has a stepmother, too, and his four parents have a good working relationship. He still senses some tension between his natural parents, but each of them likes the other's new spouse. The four of them have gotten along smoothly at Ben's recitals, plays, and special school-related events. Ben feels he has gained good qualities and interests from each of them. He was eager to relate the best qualities of each of his four parents.

Ben's mother and stepfather have taken him on many trips—to Europe, out West, and to California—and his father and stepmother have helped him appreciate nature through their many camping trips. His mother has taught him to appreciate unusual foods, and his stepmother has introduced him to films and literature. His stepfather has helped him know the world through their many excursions, and his dad has been a good listener who has helped him know himself. Ben really feels he has twice as much parenting (in the best sense) as kids in intact families. He has also enriched each of his parent's lives by being the "cultural ambassador" between the two units. He can give his father and stepmother advice on the best restaurants in Cincinnati when they come down, and hc comes home from his father's with great film suggestions for his mother and stepfather.

Ben has shown great social skill in getting the best of all worlds. He can talk to his stepmother about adjusting the visitation if his father is being too sensitive about it, and he can complain to his dad about little things his stepfather does to annoy him without fearing his father will get over-involved. In a recent conflict about cutting his visit with his father short so that he could go home and see his girlfriend, Ben used his whole "network of consultants."

"First I talked it over with my mother and we decided what compromise I should propose to my dad. We decided she would talk it over with my dad, but actually she got hold of my stepmom when she called, and so my stepmom talked to my dad about it. Then I got to make the final decision. My dad said he was disappointed that I was cutting my visit short, but was glad I was able to make my own decisions."

Ben has a very strong sense that the four adults in his life let him make his own choices most of the time. Ben's four parents have practiced mature cooperation and possessed the ability to let him love and attach to others. It is not an easy task to share a child's love, but the positive outcome for the child is well worth the effort.

STEPFATHER PROBLEMS

Studies show that very young and post-adolescent children accept stepfathers much more readily than adolescents, and these children can make a good adjustment with a "fill-in" dad. But this does not mean that stepfathers of even very young children are an overnight success. There is an old myth that as soon as one becomes a parent, he or she will love the child. This might be true in the birthing room, but any self-aware stepparent knows that your step-child is still "somebody else's child" after you wet the marriage license with the ink. It takes living together and sometimes a lot of patient coaxing to make that child responsive to you.

In addition to the loyalty conflicts the child might feel about loving another dad, the stepfather moves in and takes up most of Mom's attention for awhile. That does not make anyone popular with kids. They see themselves as having "first dibs" on Mom and will resent any attention the mother pays to the stepfather. When one of the boys has seen himself as Mom's Main Man, there is great potential for trouble. Unless the stepfather makes a conscientious effort to pay at least as much positive attention to the kids as they have lost from their mother on his arrival, he will be seen as a "loss" in their lives. Also, stepfathers often step in and begin to make some much needed rules. This does not add to their popularity.

When we consider how many men have difficulty with intimate relationships, we are not surprised to learn that few realize how much time it takes to establish a relationship with a stepchild. Psychologists have found that men are surprised by their step-children's reluctance and suspicion and are not prepared to let the child approach them gradually.[2] Instead, they rush the relationship and sometimes double the child's resistance by frightening them. Both Mom and the new stepdad may forget that even though they might be used to kissing each other, it doesn't mean that the kids are ready for a goodnight kiss from this man whom they "hardly know" and might even be feeling hostile toward.

The myth of the instant happy family has ruined many step relationships, as either kids or stepparents rush the rituals of close-ness before the feelings that go with hugs and kisses have developed at their natural pace. We can forget how frightening strange adults can be to children. Debbie related how she felt when she first met Aaron, the "stepparent" she grew to love deeply over the years:

> "I was about eight when my mom moved in with Aaron. I was very upset at first and I had a huge temper tantrum. He is really tall, and I was scared to death of him. When we moved in with him, I had to leave my cat and my pony behind and change schools and leave all my friends. I was determined to hate that man with every fiber of my being. I ranted and raved at him and he still reminds me of that from time to time, now that we're really good friends."

The relationship between Debbie and Aaron did not develop overnight. Aaron patiently stood by while Debbie and her sister got used to him being around. The trust was built up slowly and gradu-ally, rather than the mother insisting that the girls love and kiss their new daddy so he'd feel like part of the family.

DANGERS OF PUSHING

Fortunately, we've begun to raise our awareness about pushing children to show affection just to please the adults around them or to do what is expected socially. We can probably all remember times when we were expected to kiss some distant relative we hardly knew because this was how to greet kin. But these coercions take on darker meaning when we consider how vulnerable we make our children to sexual abuse by pushing them to show physical affection when it makes them feel uncomfortable, or by conveying that sometimes we kiss or hug people we don't know very well because our elders expect it of us. When it comes to stepfathers, men who live in our homes with our children and who may frequently be home alone with them, we must be careful about the "messages" we send our children about our expectations.

Unfortunately, stepfathers are the most frequent sexual abusers of children. Studies show that stepfathers are five times more likely to abuse a child than the natural father.[3] When the biological taboos are not there, men no doubt see it as less of a sin to fondle a stepdaughter than to molest their natural daughter. Some tell themselves that the stepdaughter is simply a young woman who is attractive to them (and they convince themselves that she must find them equally attractive).

However, even though the stepfather is not a biological father, he is still an adult in authority, and as such, he has an unfair psychological power advantage over the stepdaughter. Like the teacher, counselor, or minister who seduces a student, counselee, or acolyte, the stepfather is taking advantage of a situation, even when the child is an adolescent and seems to be "willing." Indeed, some teen stepdaughters do act seductively toward their stepfathers, just as many teen daughters try out flirtatious routines on their fathers. Real fathers can recognize these behaviors as a kind of play-acting their daughters do to try to get reassurance and compliments. But stepfathers are more likely to misinterpret these behaviors.

Therefore, children must know that they have a right to be close to or distant from their new stepfathers, as they see fit. They may need to be told explicitly which behaviors are appropriate in a blended household and which are not (don't run naked from the bathroom to the bedroom), particularly if their original family was exceptionally relaxed in front of each other. At the same time, when a child is very angry about a remarriage and hostile to the stepfather, it is okay to insist that he or she treat the stepfather civilly.

The best the parents should strive for is a cooperative and friendly relationship between the child and stepfather. If something deeper develops, wonderful! However, the child should never be pushed or shamed into "loving" the stepfather. If love does not develop, the relationship should not be seen as a failure on anyone's part. Children need to be reassured that they will still hold their full place in the family even if they choose never to love the stepfather.

RELUCTANT STEPDADS

When we let our children know that they are not expected to love the stepfather, we also protect them from possible disappointment if the stepfather chooses not to love them. If a man has had no children in the past, he may have no understanding of what is normal child behavior. Indeed, even most new biological parents are astonished at how irrational and uncooperative children can be. A man who is used to ordering adults around all day, and being obeyed without question or challenge, will probably believe the average child is pathologically resistant. Even after stepfathers are educated to understand what is reasonable to expect from children at different ages and stages, they will not necessarily *like* this "normal" behavior. It is generally at this point that either everyone learns to compromise a little or the marriage blows apart.

The stepfather may learn to tolerate the children's behavior but still not want to get very involved with them. He may be too rigid to change, too committed to his job, or be harboring a denied wound from leaving his own children. Indeed, if he is a divorced father, the prognosis may not be any better than if he has never been a father. He may have escaped his first family when the pressure to actively father his children became unbearable and unavoidable. Many fathers have felt a deep sense of failure and inadequacy and don't want to enter that dark corridor again.

Vanessa Riley worries about the way Jack treats her son Kirk. Jack brings many sad and frustrating memories to his experience as a father. Though Jack seems to be having his greatest success ever as a father in his relationship to Tiffany, his daughter by this new marriage, there is great tension over the stepson. Kirk never seems to quite "measure up" to Jack's expectations, and Vanessa is concerned about the way Kirk responds to this.

"All Jack ever seems to do with Kirk is discipline him. He's had two boys already and thinks boys need a lot of discipline. He thinks I coddle Kirk too much. But Jack was never close to his boys and they had a pretty rough adolescence, so I'm not sure Jack's way is right either. I feel like if he spent more time with Kirk, went to his soccer or baseball games, or helped him with his schoolwork, it would help his relationship with Kirk. He's very involved with our daughter Tiffany and I think Kirk feels the difference in the way he is treated."

Vanessa has spoken to Jack about his different treatment of Kirk and Tiffany. Jack hears her and can admit she is right, but he has had difficulty changing his behavior.

Jack grew up without a mother, and his father frequently went off and left him to fend for himself. The father eventually put Jack and his brother into an orphanage because he felt he couldn't take care of them. So Jack's beliefs about parenthood translate into, "The mother is responsible to take care of the children, and if there is no mother then no one is responsible to take care of the children."

Jack had had custody of his two older boys after his divorce because his wife was very unstable. However, at that time, Jack was working a night shift and supervised the boys very little. In the case of his first children, it didn't even enter Jack's mind that the father should step in and take over the parenting when the mother was absent. Now that there is a mother available in his family unit, Jack seems to feel all the nurturing should be done by her. He contributes discipline, the traditional male parenting skill. The rest is dictated by mood or impulse. He feels naturally moved to be more playful and attentive to his well-behaved daughter, so it is no effort to remember to be positive and nurturing with her. For Jack to reach out in this way toward his stepson, Kirk, he would have to really think and plan his responses.

Jack's father was so absent that he had no reasonable role model for fatherhood. Jack's concept of fatherhood starts way back at minus ten. He is already a far better father than his own because he kept his children instead of giving them away. And he has been a better father to Kirk than he was to his own boys, because he now works days and is home every evening. By disciplining Kirk, but not encouraging him, he is doing 50 percent, and that is 50 percent more than he offered his own boys. Playing ball with Kirk would seem to him like going way overboard. Jack never goes to any of Kirk's games until

Vanessa nags him to, yet Vanessa notices that many of the fathers Jack's age are there. Kirk probably notices this too.

"Jack spends a lot less time with Kirk than other fathers do. He needs to spend time with him that has nothing to do with discipline. Jack was closer to Kirk when he was smaller, but he has less tolerance as Kirk grows older and mouths off more. I'm getting to the point where I think we should go for counseling.

"Tiffany is a model child so it's very easy for Jack to get close to her. She's his adoring little girl. Kirk even complains to me that I love Tiffany more than him. And the difference with Jack is much more pronounced.

"It's not that Jack's expectations for Kirk are too harsh or too high, but the other half is missing. The affection part."

Tiffany has the advantage of being Jack's natural child, the product of a union that both Vanessa and Jack cherish after their earlier struggles. But the difference in how Jack feels about Kirk is not simply a case of blood bonds being tighter. Kirk is one of those extremely active boys who gets under everybody's skin, whereas Tiffany is easy to be with. Kirk is going to have problems with self-esteem because he provokes everyone to criticize him, and his irritating activity level is not something he can yet control. Vanessa may need to enlist a counselor to act as coach, referee, and support in retraining Jack.

What can Vanessa reasonably expect from Jack, and how can she help mitigate the damage done to Kirk's self-esteem by the disapproval that surrounds him every day? It might seem like a silly word game at first, but Vanessa could tell Jack that he must first compliment Kirk on something before he criticizes him. For example, Jack could say, "I really liked the way you picked up some of your trucks. Now would you pick up the rest?" This will not be easy. Jack's generation of parents were trained to focus on the negative. Techniques like this can take some of the sting out of the stepparent's criticism and lessen the damage to the child, but Vanessa cannot really expect Jack to care as deeply for Kirk as he does for Tiffany.

Meanwhile there is a place where Kirk can get the extra love he needs to help him get through the difficult years ahead. Kirk's natural father, Larry, cares about him deeply and seems untroubled by

Kirk's wild behavior. It is a blessing for Kirk that his father never quite "grew up" because it makes him more tolerant of Kirk. Because Larry does not feel responsible for making sure his son does well in school, behaves in church, or acts properly at the dinner table, he can more easily offer Kirk "unconditional love." Through Kirk we see the importance of helping kids stay in touch with their natural fathers, even when there is a more responsible stepfather ready in the wings to take over.

SUMMARY POINTS

- Many men who lose contact with their biological children become very involved fathers with the children of a new mate, making fatherhood a kind of serial relationship.
- Children of unwed adolescent mothers are often fathered by a group or series of men from the real father, to the mother's father, to any number of men she becomes involved with later.
- Though psychologists wisely warn that Mom should be cautious about encouraging relationships between her boyfriends and her children, when the relationship seems very stable it can be very enriching for children to know and enjoy Mom's male friends.
- When we consider how difficult it is for parents of either sex to stay close to their children when they seldom see them, we are not surprised to learn that both men and children can find themselves feeling closer to their "step" relatives than they do to their natural children or parents.
- Though there is always a longing to be like a "normal" family when the parent remarries, both the parent and new stepparent should actively encourage the child's continuing relationship with his or her natural father.
- The bereaved child may have particular difficulty accepting a new man in Mom's life. Unfortunately, the child's need to keep Dad alive in his or her memories clashes with the mother's need to try to let the past go and get on with her new life.
- It is a mistake to assume that stepfather and child will love each other as soon as Mom remarries. Intimacy and trust take

time to build and the stepfather and child may be a poor personality match. Sometimes everyone will have to settle for an atmosphere of mutual respect sought through compromise.

- Stepfathers are five times more likely to abuse a child than the natural father. Therefore, mothers should always be cautious about pushing closeness between child and stepfather especially when there is resistance. The children need to be reassured that Mom will still love them, whether or not they love the stepfather.
- As with all fathers, the stepfather is somewhat limited by the role models he has had in his life. The understanding and guidance of Mom and sometimes a professional counselor can help the stepfather to learn better parenting skills.
- When stepfathers cannot warm to the child, it is all the more important that the natural father be welcome in the child's life, for sometimes only a real father can offer the unconditional love that children need.

12

Creative Custody Choices

Your children are not your children.
They are the sons and daughters of Life's longing for itself.
They come through you but not from you,
And although they are with you yet they belong not to you.

—KAHLIL GIBRAN

Since our concern is with finding ways to get fathers involved, we must look at the evidence in favor of joint custody as a solution to the problem of father absence. I believe our society's current attitudes about child custody are symptomatic of the root of father's absence. Father has been told in many ways that he is not necessary. When we award custody to the mother 90 percent of the time, we are telling fathers that their money is needed but their nurturing skills are not. Then we wonder why the non-custodial father's feelings for his children are deadened and he withdraws from contact.

Though few families currently resemble the traditional family of several decades ago, most judges continue to award custody as though Mom were still home baking brownies in the middle of the day. As we know, most mothers now work outside the home, and certainly any divorced mother is hard put to support herself and her children on the father's required child-support amount (nor should she be using it to pay her own expenses). In the 1990s, at the moment the judge awards custody, the choice is usually between two parents who both work full-time outside the home. Yet, in 90 percent of the cases, the judge deems that naming the mother as primary custodian serves the "best interests of the child." Some social critics regard this preference for mothers as custodians as sexist and believe it perpetuates traditional gender roles.

Custody decisions are often very subjective because guidelines for determining what is in the child's best interest are very vague. They do not take into account the child's changing developmental needs in the years ahead, nor do they consider the varying needs of boys and girls to have a same-sex parent. There are serious flaws in almost any criteria that have been used. For example, should the child go to the parent who has provided the "most" care even if that parent was neglectful or abusive? Should the child go to the parent with the most money since that parent could provide the most materially? Should joint custody be presumed unless one of the parents can be proven unfit? Who is the "better parent"—a warm permissive parent or a more distant limit-setting parent?

There has been a great deal of recent research done that disproves the presumption that mothers make far better parents than fathers. Indeed, important new studies show that most boys fare better in the custody of fathers. Custody is a much more complicated issue than our presumption of custody-to-the-mother-unless-she-is-unfit would lead us to believe. After reviewing many studies on parent-child interactions and custody results, Ross A. Thompson, of the University of Nebraska Department of Psychology, came to the following conclusions:

Custody Points

1. Both fathers and mothers are significant figures in their children's lives.
2. Fathers can adequately fulfill the caretaking role following divorce.
3. Children fare better with the same-sex parent.
4. It is in the best interests of the child to ensure ongoing contact with the father, and boys especially need close continual contact with him.
5. Because infants and small children turn to the primary caretaker under stress, it may be wise to keep young children in custody of the primary caretaker, whether that be father or mother.

6. Considering the child's strong attachment to both parents, a joint-custody arrangement may prove best.
7. Once the child is school age, if the relationship between the parents is too volatile for a smooth joint-custody arrangement, the child will probably do best with the same-sex parent as custodian.[1]

In this chapter we'll be exploring how to incorporate these new conclusions into our ideas about custody as well as what changes we can make in terms of custody that may affect our children's relationships with their fathers.

But first, let us take a look at the prevailing wisdom. Most states currently award custody to the "primary caretaker," stating that this has no sexual bias. Attorneys, psychologists, or mediators determine whether the primary caretaker is the mother or the father by exploring a number of issues with each parent and, in some cases, the children. Below is a list of tasks that determine who is the "primary caretaker."

DETERMINING THE PRIMARY CARETAKER

The primary caretaker is the parent who has taken primary responsibility for the performance of the following caring and nurturing duties of a parent:

1. Preparing and planning meals;
2. Bathing, grooming, and dressing;
3. Purchasing, cleaning, and care of clothes;
4. Medical care, including nursing and trips to physicians;
5. Arranging for social interaction among peers after school: transporting to friends' houses or, for example, to girl or boy scout meetings;
6. Arranging alternative care: babysitting, daycare, etc.;
7. Putting child to bed at night, attending to child in the middle of the night, waking child in the morning;
8. Disciplining: teaching general manners and toilet training;
9. Educating: religious, cultural, social, etc.;
10. Teaching elementary skills: reading, writing, and arithmetic.[2]

As we all know (and as Arlie Hoschild has proven in *The Second Shift*), men in intact families rarely perform these tasks. This is particularly true if the man has been the "primary breadwinner." However, it does not logically follow that the man cannot perform these tasks in the future just because he has not performed them in the past. We sink to the grossest level of prejudice when we make that assumption. Is there some more objective criteria we can use to determine who is capable of caring for the child after the divorce?

FATHERS AS CARETAKERS

We can learn a lot about fathers' caretaking potential by looking at how fathers have done when they have had custody of their children. Dr. Deborah Luepnitz, a psychologist at the Child Guidance Clinic in Philadelphia, has spent a great deal of time studying various custody arrangements. She concludes that men are no less capable of child rearing than women are. Fathers who are given the chance to care for their children say that it has required them to develop empathy and emotional responsiveness, and to be less compulsive about their careers. The custodial fathers in Luepnitz's study found themselves softening their authoritarian approach after divorce. Even the harshest disciplinarians were able to respond to their children's emotional distress due to the divorce and to treat them more tenderly. When it was their sole responsibility to provide nurturing for the child, they could rise to the occasion. In addition, many of the custodial fathers were very expressive about the joys of having custody because many had not had it at first and it was never a "given." Custodial mothers, on the other hand, viewed it more in terms of their responsibility and had less sense of it being a choice freely made.[3]

In a study of forty single fathers, it was found that those who chose to have custody of their children had not participated in any more childcare tasks before divorce than the average father, had not been exceptionally close to their children, and were no more "feminine acting" than average men. The only common trait these custodial fathers shared was that most had been close to their mothers and had wished their fathers had been more involved with them. Also, the fathers who sought custody had had, as a group, more hostile breakups with their wives than fathers who had not sought custody, so they may have originally been motivated by "revenge" or the fear that their ex-wives would make visitation difficult. Regardless of this "negative" motivation, these fathers parented as well as custodial mothers, once faced with the task.[4]

The level of chaos in these custodial fathers' homes during the first difficult year following divorce was no better nor worse than the level of chaos in mother-custody homes. After the first year or so, life settled down for these custodial fathers, and they were functioning as smoothly as custodial mothers during their second year. Very few of these fathers had hired housekeepers; most managed it all themselves, though most of these fathers had had very little homemaking or caretaking experience prior to the divorce. In fact, most had functioned as traditional fathers, with minimal involvement in caregiving or domestic tasks.[5]

There is mounting evidence that men are as capable of parenting as women are of becoming doctors, lawyers, and soldiers. They just need to be trained. A series of studies of parents in intact families showed that although mothers traditionally did more of the caretaking tasks, the father's interactions with the babies were as high quality as the mother's interactions. Fathers of all socioeconomic levels held, rocked, kissed, looked at, explored, and talked to the babies as much as the mothers did when they had the infants alone. When fathers and mothers were each observed feeding their babies, they were equally observant and responsive to the baby's signals. The infants ingested the same amount of milk with either parent. Though fathers generally choose to spend their time playing with their infants, they are perfectly capable of performing the caretaking tasks.[6]

Infants also showed emotional attachment to the fathers similar to their attachment to their mothers. A random sampling of thirty-two one-year-olds showed twenty very attached to fathers, twenty-one very attached to mothers, and sixteen very attached to both. Most of the infants preferred fathers as play partners but turned to their mothers under stress.[7]

Therefore, the argument about who should have custody seems to be primarily political. Will we keep men out of the "parenting market" as we have kept women out of the "job market" by saying they can't have the job if they have no previous experience? We need to be tough on ourselves about having double standards that cut men out as parents.

SHARING CUSTODY

Though fathers are capable of parenting alone, I maintain that shared-custody arrangements are ideal, and fathers should not be sole custodians unless the mother is unfit, needs her independence for some reason, or the child clearly prefers or has some special need for paternal custody. The parameters and definitions of joint custody vary from state to state. Some states use the term to mean that the children live with the mother, and the father pays child support, but that the father must be consulted on all important decisions. Court-ordered joint custody in these instances means the father has certain legal rights. His signature may be required on health or school forms that pertain to any important decision. This legal re-empowering of fathers is becoming very common.

The form of joint custody that addresses the children's living arrangements is sometimes called "shared custody" or "split custody." When the parents live in close proximity, shared-custody children may spend half the week at Mom's house and the other half at Dad's. Some parents prefer a weekday/weekend split, where Mom might have the kids on weekdays, and Dad has them on the weekends. When the parents live far apart, split custody may mean the school year at Mom's and the summer at Dad's, or this year at Mom's and next year at Dad's. Parents may also "share" children by having one live at Mom's house while the other lives at Dad's.

Sometimes the custodial children in one family are split between two households because neither parent feels capable of taking care of them all. In deciding what child should go where it is good to keep in mind that recent research shows that, if all other factors are equal, boys generally do better in father-custody homes, and girls do better in mother-custody homes. Boys living with fathers were more mature, social, and independent than girls living with fathers, and girls living with mothers were more competent than boys living with mothers.[8] One reason for this may be that same-sex parents can draw on their own personal life experiences as they try to guide their children. Also, opposite-sex children often remind the custodial parent of the despised divorced spouse, and this may cause the custodial parent to be too critical. As we can see, there are many ways custody of the children can be shared, but many mothers still oppose joint custody, and some psychologists and lawmakers still question if it is good for children.

JOINT CUSTODY—THE DEBATE

When we consider the four great barriers to fathers being involved with their children after divorce—pain, conflict, feelings of inadequacy, and indifference—we have to give joint custody serious consideration as a solution. As we will see, studies of parents in various custody arrangements show that men experience the least pain, conflict, and disinterest when they have regular ongoing contact with their children. Also, the experience of caring for his child without either the watchful eyes of another parent (and the fear of criticism inherent in that situation), or the ready presence of someone more skilled to bail him out, gives a man the chance to become a very adequate caretaker who can be proud and confident about his new parenting skills. But there are many who oppose joint custody as being too disruptive for children.

Providentially, I met separately with Bob and Gina after a weekend blow-up over the kids. Gina, who works rotating shifts as a nurse, dropped Leslie and Carl off at Bob's house at 3 A.M. Saturday morning. The kids were still in their pajamas, mostly still asleep, and she had brought clothes for them to put on the next day. She didn't realize that she had forgotten their shoes. She told Bob that the kids were to be at the church at 9 A.M. to leave for a weekend camp-out. By 8:30 he realized the kids had no shoes, and they sped off in the car to look for a discount store where he hoped to buy two cheap pairs. No stores were open.

He pulled up to the church at 9:15. Everyone had been waiting for Leslie and Carl. The kids were so embarrassed that they stayed in the car while Bob went and confessed to the leaders why the children were not able to go. The disappointed kids fought with each other all day, and sulked throughout the next day as they thought about all the fun they were missing.

When Gina arrived to pick up the kids Sunday night, Bob was livid. Gina reminded him that he still owns the house they live in, and he could have gone in and gotten the shoes. Bob retorted that he had lost the key (since it's been a year since he had to use it) and that he wasn't about to break into the house.

Bob blames Gina; Gina blames Bob. The kids are disgusted with them both. Bob and Gina have joint custody. They each love their kids and don't want to give them up.

This is the nightmare scenario of joint custody, the kind of scene that offers proof for many that joint custody simply cannot work. However, like all else in post-divorce child arrangements, the success or failure of joint custody depends on how willing the parents are to resolve their conflicts. Though Bob and Gina are furious with each other, the mistakes they made that disastrous weekend were without malice. We can look at the incident as proof that joint custody can never work, or we can honestly admit that mishaps like this can happen even in intact families when compatible parents have work schedules that are poorly coordinated. Nothing with children is easy. A child in any home could have "lost" his or her shoes in a messy bedroom and not been able to find them in time to take the camping trip. It's how the parents react to the situation that becomes significant.

Difficulties notwithstanding, Dr. Luepnitz, in her book *Child Custody: A Study of Families After Divorce*, concludes that *physical* joint custody, where children spent part of the time living at Mom's and part of the time living at Dad's, is often the best arrangement for the psychological well-being of the child. Most of the joint-custody families in her study had split the child's week between the parents. Luepnitz conducted extensive interviews with single-custody fathers, single-custody mothers, joint-custody parents of both sexes, and the children in each of these situations. Both the children and the adults showed the greatest satisfaction in the joint-custody families when compared with the children and adults in single-custody arrangements. They cited a number of advantages that joint custody offered:

Advantages to Joint Custody

1. Children maintained significant and down-to-earth contact with both parents. Neither parent became the "party parent" who merely entertained and treated the kids every few months.

2. Children learned the workings of two households, thus learning that there is more than one "right way" to do many things. This can make them better-rounded, more flexible people.

3. Children kept contact with both extended families and sets of parents' friends. This gave them a sense of continuity, the security of belonging to a larger group, and the knowledge that community is sustaining.

4. Both parents had an opportunity to be a meaningful part of their children's lives, to teach them their cherished values, and to feel the satisfaction of children's small acknowledgments.

5. Each parent got frequent breaks so they could pursue their own interests such as further schooling, dating, or just relaxing. Therefore, parents were less harried and overwhelmed when they had the children.

6. Using the other parent for childcare saved money, was more satisfying for the kids than a "paid stranger," and gave the parents more peace of mind.

7. Parents had more opportunities to discuss important decisions.

8. There were fewer conflicts over money.

9. Children had a balanced relationship with both parents, thus breaking the over-involved parent vs. under-involved parent cycle.

10. Each parent became a more balanced authority. Fathers found themselves softening their approach, and mothers became stricter.

Some parents even felt a great deal of pride about modeling good conflict resolution for their children. For, though they had been involved in one of the deepest conflicts most people experience in their lives (divorce), they were working cooperatively with one another. When the parents had frequent contact with each other and could see each other's living conditions, they also tended to empathize with each other more.

There were relatively few disadvantages. The parents had to constantly contend with the logistical problems of moving the children and their belongings back and forth, they had difficulty getting a clear sense of separation from one another, and the arrangement often made it impossible for them to pursue career advantages in other locations (or to marry a new spouse who would need to relocate).

However, though joint custody offers more advantages than disadvantages, Luepnitz is opposed to joint custody becoming mandatory. A decade of clinical experience since the publication of her book, *Child Custody*, has led her to take a more pessimistic view of the joint award. In particular, she is distressed that abusive fathers might gain custody of their children, or that mothers who had been abused by their ex-husbands would be forced to give up custody of their children or have continued contact with the abusive ex-husband.[9]

As mentioned in Chapter 3, I emphatically agree that fathers who are physically abusive, or who have sexually abused any of the children and have not been through a rehabilitative program and shown genuine remorse and a willingness to change, should be barred from seeing their children. The courts should also be careful about awarding custody to any father who has a history of alcohol or drug abuse and is not in a program of recovery. Unfortunately, these fathers often continue to have visitation rights, but it is hoped that judges will not make the mistake of placing children in even more serious jeopardy by granting these fathers custody.

On the other hand, if a father has abused his ex-wife, but not his children, there are measures that can be taken to allow him joint custody of the children without endangering the ex-wife. The mother can use a calm neutral party both as a location for drop-off and pick-up and as a vehicle for necessary communications. For example, the paternal grandparents might have the best interests of the child in mind as well as an amiable relationship with the father. Their home could be used as a drop-off and pick-up point. Other possibilities are mutual friends or brothers or sisters of either spouse who have managed to remain friendly with both parents. If the joint-custody arrangements are kept simple, this can be very workable. The child might change homes once a year, for summer vacation, or to spend alternate years with each parent. School can also be a great place to transfer the kids when the joint-custody arrangements involve a shift of homes on a weekly basis. One parent can pick the child up from school to begin his or her visit (without having to see the other parent at all) and then drop the child at school the morning of the end of the custody time. Notes carried by the child can convey a lot of information between the parents without them having to have face-to-face contact. I feel that for the child's sake, it is good for the mother to overcome her fear of the ex-husband enough to try to find such a solution.

Despite Luepnitz's misgivings about the potential abuse of a mandatory joint-custody policy, her original study showed that the most frequent criticisms of joint custody were largely unfounded. Psychologists and legal advisors had speculated that joint custody would be traumatic for children as they adjusted to two households in rapid cycles, and that the amount of conflict between the parents would increase since they would have so many opportunities to fight. When questioned about the difficulties of transition and adjusting to new rules, all the joint-custody children and parents felt these hardships were insignificant. In the most "severe" case (a girl caught in a battle between two parents over what food she should and shouldn't eat), the child still felt that the benefit of having a lot of contact with both parents far outweighed the discomfort of the conflict.

Some professionals have criticized studies that show joint-custody families as having less conflict as being biased, on the grounds that only the most compatible parents would even attempt such an arrangement to begin with. However, prior to divorce, the joint-custody parents in Luepnitz's study had conflicts as deep and vehement as the single-custody parents had. Following the divorce, the joint-custody parents had no more frequent conflicts with the ex-spouse than the single-custody parents. As one mother in Luepnitz's study pointed out:

> "The need to communicate with the ex-spouse is a difficulty. You can't cherish your anger. You have to continue to work things out with him, so you have to continue to confront the part of yourself that made the marriage not work. . . . When you think of the alternative to joint custody, however, it makes this difficulty seem small."[10]

Other joint-custody parents concurred that frequent contact with the ex-spouse forced them to learn to get along with the other parent.

So joint custody also addresses two other important factors in the child's post-divorce adjustment. As we learned earlier, studies have shown that the less conflict between the parents after the divorce, the better the children do. Joint custody seems to force the parents to get along with each other: they work things out rather than avoiding problems and letting them fester. A second factor that affects children's post-divorce adjustment is the amount of contact they have with each parent. Children suffer when they do not have enough contact with both their parents. Most of the children in the single-custodian homes complained that they did not see enough of the other parent. More than three-fourths expressed a desire to live with the non-custodial parent at least some of the time. Some even stated that they would prefer to live with the other parent, but could not bear to hurt their current custodial parent. By contrast, the children in joint-custody homes felt very satisfied with the amount of contact they had with each parent and considered themselves very fortunate to see so much of both parents. One mother I interviewed, whose ex-husband was very reluctant to take any responsibility for the children after the divorce, commented,

> "Some friends of mine are getting a divorce. It's been very bitter and antagonistic with a lot of attempts at trying to use the child as a bargaining tool. They are both very good friends of mine and I've had a lot of talks with each of them. They've been friends of mine since before my husband and I divorced. I've told them that the child is getting hurt, and they know I know what I'm talking about, because I've been through it. I've tried to tell them what a wonderful situation they have. The mom has the boy four nights a week, and the dad has him three. It gives them each time to themselves to build a new life. And it's good for their son. He knows that he can count on seeing Daddy even when Mom is mad at him. I wish my kids had had a responsible father who wanted to take care of them."

CUSTODY BATTLES AND $$$

Mary Ann Mason, author of *The Equality Trap*, feels that joint custody has been used as a way for men to get out of paying child support. In the case of joint custody, the court often rules that each parent will pay for the children when they are with them; therefore, no child support will be paid by either party. Of course, there are some obvious problems with this logic—such as who will buy the children's clothes, or pay for hair cuts? We would hope that the parent with the greater income would pick up these expenses, but power struggles between parents can make such issues a constant battleground. Even more tragic is the fact that the growing acceptance of joint custody has set into motion dangerous bargaining practices. Fathers who may have little real interest in having custody of their children will threaten to ask for custody if the mother will not give up her claims to child support. Attorneys acknowledge it's a good bargaining position. In California any divorce that took place after 1980 can be reopened on the issue of joint custody. According to Mason, men who are tired of paying child support jump at the chance to use this easy out. Even if they have no interest in actually having custody, this looks like a good way to beat out the new child-support enforcement laws.[11]

However, we also know that fathers who have more contact with their children generally feel more connected and accept financial responsibility more readily. Many fathers report that the mother makes visitation difficult, so they are very dissatisfied with arrangements where the mother has custody and the father must get her "permission" to see his own child. Psychologists have verified that many of these claims are true, even when the mothers don't consciously mean to prevent visitation. The mothers succumb to an understandable urge to forget the past, and that includes Dad's relationship to the kids. It is equally understandable that a father who has had difficulty seeing his kids, and keeping his bond with them alive, will either withhold funds out of resentment or out of a diminished sense of responsibility for his estranged children.

Luepnitz also discovered that joint-custody parents have fewer conflicts over money and rarely take these disagreements to court. Thus these parents also avoid adding lawyers' costs to their financial troubles. Contrary to popular belief, this was neither because the parents had a more cooperative attitude to begin with nor because they were better off financially. Though joint-custody mothers were as strapped financially after divorce as the single-custody mothers, few of them felt the financial arrangement was unfair. Why was this? Luepnitz believes that the proximity and constant contact of the split-custody parents caused the mothers to have a more realistic view of the whole family's finances.

With Dad nearby and helping out with the physical care of the children, the mothers were less likely to have unrealistic fantasies about Dad's financial state and had less resentment than the women who were burdened with all the physical care of the children. Also, Dad would have a much better idea of what children cost, and therefore he may have been less argumentative when Mom pointed out the kids' increasing financial needs. At the same time, Dad would have felt control over money spent on the children, satisfaction at being able to provide for the children directly (and experience their gratitude), and inescapable guilt when he was there to see the children do without.

With all this to recommend joint custody, we might wonder why more people aren't trying it. In Luepnitz's study, 75 percent of the single-custody mothers said that it was just assumed that they would get custody of the children. Indeed, one-third of these mothers said they could not have pulled through emotionally without the children. As one mother stated:

> "He is an excellent parent, but they are the most important thing in my life, and I would not have survived without them. They would have been happy either way, but I wouldn't have pulled through if I had lost them."[12]

Unfortunately, even feminist sources support the mother's need as justification for her getting custody. Mary Ann Mason in *The Equality Trap* sees the mother's emotional need for the child as grounds for her receiving custody. But by well-accepted psychological principles of the need for the child to separate from the mother emotionally, this should, in fact, be grounds for her to lose custody! Any mother who feels that strongly about needing her child should make a move towards joint custody for the mental health of her child, especially if she considers the father to be an "excellent parent."

In our present system of favoring mother as custodian, the mother's feeling of isolation (which often begins before divorce as father becomes overinvested in work or other interests) is further aggravated by her exhaustion from single-parenting. Many single mothers do not have the money or time to get out and be with other adults, date, or keep up friendships. Naturally, this "over-involved" mother will become even more enmeshed with her children in her post-divorce isolation. Hence, an unhealthy psychological situation is magnified by divorce when the mother receives sole custody.

Luepnitz feels there has long been an unreasonable bias toward mother-custody and that joint custody is the inevitable trend of the future. Many single-custody mothers in her study said that they were not aware of joint custody as an option, and 43 percent said they would have agreed to it if their husbands had requested it. Unfortunately, in more than 20 percent of the cases, the lawyers or judge tried to talk the parents out of joint custody, even when both parents agreed they wanted it! Luepnitz could find no evidence to support the idea that kids are better off in sole custody of their mothers.

CONSIDERING A CHANGE IN CUSTODY

Change is slow and new ideas are frightening. How can a mother who has the power to have sole custody even begin to consider sharing that power with her "enemy"—the father? Yet it may well be the mother who must make the first move. She must trust her adversary to do what is right once she has made the first gesture of good will. Impossible? Remember when Mikhail Gorbachev astonished the world by announcing he was going to reduce his army by 500,000 soldiers? We had been engaged in a cold war with the Soviet Union for forty years, each wasting our resources stockpiling weapons, while children went hungry in each of our countries. Gorbachev began an end to that cold war by the only method that works when a conflict has been harbored so long—he made a clear, first conciliatory move. He didn't say, "I'll give up 500,000 troops *if* America gives up 500,000 troops." There were no "ifs" about it. He made himself more vulnerable by giving in a little bit, without a guarantee of reciprocation.

Mothers who are concerned about the fathers' minimal involvement in their children's lives could take a bold first step toward bringing them back into their children's lives by initiating a joint-custody arrangement. However, for many mothers the thought of sharing custody with the father is like sending their kids to stay with an irresponsible stranger. After all, if he cared about the kids or wanted to be with them, why didn't he spend time with them before the divorce? And how can he possibly take good care of them when they are with him if he has never learned how—if he has never wanted to know who their friends are, what activities they like, or how to best comfort them when they are upset? Some mothers worry that when a father does ask for joint custody it is only because he wants to avoid paying some child support. What good mother would agree to sharing custody with such a father? How can this be good for the children? Yet, is the alternative—seeing little of the father—healthy for the child in the long run?

The importance of our connections to both our parents cannot be ignored. We all have a deep-rooted, inescapable need to love our parents and resolve our conflicts with them. Every day psychologists see people as old as fifty, sixty, or even seventy, who are still wrestling with unresolved conflicts with their parents! Studies have shown that children who have been abused or neglected by their natural parents, and have had to be removed from the home by social services, do poorly when placed in the most loving foster homes. When the parent can be re-educated, and the parent and child can be reunited, the child will achieve better psychological adjustment and be more successful. This is true even when the natural parent is still a far poorer parent than the foster parent. Unless your child is being physically or sexually abused by the father, the child needs to spend enough time with the father to form a comfortable relationship. All things considered, this is best achieved with a joint-custody arrangement.

It's true that the father's first motivation in seeking joint custody might be a move to obtain a reduced child-support payment, but this selfish motivation can prove to be a blessing in disguise. As long as it is clear in the divorce contract that he will have the children regularly, and there is some provision written in about the amount of child support that would change hands if he were no longer able to take the kids for some reason, the formal, legal, public commitment to take responsibility for the children on a regular basis should set the stage for the father to bond with his children.

Mothers must also consider the changing attitudes toward custody. Even if the mother is vehemently opposed to the father having custody, this no longer means she can totally prevent it. Many states are giving the father greater consideration as a parent. If the mother does not give custody to him voluntarily, the father may be pushed to fight to gain custody. Not only would this be a waste of financial resources that could be used on the child (instead of being paid to lawyers), but it is also traumatic for the child.

Many fathers have secret longings for custody of their children and are seeking responsible, low-conflict ways they can approach this subject with their children. David, whom we met in Chapter 2, didn't even ask his ex-wife for custody of their child when she announced she was leaving, though he had longed for a child for years and had been very involved in his care. He knew no other men with custody and his lawyer advised him that it was a waste of time and money. He believed he could never win custody, and at that time the assumption was probably sound. But viewpoints and even laws have changed. When David realized that he had a good chance of winning custody if he reopened the case when his child was old enough to testify, he wrestled with the unsavory notion of putting his son on the spot to choose.

> "By state law Ben could have made his choice on where to live when he was fourteen years old. It was a tremendous temptation to really work on him and try to get him to come live with me. I did let him know it was an option but I tried to be very low-key about it, because I didn't want to put him on the spot about it. He never took me up on my offer to live here."

In my interview with Ben, he volunteered a piece of advice he wanted to offer to divorced parents that speaks to this subject.

> "Parents shouldn't be selfish with the kid. They shouldn't try to keep the kid to themselves. I really appreciate that my parents didn't compete with each other. I was never forced to choose. That would have been awful."

As I listened to David and Ben, I was reminded of the same process that my husband went through with his boys when they were of age to make their own decisions. We extended an invitation to each of them to come spend a year with us when they were twelve years old. When the first one came, we let him know we were willing to keep him beyond the year if he wanted to stay, and we would negotiate it with his mother. It was very touchy, and we tried to give him access to some neutral adults to discuss it with. We suggested he could talk to his Sunday School teacher or a family friend who was a counselor, but he never chose to talk to anyone about it. He gave us no indication of whether or not he would want to stay on longer, and we ended the agony of indecision by naming a date on which he had to tell us his decision. He decided to go back to his mother, and we were crushed, but we tried not to show it. However, I think we handled it badly and made this all very hard on him.

When we extended the invitation to his younger brother, we had lower expectations and higher sensitivity, so I think we handled it better and let him go without making him feel guilty. But it is a very gnarly moment in the custody drama. Children really need to know that we will love them even if they say no. I think the key to why I felt better about it with the younger child is that I explained to him how our lives would be better if he stayed with us and how our lives would be better if he left. In other words, I let him know that either way we had some sadness and some things to look forward to, so he should do what was best for him and not worry about us. We would survive and be happy either way. This relieved his burden when he, too, told us no. Both this son and the first son chose to return to us when they had graduated high school, presumably because they could then leave without hurting their mother or implying any negative judgment of her parenting.

FATHERS IN TRAINING

If a mother does decide to try sharing custody, she must keep in mind that, if the father has had very little involvement with the children prior to the divorce, he's bound to make a mess of parenting for awhile. Remember, studies showed that both custodial mothers and custodial fathers ran chaotic households during the first year of solo parenting. This will be hard on the children, hard on the father, and perhaps hardest on the mother who must release her children into his custody every week, fearing that her children will not be receiving the "best" care. But suffering can be reduced all around if there is a clause in the custody agreement that says the sharing of custody is contingent on the parents taking a parenting course. I say the *parents*, not just the father, because we can all learn something about parenting and things work much more smoothly if the parents share the same parenting philosophy and techniques.

Before a mother signs a contract agreeing to joint custody, she might check out all available parenting courses in the area. Many family counseling centers offer extensive in-depth courses. Child protective services often have information about parenting programs in the area, since parents who have lost custody of their children due to neglect or abuse are usually required to take a parenting course before they can regain custody. Parents should call each program and select a very thorough one. It's helpful to talk to the instructor and explain the situation and what you hope to accomplish. Ask how well the instructor feels he or she can handle divorcing or divorced parents. It is good to be able to offer a choice of three parenting programs so your ex has some say in the selection.

Your school psychologist is another source of guidance, advice, and knowledge about local resources. As a matter of fact, all mental health professionals who work with you and your child in post-divorce adjustment problems should be making an effort to include the non-custodial parent in their therapeutic plan.[13] In addition to providing good advice on parenting courses in your area, your school psychologist may act as an important bridge for the child to have access to both parents.

If you and your ex are not in a state of declared war, it is ideal to attend these classes together, because you may have opportunities to discuss some of your concerns and differences in class. But if you two are in such strong conflict that you would be a distraction to each other, and inhibit each other's ability to admit to problem areas, you might do better if you each attend different sections of the same course. You might even offer to babysit for each other. Be firm in your insistence that you both take a parenting course, but flexible about making it happen. If you hear about your ex using the recommended parenting techniques with the kids, make a supportive comment and ask if there is something he would like you to do in your home to reinforce what he's trying to do with your children.

ONE LUCKY KID

Crystal, now twenty-one, was six years old when her parents divorced with a split-custody arrangement. Contrary to popular belief, her parents did not select joint custody because they had a "peaceful divorce" and looked forward to further contact with one another. Rather, they did it for the sake of the children. Crystal explained,

> "My mom really doesn't like my father all that much, but they can get along if they have to — like if they both have to attend the same wedding. They've never had a lot of contact. It wasn't a real bitter divorce, but they weren't friends either."

On Tuesdays, Thursdays, and Saturdays the father would come to pick up Crystal and her older brother, Ronnie. The mother arranged a neutral transition by going to a neighbor or staying at work when the father was due. At first they visited for the evening only on weekdays, but as they got older, they spent three nights a week at their father's. When her brother was sixteen, he chose to move in with the father. According to Crystal,

> "Ronnie wasn't getting along with my mom and he was getting in trouble at school all the time. My mom and my brother tried really hard to work things out for two or three years and my father was really good about being supportive of my mother while my brother was living with her. He would tell Ronnie he had to try harder to get along with my mother. Then my mom and dad finally agreed that it might be best for Ronnie to live with my dad.
> "My parents sort of got together with my brother's school counselor to help him get his act together. Everyone in his little world knew what was going on and he had to shape up. My brother has a really good relationship with my mom now."

Both parents have shown remarkable maturity through difficult periods with the children. Crystal's father could have taken advantage of the situation when her brother first began to complain about the mother. Instead, the father pushed the son to try to work things out with the mother. He was supportive throughout, and even his finally agreeing to take the son into his primary custody is supportive of the mother. The mother felt she couldn't handle Ronnie, and the father was willing to step in and give the son the extra structure he needed. All this was done without giving the children the impression that he judged their mother to be an inferior parent.

Crystal had always felt closer to her dad but never requested to live with him because she knew it would hurt her mom unnecessarily, especially after her brother's departure. Things became most rocky between Crystal and her mom when she began talking on the phone too much during puberty. Then her grades dropped, and her mom got upset.

"My mom has always been more hysterical than my dad. He would have sat down and talked about it calmly, but my mom is more of a screamer. That's her first reaction, then she'll sit down and talk, too.

"I remember one time we had this big fight about something—I don't even remember what—and my mom yelled, 'You can just go live with your father!' And I said, 'Okay.' And then she said, 'No, you can't go live with your father.' Like I might enjoy it too much. And we both just started laughing.

"I've always been really close to my dad. I'm more like him than I am like my mom. It was actually hard living with my mom, but I could complain about my mom to my dad and he would never badmouth her. He would just tell me that I needed to work out my arguments with her."

Crystal still likes to talk to her father about everything.

"I talk to my father just about every day. I'll talk to my dad about my job and then we talk about his job. I've always got some little plan or goal I want to achieve and he likes to discuss it with me. He gives me suggestions about how to achieve what I want to achieve—what little thing I have to do now to get where I want to go. We talk about finances and he gives me advice. Or he just listens to me when I need somebody to listen.

"My dad has had a lot of experiences growing up that are like things that are happening to me and he'll tell me how he worked it out. He empathizes with me and I know he really understands. We think so much alike that we perceive things in the same way. We have a lot of the same interests and we've spent a lot of time together. He's always been supportive. He's always been the kind of father I would want for my own kids.

"When I'm really upset I can call him up and talk to him. Like when my grandmother died. I had felt really close to her and she was the first person I knew that died. I started crying and then he started crying. He said to me that I was the first person he'd been able to cry in front of for a long long time."

Crystal's closeness and comfort with her father is exemplary. She has the relationship that every child longs to have with his or her father. I cannot help but believe that this ease between them is a result of the great deal of time she has spent with her father despite the divorce. Of course, the parents made this possible and pleasant on a daily basis by their cooperative attitude. I marvel at their ability to each let Crystal love the other parent—their lack of the need to be her favorite parent. The mother gave the father lots of space to love and be loved by his children.

What made Crystal's parents so open to sharing her with each other? First, Crystal's parents have lots of access to kids' feelings and problems through their work. Her mother is a teacher, and her father is a school administrator. They have also had experience sharing Crystal with others. Since they both worked full-time, Crystal was cared for by an elderly couple during the day. This couple served as surrogate grandparents and Crystal still visits the family. She has always spent part of the holidays with these surrogate grandparents, affectionately nicknamed "Nonnie" and "Bumpa," just because they feel like family to her. This was fine with her parents, who have always had a healthy ability to "let go" and let her love others. Crystal was so close to this couple that they became part of the shared-custody arrangement! Crystal spent one night of the weekend at Nonnie and Bumpa's house. She now has Sunday dinner with them every week.

"I have three Christmases," Crystal tells me. "Christmas Eve I would spend with my dad and his parents; then I would spend Christmas day with my mom. Then at night, my brother and I would go down and have dinner with Nonnie and Bumpa."

Crystal's life is rich with love. She has been a truly fortunate child—possessed by none, but shared by many.

SUMMARY POINTS

- In most states, the mother automatically gains sole custody, unless the decision is challenged and she is extremely unfit.

When judges award custody to the mother 90 percent of the time, it becomes a message to fathers that their money is needed but their nurturing skills are not.

- Studies show that fathers who have gained custody were as capable caretakers as custodial mothers once the trauma of divorce and its attendant chaos had settled down. Many of these fathers had not been at all involved with caretaking tasks prior to the divorce.

- There are many types of shared-custody arrangements: from splitting the week between parents to having the child live with one parent one year and then the other parent the next year. A creative joint custody plan can be arranged to meet the needs of any family who sincerely wishes it to work.

- Some oppose joint custody because they worry that it will be too confusing for the children. However, one study which intensively interviewed children and parents in various custody arrangements showed that both parents and children found it was well worth the effort.

- Studies show there are many advantages to joint custody. For example, children maintain down-to-earth contact with both parents, children are able to keep in touch with both extended families, parents get much needed breaks from the children while they are trying to rebuild their lives after divorce, and the forced cooperation between the parents increases their understanding and sympathy for each other's difficulties.

- Unfortunately, there are men who have used the threat of joint custody to "bribe" their ex-wives into accepting less child support, and some have taken the children part of the time primarily to avoid paying out so much money for them. However, the increased time with the children has made many of them more responsive to their children despite their original motivation.

- Joint custody is the natural antidote to the "overinvolved mother/underinvolved father" syndrome cited by psychologists as most damaging to the child. Sole custody not only fails to loosen the mother's bond, it often leaves her trapped in the house without an alternate caretaker who could free her to pursue her own interests.

- Many mothers are naturally concerned about fathers who have had little contact with the children and have shown no interest in caretaking skills being given full charge of the children even for a few days at a time. One way to relieve mother's stress and push the father to sharpen his skills is for both to agree to take a parenting course as a joint-custody contingency.
- The most fortunate children are those whose parents can share them peacefully, for studies show that all children need contact with both parents, and boys, especially, need more contact with their fathers as they grow older.

13

Moms on Their Own

"My mother worked and she loved me. I never felt like the kid that had screwed up her life. As a matter of fact, everybody in my family made me feel special. If anything, they spoiled me."

— AN ADULT CHILD OF DIVORCE

Gabriel's parents married in their early twenties when they learned that Gabriel's mother was pregnant. The father did not have a job that would support his wife, so the couple moved in with the mother's parents. The father was not ready for marriage and spent less and less time in his wife's parents' home. Gabriel's mother would run into her husband in town, sometimes with another woman. When Gabriel was two years old, her mother decided to give up hope for reconciliation and filed for divorce. The father had never paid much attention to Gabriel and now he seemed to see himself as divorced from the daughter as well as the wife, though he agreed to pay nominal child-support payments.

Though the father lived within a thirty-minute drive from his former family, Gabriel does not ever remember him visiting. Fortunately, Gabriel's mother stayed in touch with the father's family, and Gabriel spent a great deal of time with her paternal grandparents, her paternal aunt, and her cousins on the father's side. She visited their homes often, and occasionally she would run into her father there at family gatherings though he paid her no special attention. Gabriel told me,

"My mom never tried to influence me negatively or manipulate my feelings about him one way or the other. When I was younger and I would ask her questions, about him not seeing me and all, she would just say something like, 'Well, I don't know about your father, but your grandparents love you very much.' She would always stress the positive. And I always knew that she had been very much in love with him. My Mom also said good things about my father's family and encouraged me to visit them.

"I really respect the way she handled all this while I was growing up. I wanted to believe good things about my dad and I think it was good that my mom let me do that. I was really a happy high-spirited kid. I think my family helped me preserve my sense of self esteem.

"I learned recently that my father once called up and said he wasn't going to pay my medical bill because it was too much. He actually got quite nasty with my stepfather about it. The gist of the matter was that he didn't want to accept financial responsibility for me. I didn't need to know about all that when I was little, and I appreciate my mother protecting me from it."

During Gabriel's childhood, her mother was not guided by her own need to justify herself or prove how bad the father was. Instead she was sensitive to Gabriel's ability to take in certain details and considered what knowing those details would do to Gabriel when she was young. Even the father's relatives were careful to respect Gabriel's need to have a childhood that was not burdened by adult problems she hadn't caused and couldn't solve.

"If I were going to give advice to the relatives of a child whose father was absent, I'd tell them, 'Always be aware of the child's level of understanding and emotional needs. Don't give the children information that will burden them, confuse them, or sadden them. Just provide a lot of support. Then as they become an adult they will be ready to know more of the truth.' Now my mom will admit that there are really no excuses for my father not seeing me because she knows I need that kind of honesty now.

"As I grew older I started to feel angry and resentful about my father never wanting to be with me. Even so, when I began to talk to my mom about it, she didn't criticize my father. She just apologized to me for being foolish enough to get involved with someone who would be so uninvolved with me. She felt embarrassed that she had gotten pregnant when she was unmarried. But I felt so proud of her that she had been through that.

"My mother worked and she loved me. I never felt like the kid that had screwed up her life. As a matter of fact, everybody in my family made me feel special. If anything, they spoiled me. My grandfather would take me everywhere with him. When they had company he'd come wake me up and get me out of bed because he wanted to show me off. He didn't try to hide me. He was proud of me like a father would be. My grandmother took care of me during the day when my mother worked.

"It's made me realize that when everybody kicks in and helps out it can even make up for an absent father. But you've got to have all that help—the stepfather, the grandparents, the aunts, the uncles, and the cousins—then it makes it feel okay."

I am struck by how Gabriel *only* lost her father. Usually when a father deserts, the children lose the father's whole side of the family, half their heritage. Gabriel has had everything in the picture except one man. Against this background of supportive relatives, participation in family events on both sides, and lifelong contact with her cousins and aunt, the father seems a small loss.

For a variety of reasons as different from one another as the men who have them, some fathers simply won't become involved with their children. If no effort is made to compensate for the father's lost affection and attention, the children are likely to have school problems, low self-esteem, confusion about their attractiveness and sexuality, and problems with authority.

Single mothers can certainly improve their children's chances of growing up "whole" by analyzing what men provide and trying their best to provide it themselves. I believe women can go a long way in their efforts to make up for the loss of a father's attention, but I also feel that it is essential for mothers to make the time and opportunity for their children to have contact with men. To get a hold of what a man's influence might be, let's take a look at what Dad has typically contributed to the child's life when he was at his best:

Dad's Critical Early Influence

- *Conception:* Father contributes half the gene pool. The child may have inherited both Dad's talents and his hereditary medical or psychological problems.
- *Newborns:* Father's help can relieve stress on mother and give the child a sense that the world is a safe, supportive, dependable, responsive place.
- *Infancy:* Fathers are inclined toward rough-and-tumble play. Such sensory stimulation often increases the child's IQ.
- *Age 1:* Father's relationship with his child gives the child an alternative to Mom and helps him or her break the now too-close symbiotic tie.
- *Age 2-3:* Father's presence helps the child sort out the difference between maleness and femaleness. Mother and father model male/female interaction.
- *Age 4-5 (or Oedipal stage):* Father's presence helps boys realize they cannot "marry Mom" and thus moves them toward autonomy. Girls gain self-esteem and feel attractive to the opposite sex when Dad pays attention to them at this stage.

If the father became distant, uninvolved, or totally absent before the child turned six, the mother has some rebuilding to do. When a child's life is disrupted by a major change such as divorce or the death of a parent, he or she will often become arrested at that stage or even regress to an earlier stage. This is a common reaction to trauma. The child may go on exhibiting the characteristics of a two-year-old for years, until someone helps him or her work through that developmental stage. Here are some suggestions for mothers whose children lost their fathers during those crucial early years.

STEP BY STEP

Step 1: Conception. We can do nothing about the father's genetic contribution except to note it before it is forgotten. It may become important much later. What medical problems did the father's parents have? Did either of them have heart disease, diabetes, cancer, glaucoma, or any other hereditary health conditions? Did alcoholism or mental illness run in his family? Was the father ever hospitalized for any reason? What special talents did the father have that your child might have inherited? If you have lost touch with the father, try contacting the paternal grandparents or sympathetic siblings to get this information. Write it down and put it away for your child along with the baby pictures and birth certificate.

Step 2: Infancy. During infancy an involved father provides support to the mother and stimulation for the baby. If you are parenting alone, try to make sure you have plenty of emotional and physical support. Involve your relatives as relief babysitters and try to set up babysitting exchanges with friends who provide you with an occasional night out as well as expanding your child's social contacts. As children grow older they will need to have other adults they feel they can depend on so that they can feel safe to break the symbiotic bond with the mother when the time comes. At that stage, the alternative adult can be either male or female, as long as the adult is dependable and attentive.

Step 3: Preschool. At the Oedipal stage, Mom will need to show her son that she has other people in her life who are deeply important to her. She must somehow convey to the son that although she loves him very much, they both need other relationships. The child's quick adjustment to school is possible only when he is not overly attached to mother.

At the same time, moms must encourage rough-and-tumble play. Single moms are perfectly capable of tossing babies up in the air or rolling around and wrestling on the floor with their toddlers. My son and I used to play a game we called "bulldozer." I would lie in the center of the double bed and he would roll across me and onto the floor. (I sort of leaped over him when it was my turn to be the bulldozer.) The "dirt heap" would moan and groan and occasionally scream to increase the bulldozer's excitement, and the bulldozer would make lots of loud engine noises. We always ended up giggling hysterically. This kind of physical play is very relaxing and stimulating at the same time—a real after-work "icebreaker."

Mothers not only habitually shy away from this type of play with their children, they often become fearful when children wrestle or tumble. Boys especially need to tumble around with other boys their age. It's the way males communicate. If a boy is reluctant to chase and "take his knocks," other boys will shun him. Little girls who are not overprotected will later find it easier to approach normally aggressive boys and outgoing men. Kids need to develop the courage to try new things. Whether male or female, surviving a few bumps in rough-and-tumble play teaches kids that they are not made of glass. Moms should encourage this play and not make too great a fuss when the child gets hurt.

Step 4: Sex-Role Development. For some developmental functions it's hard to get around involving a man. Children need to observe men and women together to form an understanding about male and female ways of doing things. As our society moves toward androgyny, those differences seem less important, but, ironically, it is the most insignificant differences that retain their importance. Male and female mannerisms and ways of sitting and moving are different. Part of this is "in the bones"—a boy will often develop his father's walk even when he has had little chance to observe it. But many of our hand movements, facial expressions, and habitual word choices come from unconscious imitation of those with whom we spend a lot of time. Girls with masculine mannerisms and, to an even greater extent, boys with feminine mannerisms, will often be taunted by their peers. When boys spend so much time with women that they do not know what men talk about, they become increasingly distanced from their own sex. This is when it is essential for Mom to inspire a male relative to be with the kids more or to make space in her crowded schedule to help her children connect with groups or organizations where they may have close contact with men.

MOMS COPING ALONE

Although dads can make significant, irrefutable contributions to a child's development, and studies have shown that Dad's absence can be very damaging to a child, how much and how deeply the child is affected depends a lot on Mom's coping skills and attitudes. Unfortunately, while Dad is absent, Mom is experiencing her own sense of loss whether Dad's absence is due to abandonment, divorce, death, or workaholism. She is without a workmate and companion. She may be quite stressed as she tries to cope with both parenting alone and pursuing a career. Many women parenting today were raised to expect the breadwinner/homemaker lifestyle and are still in shock over the expectation that they should work and raise a family simultaneously. Though it may be easier for the next generation, who have been raised with different expectations, in this generation of moms there are many who are still struggling with not only a lack of confidence in their ability to achieve rewarding careers, but also a lack of marketable skills.

Betsy is a mom who exemplifies these struggles. She felt very overwhelmed after she was widowed, although she was only thirty-eight years old. Betsy had been comfortable in the role of homemaker, and her thoughts had always been wrapped up in her children. The traditional family "worked" for her with a dad there to set limits for her son. In the five years since her husband's death, Betsy has not been able to get a steady full-time job, and her financial resources are shrinking steadily. Now she not only feels the loss of her husband as breadwinner, she feels she is doing a poor job as a nurturer.

"Because I went back to school right away, I feel like I wasn't around enough for Mark. Even when I got sick and was at home more, I wasn't here for him emotionally. We all started drifting apart.

"We had always sat down to the dinner table together but after their dad died, they didn't seem to want to eat at the table anymore. They wanted to have their dinner in the living room in front of the TV. I think the table brought back too many memories. I would try to hug Sylvie and she would shrug me off. I felt like she was not ever going to let me get close to her again.

"I was worried about Mark, and his teachers would tell me what to do, but I just couldn't follow through. I feel like I was in a fog for three years. I was all stressed out and I kept getting sick. I was in a bad car accident, and I had to have major surgery. I just couldn't be there for Mark very well. I started coming out of it the fourth year.

"Still, I often feel like I just can't handle Mark. If there was anyone who could take him and help him I would let him go. I love him that much. I would miss him terribly but I just don't know if I can help him. I don't want him to sink and go down the tubes. I want him to grow up to be happy and find someone to love and care for and have a good life. That's all I want for my kids."

The generation who grew up in the fifties is often ill-trained to break away from traditional roles. Not only were the women trained to wait on men, their mothers' modeling taught them to wait on their children hand and foot. Many feel guilty asking their children to help. Instead they become overburdened trying to do it all, while resenting not only their ex-husbands, but also their children. This is another source of emotional conflict for children. They become confused by Mom's "mixed messages," asking themselves, "If my mom is doing my laundry because she loves me and wants to take care of me, why does she seem so mad at me all the time?"

Children are much better off when single mothers push them to help out more and become more responsible for themselves. No one wants the resentful "love" that is the price of sacrifice. Besides, the men and women of tomorrow will find it easier to do their shares of housework if they are expected to do so as children today. When a single mom demands that her children help more, she transforms her problem into an opportunity for her children.

WHEN FATHERS WON'T

Though many men feel inadequate with children, there are also men who are willing to step in and give their male attention to someone else's forgotten child. Many stepfathers have contributed not only time, but money to children who are not their biological offspring, and many older brothers, uncles, grandfathers, and male family friends have shown a special saving interest in a needy child.

Organizations like Boy Scouts and sports groups have long provided male role models for boys, and some have even brought girls into contact with men. Even so, sometimes a mother's location, personal contacts, or work schedule may bring no men into her or her children's lives. Then it is up to her to be aware of what is missing and try to bridge the gaps as best as she can.

Before we can look at the effectiveness of different avenues for bringing children into contact with men, or trying to give them the special stimulus that fathers have traditionally provided through some other means, we need to take a look at the ways good active fathers influence their children.

A Father's Influence

Direct
- Modeling
- Reward and Punishment (Reinforcement)
- Establishing Rules
- Expressing Expectations for Behavior
- Instructing or Training
- Reasoning and Rational Persuasion (Cognitive)

Indirect
- Support of Mother's Positive Behavior
- Inhibitor of Mother's Negative Behavior
- Provides Alternate Network of Family and Friends
- Material Contributions

Ongoing Circular Transactions
- Synergistic Stimulus
  (The sum of Mom + Dad + Child = More than the wisdom of the three minds and personalities combined.)[1]

Fathers have direct influence over the child's sex-role development by modeling male behavior and male-female interaction. This is most important in "traditional societies." As we learned in Chapter 8, the father's direct attention also strongly affects the child's cognitive development. Studies focusing on math scores show that boys with nurturing, encouraging fathers are generally high academic achievers, and the more a father is available, the higher the math ability a boy will have. On the other hand, inadequate, powerless-feeling fathers have a negative affect on boys. The father's effect on girl's achievement is much less noticeable, but girls do better in math if the father has been very involved with them between the ages of one and nine.

The child's social competence is also noticeably influenced by both the father's parenting style and degree of involvement. Involved, nurturant fathers produce well-adjusted, socially competent boys; uninvolved, weak, or neurotic fathers produce boys with few friends; and rejecting, hostile fathers produce delinquent sons. Girls grow up to be independent and self-motivated if their fathers are demanding, challenging, or even abrasive, but overall, girls are not as much affected by their fathers as boys are.[2]

Fortunately, any man who is willing to get involved with the children can learn how to relieve stress on mother, encourage independence, demand that kids behave, treat them respectfully, and talk to them about the world outside their home. Indeed, any mother can learn to do most of these things on her own if necessary. One study which compared matched families of single fathers, single-mothers, and intact parental units, found that boys in father-custody families were more socially competent, warmer, higher in self-esteem, more mature, and more independent than boys raised in two-parent families. However, girls raised by mothers were more socially competent and mature than girls raised by a father alone. The most promising observation of this study was that both boys and girls raised by authoritative, warm, supportive, and demanding parents of *either* sex did better than children raised by authoritarian, traditional, or permissive parents. Thus a mother with a secure, supportive, but firm parenting style can raise more competent boys and girls than many two-parent families.[3]

Though stepfathers are likely candidates to call on as replacement fathers, few mothers have an extra father in the wings when they become divorced, separated, widowed, or pregnant outside of marriage. In fact, all of these life transitions are usually so disruptive that Mom will not find a new mate for quite some time. Mom needs to look around her for people who are obviously interested in kids.

CALLING IN REINFORCEMENTS

Many responsible men are aware that they will be better fathers if they have some experiences with children before they make that final, total commitment. Though men who are interested in children are still fairly scarce, mothers who use their social network and take advantage of organizations such as Scouts, soccer leagues, church groups, and YMCA programs can generally find an older male who will take an interest in their child.

Rae Ann, whom we met in Chapter 3, helped her son Jesse through the difficult teen years without a father by becoming very

involved in 4-H Club and committing a considerable amount of her
meager income so that Jesse could have his own horse. The men he
met at the stables welcomed him into manhood.

> "I know this may sound really frivolous but I used horses to
> help me rear Jesse. The family who owned the horse farm had
> two boys who were about ten years older than Jesse and they and
> their Dad just took Jesse under their wings. He spent a lot of time
> with them doing whatever it is that men do.
>
> "They went hunting, they rode horses together, and I guess
> they told him whatever it is that men are supposed to tell their
> sons. Whatever they did, it must have been the right thing. Jesse
> has grown up into a wonderful young man. He's gentle and
> polite. He's got a lot of self-confidence. I was at a loss myself
> during Jesse's late teens, so I feel like those men should get
> credit."

Rae Ann was especially grateful to these men for helping Jesse
through his late adolescent confusion. Jesse had pulled out of the
college-bound program (although he had been classified as gifted)
and chose the "easy route" of vocational education. Following high
school, Jesse got a job for UPS, where he rose rapidly toward a
management position. Those times were difficult for Rae Ann. Proud
though she was at his achievement in the work world, she felt her son
was failing to work up to his full potential, and she worried about
his future.

Fortunately, Jesse had continued to work at the horse farm at
night. When Rae Ann couldn't be calm with Jesse, these warm,
concerned men at the stables could. They were a steady influence on
Jesse throughout his early and late adolescence. With their acceptance firmly under his belt, Jesse eventually decided to go to college
and head for a professional career.

As the men's movement gains momentum, more and more men
are willing to get involved with kids in a fathering role. Robert Bly
tells the men who attend his conferences:

> "What I'd like you to do is to go out and find a young man who
> doesn't have any father in the house. I'd like you to hold that boy
> in your heart. Which means that you may write him once a

month, you may take him somewhere once a month. He knows that he has a heart-link through you with the male world.

"And that's a responsibility that the men have got to take in this country. They've got to take more responsibility for the younger men, for encouraging the younger men, admiring the younger men and holding the younger men in their hearts."[4]

Boys need to link up with older males even more than girls do because they have more overt symptoms of disturbance. As we know, they are more likely to get in trouble with the law or drop out of school when there is no male influence in their lives. On the other hand, when I interviewed Mary, the unmarried mother who adopted a daughter, I became aware of the special problem girls have developing a bond with a father figure. Many girls desperately need casual contact with warm, concerned men so that they can learn how to be at ease with the opposite sex.

However, even if there were enough interested men to play father to all the boys and girls in need of a father figure, there would be certain logistical problems with girls having, for example, a Big Brother. Similarly, it is simply not wise to hire a boy babysitter for a pre-adolescent daughter, or to send her off alone with a man. The potential for sexual abuse is too great. It is better for mothers to plan activities for her daughter to be with men or much older boys when the mother or some other appropriate person can accompany them. Church outings and other intergenerational activities are ideal. A large group gathering allows individuals to divide up casually for games and social activities, so that the daughter may have a special man all to herself while Mom is stationed out of earshot but in easy reach.

Surprisingly, Mary has managed to make the Big Brother/Big Sister program work for her adopted biracial daughter, Rachael. In addition to the single adoptive parents' group which provides moral support for Mary's family unit, the Big Sister group in Mary's city provides Rachael with a much-needed extended family. Mary's dysfunctional family of origin never showed much interest in Rachael, and Mary hoped to find an older black girl who would be a good role model for Rachael. Although Rachael already has a caring woman in her life and could use a caring man, the Big Brother/Big Sister programs always match up the child with a same-sex sponsor. Mary feels the alliance between Rachael and her "big sister" Zena has been very worthwhile.

> "It's a valuable experience. Rachael needs someone else's perspective and some other people who love her unconditionally and are proud of her accomplishments. Her big sister Zena has helped with other small but important things. Rachael has very textured hair and I didn't know what to do with it, but Zena taught us how to work with her hair."

Rachael really has acquired a whole family through the program. She visited Zena at her home and got to know both the mother and father of her big sister. Last spring Rachael was the flower girl at Zena's wedding, and Rachael is getting to know Zena's new husband (who also has a "little brother" through the program).

Even if there were no man in Zena's life, Rachael had already acquired a "grandfather" through her big sister, as Zena's dad took a spirited interest in Rachael. In addition, the relationship has provided several other advantages usually supplied by an interested father. Zena provides a different perspective than Mary and can be a sounding board if Rachael needs to talk through a conflict she has with her mother. Zena broadens Rachael's experience with other people and shows her a little more of the world outside her home. And Big Brothers and Big Sisters see their sponsored child about once a week—more often than many divorced fathers see their children.

NEIGHBORS

Neighbors or fathers of your child's friends can also be a wonderful source of "father energy." My own father was seldom home, never spoke to us in a conversational way, and was frequently in a violent rage. Although my parents never divorced or separated, my father met few of the criteria for the active father. He never reduced my mother's stress or gave her a break during a crisis. He generally was the crisis! In fact, he treated us all so badly that every child in my family had problems with authority. We were either terrified of people in authority, pugnaciously rebelled against authorities, or somehow attracted lots of negative attention to ourselves from those in charge.

It is a near miracle that I survived the treatment of my father during my childhood and have been able to capture psychological health. What saved me was the attention of my best friend's father. Since I was always at her house (in order to escape my own as much as possible), her father treated me just like one of the family. If we did something wrong together, we both got talked to and punished. He never hit me because he never hit his daughter. We were grounded or we lost privileges. But it seldom came to that because we both adored and respected her father. He encouraged our independence by teaching us things but refusing to help us beyond a certain point. He was a warm, firm authority, and by knowing him I knew a whole new world of choices about human relationships. Having this man as a "back-up Dad" made me come out ahead of the kids with ordinary dads, despite my own father's very negative effect on my psyche and my self-esteem.

EXTENDED FAMILY

In many families uncles or much older cousins can be a wonderful source of interested males who may take a special delight in your child's accomplishments while keeping their "egos" uninvolved in what the child does or doesn't do. Grandfathers, too, often have an objectivity and perspective that allows them to be even more supportive than a child's parent. If your child has lost the attention of his father, but can capture that of his grandpa, he may be more fortunate than most kids with dads in their homes.

Robert Bly enjoys retelling this story of one of his workshop participants. When this young man was about fifteen and wearing the ritual rebellious long hair of the sixties, his parents tied him down and cut off his hair. His grandfather, who arrived shortly afterwards, came and found the young man weeping inconsolably. So the grandfather took him out to the ocean and said to the young man, "You see this ocean? Now, this is for you. This ocean is going to be here whether you have long hair or short hair."[5] The young man related that he found comfort in the ocean ever after that, as if his grandfather had given him the ocean. Whereas the father's message may have been too harsh, the grandfather gave the boy the perspective he needed to become a man.

Shirley O'Rourke, whose husband died when her children were five, nine, and eleven years old, feels deeply grateful to her father-in-law, who was willing to step in and fill the gap in her children's lives. The father-in-law has been significantly emotionally supportive of her and her children since before her husband's death.

> "Mickey's father is a very warm person. He has come over every Saturday to visit ever since Mickey became ill. The night that my husband died, my father-in-law came back from the hospital with me. I told the kids that their father had died and we were all crying. Michael said, 'Does that mean that Grandpa won't come and visit us anymore on Saturdays?'
>
> His grandfather said, 'Oh, no. I will always come and visit you on Saturdays.' And he has. Every Saturday, just like clockwork, he comes to visit."

As I listened to Shirley I felt deeply moved by this one small but so significant commitment. Here was the next most important man in these children's lives saying, "I will always be there." When a parent dies, kids feel like there is nothing they can count on, but this loving grandfather came every Saturday, as sure as the sun rose each day. This dependability and consistency provided a life-long base of security for the O'Rourke children. Melody told me,

> "My grandfather has always been there if we ever needed to talk or anything. Even since before my father died. He's such a good role model. He's an attorney but he doesn't work to make money, he works to help people. If you're in trouble, he'll go out of his way to help you. He's been very supportive of anything we wanted to do.

Michael added his praise,

> "My grandfather has been a real influence on my doing well academically. He was like a father to me. I think he really felt for me because his father died when he was ten, too. I think I'm probably more like him than I am like my dad."

Katy also describes the grandfather in tender terms.

"My grandfather is so loyal. He's perfect. I'd like to marry someone who is like him—loving, like my dad was too."

She remembers fondly that when she was small, her grandfather would take her shopping and buy her a gift. Each holiday their grandpa takes each of the three children out to eat with him and just chats about their life and plans.

Since so many young, unwed mothers live at home, grandfathers often find themselves fathering their grandchildren, and they find that their parenting experience makes them better at the job this time around. Kim, whom we met in Chapters 4 and 5, has lived with her parents since her five-year-old son Brian was born. She fondly stated,

"Brian has got my dad wrapped around his finger. I think he's been really good for my family. I think he's helped my dad stay sober because my dad spends a lot of time with him and really seems to enjoy him. I feel like Brian brought my family back together again."

Kim's dad is a much better father to Brian than he was to Kim. He had been a quiet drunk who would withdraw and pay little attention to his kids.

"He's a much better grandfather than he was a dad. He's still not super-dad, but they do things together all the time. They go to the mall; they go out for hot dogs; and my dad watches Sesame Street with Brian."

Perhaps even more important is the fact that Kim's father has helped her provide a stable home for Brian during those very crucial early years. Research shows that children who have a father or stable father-figure in their lives during the first six years will generally not develop the problems that plague children of absent fathers.

FANTASY FATHERS

Imagination, wisely used, is a powerful tool. When I interview people who have overcome problems, they often talk about fictional book or TV-show characters who have not only been models for them, but have also been a source of comfort. From *Father Knows Best* in the 1950s, to *The Waltons* and *Little House on the Prairie* in the 1970s to the eternal *Bill Cosby Show*, little viewers have been watching TV fathers do the right fatherly thing week in and week out and gaining a sense of security that life can be fair, gentle, and just. Atticus Finch, the widowed father in the acclaimed novel *To Kill A Mockingbird*, is the epitome of the strong, wise, morally exemplary father. Your local librarian can help you find some books to read to your children, or that your children can read to themselves, to develop warm images of fathers or to work through feelings about absent or abusive fathers.

Books about Fathers to Read to and Be Read by Children

- *Toddlers*

  Dad's Back; Reading; and *Sleeping*, all by Jan Ormerod.
  New York: Lothrop, Lee & Shepard Books, 1985.

- *Pre-School*

  Just Me and My Dad by Mercer Mayer.
  New York: Golden Press, 1977.
  Owl Moon by Jane Yolen.
  New York: Philomel Books, 1987.
  The Summer Night by Charlotte Zolotow.
  New York: Harper & Row, 1974.
  Do I Have a Daddy? by Jeanne Warren Lindsay.
  Buena Park, CA: Morning Glory Press, 1991 (with an excellent special section for parents).

- *Early Elementary*

  Bea and Mr. Jones by Amy Schwartz.
  Scarsdale, NY: Bradbury Press, 1982.
  Daddy Is a Monster . . . Sometimes by John Steptoe.
  New York: J. B. Lippincott, 1980.
  Play Ball, Zachary! by Muriel Blaustein.
  New York: Harper & Row, 1988.

- *Late Elementary*

  The 25c Miracle by Theresa Nelson.
    New York: Alladin Books, 1986.
  Danny the Champion of the World by Roald Dahl.
    New York: Alfred A. Knopf, 1975.
  Where the Red Fern Grows by Wilson Rawls.
    New York: Bantam Books, 1961.
  The Education of Little Tree by Forrest Carter.
    Albuquerque: Univ. of New Mexico Press, 1986.
  Tiger Eyes by Judy Blume.
    Scarsdale, NY: Bradbury Press, 1981.
  Onion John by Joseph Krumgold.
    New York: Harper Trophy, 1959.

My father had withdrawn from me totally by the time I was five, but I had male TV heroes who pulled me through. Gene Autry and Hopalong Cassidy were strong, dependable men, and I would lull myself to sleep at night imagining one of them carrying me in his arms (across the chest, daddy-style, with my arms looped around his neck) into the proverbial sunset. As a teenager I was soothed by the gentle image of Jean Valjean, the fatherly guardian to poor Cosette in *Les Misérables*.

Whether the source is books, TV, movies, or relatives' anecdotes, fantasies about fathers are good medicine for the child with an absent father. Dr. Carol S. Michaels, a professor in the Department of Educational Psychology at New York University, has done extensive research on father fantasies.[6] Many psychologists have discovered that children persist in fantasizing about their fathers even if they have not seen them in years and have no real memories of them.

In a study done during World War II, when fathers were absent due to the war, the children's fantasy fathers were more affectionate, more fun, more predictable, and less hostile toward the family than the fantasy fathers created by children whose fathers were still at home. However, in order to determine how modern children are affected by the absence of their fathers, Dr. Michaels conducted an extensive study in the early 1980s to determine how father-absence affected preschoolers whose fathers had left due to divorce, permanent separation, or abandonment.

Michaels wondered how the attitude of the mother toward the father or men in general would affect the kind of fantasies the children had about Dad as exhibited in their play with dolls. She defines "good" fantasies as ones in which Dad is affectionate and heroic; "bad" fantasies as ones in which Dad is aggressive, authoritarian, withdrawn, sad, or depressed; and creates a third category of "silhouette" fantasies in which Dad acts like a prop during the child's fantasy play—simply saying "Good morning," as he leaves for work, and "Hello," when he returns, but having little impact on the family drama.

Almost half (45 percent) of the children's fantasies included a father and most of these were "good" father fantasies. The next most frequent category of fantasy was the "silhouette" father (who to me represents the typical father in the last generation in America!). When compared with other factors, the researchers learned that the more positive the mother felt about the nonresident father, the more positive the child's fantasies. However, the children of mothers with bad attitudes toward the nonresident fathers had fewer positive responses but not necessarily more negative responses. Many of these fell into that nebulous "silhouette" category. Boys more often than girls imagined Dad as a heroic figure. The girls' play showed them having more fantasies about mothers, and the boys' had more fantasies about being with their fathers.

Dr. Michaels feels that one of the most significant outcomes of the study was to show that even absent fathers are very much on the minds of children. The fantasy father they choose for their play is good more often than not, and they seem to need to form an attachment to this abstract figure of the good father. She feels that this good father who lives on in the imagination of the children provides them with a sense that Daddy is with them during the challenges of their childhoods. The many times that children chose to act out scenes with father in their doll play also shows how much they want and need a father in their lives. Since many of these children seldom saw their real fathers, this fantasy play may show their need to forget their neglect and soothe themselves with a better fantasy. However, Michaels also felt that the fantasies of the good father served to keep the children open to relationships with good men who might come along in their lives. At the very least, the children did seem to find gratification and comfort while fantasizing about good fathers.

On the other hand, these good fathers were so good they could be said to have outperformed most real fathers by a mile! The fantasy fathers were seldom bossy, harsh, or punitive, and were more affectionate and nurturing. The fantasies don't show the children as being very ready to accept most mortal men as replacement fathers. In addition, if the children do not gain a more realistic conception of men, the boys will have a hard time measuring up to their idealized image of Dad, and the girls will be hard-put to find a mate who can compare to "dear old dream Dad." The book *Daddy Is a Monster . . . Sometimes* (see booklist) presents a realistic dad and would entertain any child from age four to eleven.

Considering the actual experiences of the children in this study, the relatively small percentage of bad father fantasies show that the children are generally afraid to think bad thoughts about their fathers and may have repressed the image of their real fathers. These children may need a safe outlet for discussing negative feelings and disappointments they may feel about their fathers.

Books with negative father images can be valuable for sorting out feelings about an abusive or neglectful dad's past acts. For the young child, the story of Huckleberry Finn on videotape or read aloud can open up a lot of conversation about alcoholic fathers. For teens, Pat Conroy's *Prince of Tides* offers a descriptive account of a harsh, violent father and his transformations across a lifetime. This book or video would be too strong for younger children, but Mom or the teenagers may want to read it to take a hard look at how children respond to an abusive father. Also, the video *Desert Bloom*, with Jon Voight, presents a stirring story of an earnest but difficult stepfather.

Mom may want to view some of these films to work through feelings about her own father first, so that she can be more objective, and teenage children may be able to cope with discussing or thinking about a fictional violent father more easily than they could deal with memories of their own abusive fathers. Any experience you can share with your child that encourages talking about the father can be good therapy.

FINAL THOUGHTS

Ultimately, what every mother wants to know, when the father of her children has been less than ideal is, will my child be irreparably damaged? Do all my good efforts amount to nothing if the child's father is unresponsive or abusive? When kids are at their worst right before dinner, or for months on end when they hit their teens, we all want to find one handy reason/person to blame—preferably one that has nothing to do with us. Intact parents blame the family genes or the child's friends. When a father is absent, it's convenient to put all the blame on him. But the good news is that the father doesn't decide the child's fate, and the bad news is that the father doesn't decide the child's fate. Like it or not, he is just one factor.

As Mary and her daughter Rachael make us aware, there are many hurdles for our children. Rachael was born prematurely and she has learning problems as a result. She will have to cope with being half black and half white, as well as with the social stigma of being adopted. Mary knows she ought to be worrying about providing a male influence in Rachael's life, but for now that seems like a low priority. Every child has something to struggle with. If your child has a disinterested father, in addition to following the suggestions in this chapter, consider how you will help your child solve the other challenges in his or her life.

And if an absent father is *all* your child has to cope with, then thank God your child has this opportunity to deal with at least *some* adversity!

SUMMARY POINTS

- Now that we are no longer a homemaker/breadwinner society, moms can fill in as a "link to the outside world" and dads can take over more nurturing roles. When each parent is a "whole" person, the loss of one parent is less damaging to the child.
- The father's contribution is especially important during the first six years of life. When fathers are absent, mothers need to know about the father's hereditary contributions, provide children with plenty of stimulation, and make sure they have enough support from friends and family so they can learn to distance themselves from their children in a healthy way.
- Moms must help children move toward independence by expecting them to care for themselves and help around the house as is appropriate for their ages.

- Studies of successful, competent children and their parents show that the most important factor is the parenting style used. A single parent, of any sex, who uses a warm, authoritative style can raise happy, healthy children.
- Though moms can provide much of the stimulation that children need, it is best for children to have some contact with warm, interested men. Scouts, team sports, church groups, and YMCA's are just a few places moms can find men who are interested in children.
- Male neighbors, fathers of children's friends, and male relatives are important sources of male nurturance for children with absent fathers. Grandfathers, because of their wisdom and perspective, are often better "fathers" to their grandchildren.
- Books, films, and other stimulants of imagination help children sort out what fathers do, or what they wish their own fathers had done. When Mom reads books or views films about fathers with her child, it opens up an easy avenue for talking about the child's feelings and questions about the absent father.

Notes

CHAPTER 1: THE ROLE OF THE FATHER

1. Arlie Hochschild with Anne Machung, *The Second Shift: Working Parents and the Revolution at Home* (New York: Viking, 1989.), 238.

2. Frank F. Furstenberg, Jr., "Good Dads—Bad Dads: Two Faces of Fatherhood" in *The Changing American Family and Public Policy*, ed. Andrew J. Cherlin (Washington, DC: The Urban Institute Press, 1988), 201.

3. Furstenberg, "Good Dads—Bad Dads," 201.

4. Geoffrey L. Greif and Mary S. Pabst, *Mothers Without Custody* (Lexington, MA: Lexington Books, 1988), 103–4.

5. Furstenberg, "Good Dads—Bad Dads," 203–4

6. Andrew J. Cherlin, ed., *The Changing American Family and Public Policy* (Washington, DC: The Urban Institute Press, 1988), 9.

7. Theodora Ooms and Todd Owen, *Encouraging Unwed Fathers to Be Responsible: Paternity Establishment, Child Support and JOBS Strategies* (Washington, DC: Family Impact Seminar, American Association for Marriage and Family Therapy, Research and Education Foundation, 1990), 3. Background briefing report and meeting highlights for the seminar "Family Centered Social Policy: The Emerging Agenda."

8. L. Eugene Arnold, *Childhood Stress*. (New York: John Wiley), 409.

9. Stanley H. Cath, Alan Gurwitt, Linda Gunsberg, eds., *Fathers and Their Families* (Hillsdale, NJ: The Analytic Press, 1989), 5.

10. Tamar Lewin, "Father's Vanishing Act Called Common Drama," *The New York Times*, 18 June, 1990, sec. A 18.

11. Furstenberg, "Good Dads—Bad Dads," 202–3.

12. Cherlin, *The Changing American Family*, 9.

13. Mary-Joan Gerson, "Tomorrow's Fathers: The Anticipation of Fatherhood," in *Fathers and Their Families*, ed. Cath, Gurwitt, and Gunsberg, 127–39.

14. Hochschild with Machung, *The Second Shift*, 228.

15. Michael E. Lamb and David Oppenheim, "Fatherhood and Father-Child Relationships," in *Fathers and Their Families*, ed. Cath, Gurwitt, and Gunsberg, 11–22.

16. Furstenberg, "Good Dads—Bad Dads," 196.

17. Carol Lawson, "Tracking the Life of the New Father," *New York Times*, 12 April 1990.

CHAPTER 2: WHY DON'T DADS GET INVOLVED

1. Furstenberg, "Good Dads—Bad Dads," 203–4.

2. Cherlin, *The Changing American Family*, 9.

3. J. A. Fulton, "Parental Reports of Children's Post-Divorce Adjustments," *Journal of Social Issues* 35 (1979): 126–39 as quoted in *Fathers* by Ross D. Parke (Cambridge, MA: Harvard University Press, 1981), 86

4. Cath, Gurwitt, and Gunsberg, *Fathers and Their Families*, 428

5. Greif and Pabst, *Mothers Without Custody*, 104–10.

6. Judith Wallerstein, "Introduction," in *Impasses of Divorce: The Dynamics and Resolution of Family Conflict* by Janet R. Johnson and Linda E.G. Campbell (New York: Free Press, 1988), ix–xv

7. Johnson and Campbell, *Impasses of Divorce*, 24–52.

8. Judith S. Wallerstein and Sandra Blakeslee, *Second Chances: Men, Women and Children a Decade After Divorce* (New York: Ticknor & Fields, 1989), 141–3.

CHAPTER 3: INVOLVING DAD

1. Parke, *Fathers*, 80–81.

CHAPTER 4: UNCOMMITTED FATHERS AND UNWED MOTHERS

1. Ooms and Owen, *Encouraging Unwed Fathers to Be Responsible*, 3.

2. National Center for Health Statistics, *Monthly Vital Statistics Report. Advanced Report of Final Natality Statistics, 1982*, vol. 33 (Washington, DC: GPO, September 1984), (6) (Supplement).

3. *Teenage Fathers*. Children's Aid Society of California, 1978.

4. Arthur B. Elster and Michael E. Lamb, eds., *Adolescent Fatherhood* (Hillsdale, NJ: Lawrence Erlbaum Associates, 1986), 8.

5. Ooms and Owen, *Encouraging Unwed Fathers to Be Responsible*, 2.

6. Elster and Lamb, *Adolescent Fatherhood*, 71–77.

7. Arthur B. Elster, "Adolescent Fathers from a Clinical Perspective," in *The Father's Role: Applied Perspectives*, ed., Michael E. Lamb (New York: Wiley, 1986), 332.

8. Elster and Lamb, *Adolescent Fatherhood*, 27.

9. Ibid., 57.

10. Ibid., 142.

11. Teen Father Collaboratives were established at the Teenage Pregnancy and Parenting Project of the Family Service Agency of San Francisco; YMCA of Greater Bridgeport in Connecticut; Teenage Parent Program of the Jefferson County Public Schools in Louisville, Kentucky; Division of Indian Work in Minneapolis, Minnesota; Face to Face Health and Counseling Service, Inc. in St. Paul, Minnesota; YMCA of Dutchess County in Poughkeepsie, New York; National Council of Jewish Women Insights in Portland, Oregon; and Medical College of Pennsylvania in Philadelphia.

12. Elster and Lamb, *Adolescent Fatherhood*, 155–70.

CHAPTER 5: MOTIVATING UNWED DADS

1. Gary Kreps, Child Advocate Office, telephone interview with author, Charleston, WV, 16 September 1991.

2. Ooms and Owen, *Encouraging Unwed Fathers to Be Responsible*, ii.

3. Ibid., 13–14.

4. Ibid., 9–11.

5. Ibid., 18.

6. Ibid., 11.

7. Gary Kreps, Child Advocate Office, telephone interview with author, Charleston, WV, 16 September, 1991.

8. Furstenberg, Jr. "Good Dads – Bad Dads," 199–201.

CHAPTER 6: WHO WAS MY DAD?

1. Elliot M. Kranzler, "Parent Death in Childhood," in *Childhood Stress*, ed. L. Eugene Arnold, (New York: John Wiley, 1990), 406.

2. Edna Furman, *A Child's Parent Dies: Studies in Childhood Bereavement* (New Haven, CT: Yale University Press, 1974).

3. Kranzler, "Parent Death in Childhood," 408–9.
4. Ibid., 414.
5. Ibid., 418.

CHAPTER 7: THE CLOSED DOOR

1. Kranzler, "Parent Death in Childhood," 416.

CHAPTER 8: WHAT'S MISSING WHEN DAD'S MISSING?

1. Dotson Rader, "I Want To Be Like My Dad," *Parade Magazine,* 20 January 1991, 7.
2. Parke, *Fathers*, 38–41.
3. Ibid., 69–71.
4. Ibid., 56–58
5. H. B. Biller and R. Bahm, "Father Absence, Perceived Maternal Behavior, and Masculinity of Self-Concept Among Junior High School Boys," *Developmental Psychology* 4 (1971):178–81.
6. Parke, *Fathers*, 87.
7. Cath, Gurwitt, and Gunsberg, *Fathers and Their Families*, 462.
8. Bill Moyers and Robert Bly, *A Gathering of Men* (New York: Public Affairs Television, 1990). Transcript, pp. 4–5.
9. John Guidubaldi et al., "The Role of Selected Family Environment Factors in Children's Post-Divorce Adjustment," *Family Relations* 35 (January 1986):141–51.
10. As quoted by Robert Bly in *A Gathering Of Men*, transcript, p. 16.
11. Parke, *Fathers*, 70.
12. Ibid., 61.
13. Ibid., 74–77.
14. Lora Heims Tessman, "Fathers and Daughters: Early Tones, Later Echoes," in *Father and Their Families*, ed. Cath, Gurwit, and Gunsberg, 202–5.
15. Parke, *Fathers*, 61.
16. Tessman, "Fathers and Daughters," 199.
17. Mavis Hetherington, "Effects of Paternal Absence on Personality Development in Adolescent Daughters," *Developmental Psychology* 7 (1972):313–326.
18. Parke, *Fathers*, 67.
19. Ibid., 72–73.
20. Deborah Anna Luepnitz, *The Family Interpreted: Feminist Theory in Clinical Practice.* (New York: Basic Books, 1988), 294–5.

21. Ibid., 308.

CHAPTER 9: DAD IS MONEY

1. Mary Ann Glendon, *Abortion and Divorce in Western Law* (Cambridge, MA: Harvard University Press, 1987), 111.

2. Andrew J. Cherlin, "The Changing American Family and Public Policy," in *The Changing American Family*, ed. Cherlin, 6–10.

3. Luepnitz, *The Family Interpreted*, 9–11.

4. Hochschild with Machung, *The Second Shift*, 230.

5. Jane Lazone, "The High Cost of Living Off Someone Else," *Ms.*, 15 January 1981.

6. Deborah Anna Luepnitz, *Child Custody: A Study of Families After Divorce* (Lexington, MA: Lexington Books, 1982), 45–50.

7. Department of Health and Human Services, Social Security Administration, *Survivors* (Baltimore, MD: SSA Publication No. 05-10084, January 1991).

8. Ooms and Owen, *Encouraging Unwed Fathers to Be Responsible*, 8.

9. Mary Ann Mason. *The Equality Trap* (New York: Simon & Schuster, 1988), 68–69.

10. Glendon, *Abortion and Divorce*, 108.

11. Ibid., 89–90.

12. Bureau of the Census, *Child Support and Alimony: 1989. Current Population Reports*, Series P-60, no. 173 (Washington, DC: GPO, 1991), 1–6.

13. Spencer Rich, "Most Absent Fathers Fail to Pay Full Child Support," *Washington Post*, 21 August 1987.

14. Andrea Rock, "Can You Afford Your Kids?" *Money*, July 1990, 88–99.

15. Department of Agriculture, Agricultural Research Service, Family Economics Research Group, *Expenditures on a Child by Husband-Wife Families: 1990* (Washington, DC: GPO, January 1991), 11. To obtain this report call (301) 436-8461 or write to:
USDA, ARS, Family Economics Research Group
Room 439A, Federal Building
6505 Belcrest Road
Hyattsville, MD 20782

CHAPTER 10: CHILD SUPPORT: HOW TO GET IT

1. Dennis A. Cohen, "How to Collect Overdue Child Support," *Los Angeles Herald Examiner*, 18 February 1986.

2. Elaine M. Fromm, President, Organization for the Enforcement of Child support, 119 Nicodemus Rd., Reistertown, MD 21136. Telephone interview with author, 25 April 1991. Call (301) 833-2458 for more information.

3. Bureau of the Census, *Child Support and Alimony: 1989, Current Population Reports*, Series P-60, no. 173, (Washington, DC: GPO, 1991), 12.

4. Robert Riffle, Child Advocate Officer, Parkersburg, West Virginia, telephone interview with author, 22 March 1991.

5. Riffle, telephone interview.

6. Jackie Hyman, "The Money Chase: Tracking Child Support Evaders," *Washington Post*, 27 March 1983.

7. Kathleen Doheny, "Counsel for Collections." *Los Angeles Times*, 7 August 1989.

8. Ibid.

9. Bureau of the Census, *Child Support and Alimony*, p. 7.

10. For further information contact: Dennis A. Cohen, Center for Enforcement of Family Support, 6404 Wilshire Blvd. Suite 500, Los Angeles, CA 90048.

11. Cohen, "How to Collect Overdue Child Support.".

12. Wallerstein and Blakeslee, *Second Chances*, 156.

13. Ibid., 157–158.

CHAPTER 11: TWO DADS

1. Furstenberg, "Good Dads—Bad Dads," 204.

2. Parke, *Fathers*, 97.

3. Ann H. Tyler, "The Abusing Father," in *The Father's Role*, ed. Lamb, 258.

CHAPTER 12: CREATIVE CUSTODY CHOICES

1. Ross A. Thompson, "The Father's Case in Child Custody Disputes: The Contributions of Psychological Research," in *Fatherhood and Family Policy*, ed. Michael E. Lamb and Abraham Sagi (Hillsdale, NJ: Earlbaum, 1983), 91–94.

2. Garska v. McCoy, 167 West Virginia 59, 278 S.E.2d 357 (1981).

3. Luepnitz, *Child Custody.*

4. Thompson, "The Father's Case," 84–85.

5. Ibid., 85–87.

6. Ibid., 66–73.

7. Ibid.

8. J. W. Santrock, R. A. Warshak, and G. L. Elliot, "Social Development and Parent-Child Interaction in Father-Custody and Stepmother Families," in *Nontraditional Families*, ed. M. E. Lamb (Hillsdale, NJ: Erlbaum, 1982).

9. Deborah Anna Luepnitz, "A Comparison of Maternal, Paternal, and Joint Custody: Understanding the Varieties of Post-Divorce Family Life," in *Joint Custody And Shared Parenting*, ed. Jay Folberg (New York: Guilford Press, 1991), 105–13.

10. Luepnitz, *Child Custody*, 45.

11. Mason, *The Equality Trap*, 83.

12. Ibid., 90

13. Guidubaldi et al., "The Role of Selected Family Environment Factors," 149.

CHAPTER 13: MOMS ON THEIR OWN

1. Norma Radin and Graeme Russell, "Increased Father Participation and Child Development Outcomes," in *Fatherhood and Family Policy*, ed. Lamb and Sagi, 191–218.

2. Ibid., 195–98.

3. Ibid., 200.

4. Moyers and Bly, *A Gathering of Men*, Transcript, 23

5. Ibid., 5.

6. Carol S. Michaels, Ph.D., "So Near and Yet So Far: The Nonresident Father," in *Fathers and Their Families*, ed. Cath, Gurwitt, and Gunsberg, 409–23.

Bibliography

BOOKS

Arnold, L. Eugene. *Childhood Stress*. New York: John Wiley & Sons, 1990.

Bienenfeld, Florence. *Helping Your Child Succeed After Divorce*. Claremont, CA: Hunter House, 1987.

Cath, Stanley H.; Gurwitt, Alan; and Gunsberg, Linda, eds. *Fathers and Their Families*. Hillsdale, NJ: Analytic Press, 1989.

Cherlin, Andrew J., ed. *The Changing American Family and Public Policy*. Washington, DC: Urban Institute Press, 1988.

Conroy, Pat. *Prince of Tides*. New York: Bantam Books, 1986.

Elster, Arthur B., and Lamb, Michael E., eds. *Adolescent Fatherhood*. Hillsdale, NJ: Lawrence Erlbaum Associates, 1986.

Fassel, Diane. *Growing Up Divorced: A Road to Healing for Adult Children of Divorce*. New York: Pocket Books, 1991.

Fisher, Roger; and Ury, William; with Patton, Bruce, eds. *Getting to Yes: Negotiating Agreement Without Giving In*. New York: Penguin Books, 1981.

Fisher, Roger, and Brown, Scott. *Getting Together: Building Relationships as We Negotiate*. New York: Penguin Books, 1988.

Furstenberg, Frank; Lincoln, R.; and Menken, J., eds. *Teenage Sexuality, Pregnancy, and Childbearing*. Philadelphia: University of Pennsylvania Press, 1981.

Gilligan, Carol. *In a Different Voice: Psychological Theory and Women's Development*. Cambridge, MA: Harvard University Press, 1982.

Greenberg, Martin. *The Birth of a Father*. New York: Avon Books, 1985.

Glendon, Mary Ann. *Abortion and Divorce in Western Law*. Cambridge, MA: Harvard University Press, 1987.

Greif, Geoffrey L. *The Daddy Track and the Single Father.* Lexington, MA: Lexington Books, 1990.

Greif, Geoffrey L., and Pabst, Mary S. *Mothers Without Custody.* Lexington, MA: Lexington Books, 1988.

Hochschild, Arlie, with Machung, Anne. *The Second Shift: Working Parents and the Revolution at Home.* New York: Viking, 1989.

Johnson, Janet R., and Campbell, Linda E. G. *Impasses of Divorce: The Dynamics and Resolution of Family Conflict.* New York: Free Press, 1988.

Lamb, Michael, ed. *The Father's Role: Applied Perspectives.* New York: John Wiley & Sons, 1986.

——, ed. *Nontraditional Families.* Hillsdale, NJ: Lawrence Erlbaum Associates, 1982.

Lamb, Michael, and Sagi, Abraham. *Fatherhood and Family Policy.* Hillsdale, NJ: Lawrence Earlbaum Associates, 1983.

Lee, Harper. *To Kill a Mockingbird.* New York: Warner Books, 1960.

Levant, Ronald, and Kelly, John. *Between Father and Child: How to Become the Kind of Father You Want to Be.* New York: Viking, 1989.

Luepnitz, Deborah Anna. *Child Custody: A Study of Families After Divorce.* Lexington, MA: Lexington Books, 1982.

——. *The Family Interpreted: Feminist Theory in Clinical Practice.* New York: Basic Books, 1988.

Mason, Mary Ann. *The Equality Trap.* New York: Simon & Schuster, 1988.

Parke, Ross D. *Fathers.* Cambridge, MA: Harvard University Press, 1981.

Smart, Carol, and Sevenhuijsen, Selma, eds. *Child Custody and the Politics of Gender.* New York: Routledge, 1989.

Tannen, Deborah. *You Just Don't Understand: Women and Men in Conversation.* New York: William Morrow and Company, 1990.

Wallerstein, Judith S., and Blakeslee, Sandra. *Second Chances: Men, Women and Children a Decade After Divorce.* New York: Ticknor & Fields, 1989.

Wassil-Grimm, Claudette. *How to Avoid Your Parents' Mistakes When You Raise Your Children.* New York: Pocket Books, 1990.

Yablonsky, Lewis. *The Emotional Meaning of Money.* New York: Gardner Press, 1991.

VIDEOS

Moyers, Bill, and Bly, Robert. *A Gathering of Men.* Transcript. New York: Public Affairs Television, 1990.

Rosenbaum, Jean, and Rosenbaum, Veryl, narrators. *Single Parenting.* Durango, CO: Video-11, 1990.

ARTICLES

Biller, H. B., and Bahm, R. "Father Absence, Perceived Maternal Behavior, and Masculinity of Self-Concept Among Junior High School Boys." *Developmental Psychology* 4 (1971): 178–81.

Cohen, Dennis A. "How to Collect Overdue Child Support." *Los Angeles Herald Examiner*, 18 February 1986.

Doheny, Kathleen. "Counsel for Collections." *Los Angeles Times*, 7 August 1989.

Guidubaldi, John; Cleminshaw, Helen K.; Perry, Joseph D.; Nastasi, Bonnie K.; and Lightel, Jeanine. "The Role of Selected Family Environment Factors in Children's Post-Divorce Adjustment." *Family Relations* 35 (1986): 141–51.

Hetherington, M. "Effects of Paternal Absence on Personality Development in Adolescent Daughters," *Developmental Psychology* 7 (1972): 313–26

Hyman, Jackie. "The Money Chase: Tracking Child Support Evaders," *Associated Press*.

Lawson, Carol. "Tracking the Life of the New Father." *New York Times*.

Lazone, Jane. "The High Cost of Living Off Someone Else." *Ms.*, 15 January 1981.

Lewin, Tamar. "Father's Vanishing Act Called Common Drama." *New York Times*, 18 June 1990.

Rader, Dodson. "I Want to Be Like My Dad." *Parade*, 20 January 1991.

Rich, Spencer. "Most Absent Fathers Fail to Pay Full Child Support." *Washington Post*, 21 August 1987.

Rock, Andrea. "Can You Afford Your Kids?" *Money*, July 1990.

Sentrock, J. W. "Influence of Onset and Type of Paternal Absence on the First Four Eriksonian Developmental Crises." *Developmental Psychology* 3 (1970).

Shearer, Harry. "Caught in the Malestrom," *Los Angeles Times Magazine*, 21 April 1991.

PAMPHLETS AND DOCUMENTS

Bureau of the Census. *Child Support and Alimony: 1989. Current Population Reports*, ser. P-60, no. 173. Washington, DC: GPO, 1991.

Department of Agriculture, Family Economics Research Group, Agricultural Research Service. *Expenditures on a Child by Husband-Wife Families: 1990.* (Washington, DC: GPO, January 1991).

Department of Health and Human Services. Social Security Administration. *Survivors*. SSA Publication No. 05-10084, (Washington, DC: GPO, January 1991).

National Center for Health Statistics. *Monthly Vital Statistics Report. Advanced Report of Final Natality Statistics, 1982.* Vol. 33 (6) Supplement. (Washington, DC: GPO, September, 1984).

Ooms, Theodora, and Todd, Owen. *Encouraging Unwed Fathers to Be Responsible: Paternity Establishment, Child Support and JOBS Strategies.* Background briefing report and meeting highlights for the seminar "Family Centered Social Policy: The Emerging Agenda." Washington, DC: Family Impact Seminar, American Association for Marriage and Family Therapy, Research and Education Foundation, 1990.